Mustang
Buyer's Guide
1979–2004

Brad Bowling

MOTORBOOKS
INTERNATIONAL

First published in 2004 by Motorbooks International, an imprint of MBI Publishing Company, Galtier Plaza, Suite 200, 380 Jackson Street, St. Paul, MN 55101-3885 USA

Motorbooks International titles are also available at discounts in bulk quantity for industrial or sales-promotional use. For details write to Special Sales Manager at Motorbooks International Wholesalers & Distributors, Galtier Plaza, Suite 200, 380 Jackson Street, St. Paul, MN 55101-3885 USA.

ISBN 0-7603-1643-0

Printed in China

Edited by Heather Oakley & Chad Caruthers
Designed by Mandy Iverson

On the front cover:

The hard tonneau cover on this 1997 Saleen S-351 turns a regular convertible into a sleek Speedster.

SVT's new Cobra design was powered by a 240-horsepower 5.0-liter V-8 when introduced in 1994.

It doesn't look that sleek by today's standards, but the 1979 Mustang was an aerodynamic wonder for its time.

By 2002, Ford had turned even the V-6 Mustang into a sporty car. With a few options, the base coupes and convertibles could be made quite attractive.

Contents

Photo Acknowledgments

No matter how much you love Mustangs, this book would be pretty dry if there were no photos. The following people were kind enough to let me photograph their cars, often during the hot, muggy days of summer, and I would like to thank them specifically. The generosity of such folks is what makes the Mustang hobby such a fun place:

Daniel Carpenter (Daniel Carpenter Reproductions in Concord, North Carolina), has an unbelievable group of no- or low-mile Fox-body Mustangs in showroom condition. He's never too busy to show me his latest find. His cars in this book include: 1979 Indy Pace Car; 1986 GT; 1989 GT Hatchback; 1993 LX Convertible.

Monty Seawright is also a collector of low-mile Mustangs, but his collection runs from a 1964½ K-code convertible to a 1994 Cobra pace car replica. Because I had to travel to shoot his cars during the rainiest spring in history, Monty had to rearrange his work schedule many times while we tried to find a good weather window. His cars in this book include: 1979 Indy Pace Car; 1982 GT; 1983 Convertible; 1984 20th Anniversary Coupe, 1985 GT Twister II; 1987 Saleen.

Mark LaMaskin (Performance Autosport in Richmond, Virginia, www.performanceautosport.com) buys, sells, and collects Saleens, Cobras, and other late-model Mustangs of special interest. To say that he's an expert on these cars is putting it mildly. His cars in this book include: 1986 Saleen; 1986 Cop Car; 1989 Saleen SSC; 1993 Cop Car; 1994 Cobra Coupe; 1995 Saleen S-351; 1996 Cobra Mystic; 1999 Cobra.

Jimmy Morrison (Morrison Motor Co. in Concord, North Carolina, www.morrisonmotorco.com) also buys, sells, and collects late-model Mustangs. His interests also lie with Corvettes, Harley-Davidson motorcycles, and cars from the 1950s and 1960s. Between his collector car dealership, private collection, and museum, Jimmy has hundreds of photogenic cars. His cars in this book include: 1990 LX Coupe; 1993 Cobra; 1993 Cobra R; 1995 GT Coupe; 1998 GT Coupe; 1998 V-6 Convertible; 1998 Saleen Convertible; 1999 GT Coupe; 2000 GT Coupe; 1999 Saleen Convertible; 2001 V-6 Coupe.

Other owner/contributors include: Robert Tunney, 1984–1986 SVO; Pat Szyslowski, 1988 LX Hatchback; Keith Jones, 1987 GT Convertible; John McCauley, 1993 Saleen SA-10; Norm Demers, 1995 Cobra Convertible and 2003 Mach 1; Pat Suddeth, 1994 Saleen V-6 Coupe; Bob Cox, 1997 Cobra; Larry Vandeventer, 2000 V-6 Coupe; Rich Thacker, 1999 Saleen SA-15; Rachel Newcomb, 2002 V-6 Coupe; Richard Canter, 2001 GT Convertible; Todd Risko, 2001 Saleen Coupe; Darrell Smith, 2003 Saleen; Carol Barker, 2001 Stage 3 Premium Convertible.

Introduction

Many have compared the 1979-present Mustang to the 1955-'57 Chevrolet phenomenon, citing that both cars were great when new, became even better as used cars for performance-minded buyers on a budget and have since evolved into classics worthy of restoration and collection.

Taken as a whole, this book can be read as a drama that follows America's once-favorite pony car from just after the dark years of the Mustang II (1974-'78) to its current dominant position atop the American musclecar food chain of the 21st century. During its 26-year run the Mustang known internally at Ford as the "Fox" (and "Fox-4" beginning in 1994) evolved from a sporty coupe with adequate power to a world-class chassis capable of handling a supercharged, double overhead camshaft V-8 with 390 horsepower, backed up by a six-speed manual transmission and independent rear suspension.

It's the story of how Ford took a sedan/station wagon chassis in 1979 and created a Mustang that would survive and thrive for the next two and a half decades, gaining new enthusiasts and spinning off whole new segments of the performance aftermarket as it went.

The 1979-'04 Mustang saga is about redemption and the continuation of a love affair between a car and a country. Why Hollywood hasn't turned the tale into a summer blockbuster starring George Clooney as the president of Ford Motor Co.; Julia Roberts as the leggy, wisecracking SVO engineer; and Tom Hanks as Steve Saleen is beyond me.

FOX CHARACTERISTICS

The popular Fox Mustang was and has always been engineered to deliver average to high performance for buyers on a budget – owners who sometimes need a rear seating area for small children. In 1979 Ford had no idea the car's V-8 engine would nearly double in horsepower by the end of the next decade, so the chassis was designed for lightness and greater interior room, not road course-level handling.

As buyers drove those early Foxes hard and began boosting engine output through time-honored hot rodder techniques, it became evident that the Mustang's unibody structure was not strong enough to withstand the rigors of spirited driving. The hatchback models showed the most chassis stress over time, especially around the C-pillar, because the enormous rear opening to the cargo area removed as much load-bearing metal as a convertible top. When T-tops were installed at the factory, the bodies became even flimsier.

For cars subjected to heavy-duty conditions, such as Special Service Vehicle Mustangs bought by police and highway patrol departments all across America, floorpans had a tendency to weaken and fail if not reinforced. Over the years Ford addressed the Fox's structural weaknesses, finding ways to tweak the chassis for greater rigidity here and there. The aftermarket responded with various chassis stiffeners, braces and subframe connectors that can greatly improve a late-model Mustang's handling and ride.

There are very few other negatives built into the '79 and later Mustangs. Any car more than 10 years of age will have its share of rotted weatherstripping, faulty electronics, sagging door hinges and broken interior plastic parts; all of these are areas that should be inspected for signs of trouble before purchasing. The good news is that the late-model parts industry is as thorough as that devoted to the early Mustangs.

New techniques for cheating the wind made the fifth-generation Mustang an aerodynamic milestone by registering a then-phenomenal 0.44 coefficient of drag for the hatchback model and 0.46 for the notchback.

Chapter 1

1979–1981 Mustang

The European-influenced styling of the 1979 New Breed Mustang, introduced in September 1978, gave longtime fans of the marque reason to be optimistic after five years of lethargic performance and questionable styling. Its body was massaged again and again in the wind tunnel as designers tweaked every angle for coefficients of drag measuring 0.44 on the three-door model and 0.46 on the two-door, two of the highest ratings in the industry at the time.

Designers avoided the temptation to revisit the original 1965 pony car, fearing unfavorable comparison with the retro-styled Mustang II. New design techniques and advances in metallurgy helped produce a Mustang that was 200 pounds lighter than its predecessor but larger in every dimension (4.1 inches longer bumper to bumper and 4.2 inches more in the wheelbase), and with greater passenger space.

On paper, the new pony looked great, with MacPherson struts, front disc brakes, rack-and-pinion steering, four-link rear suspension, and a handling package built around alloy wheels and high-performance radial tires. Unfortunately, under those aerodynamic hoods Ford had largely carried over its powertrain lineup with only a few changes from the Mustang II years, resulting in lukewarm performance and strong complaints about reliability with its one new engine.

The 2.3-liter overhead cam four-cylinder ("Y" code on the VIN) performed base Mustang duty for the sixth year in a row, its noisy 88 horses hooked to a standard four-speed manual gearbox. From an owner's perspective, the only positive side to a new four-cylinder Mustang was the reasonable gas mileage. Ford advertised an EPA highway rating of 38 miles per gallon with the base model at a time when concern about gas prices still figured in buyers' decisions. It's very unlikely anyone ever saw numbers that high, as the EPA revised its mileage-rating system a few years later to be more realistic.

The optional 2.8-liter V-6 ("Z" code) produced 109 horsepower with a two-barrel carburetor and initially was only available with an automatic transmission. Production problems with the German-built V-6 that had been such a mainstay for the Mustang II forced Ford to replace it in the middle of the year with its much older 3.3-liter inline six ("T" code), which produced a meager 86 horsepower despite its greater cubic inch displacement.

Offering some hope to the performance-starved was the 5.0-liter V-8 ("F" code), which had been introduced to the Mustang line in 1968 but has a heritage going back to the car's first V-8, the 260. Because of the car's weight-loss program, a V-8 1979 coupe was certainly peppier than the 1978 King Cobra, and a realistic 8.7-second 0 to 60 time made it the bright spot of an otherwise lackluster lineup. In an incredible marketing blunder, Ford dropped the 302 for 1980 and 1981, replacing it with a de-bored version that displaced 255 cubic inches ("D" code) and rated only 119 horsepower.

Ford probably lost sight of its need for a powerful V-8, as it gambled everything on a high-tech turbocharged version of its 2.3-liter four-cylinder ("W" code), which the company considered the Mustang's flagship engine in 1979. The Turbo package could be identified externally by its short, front-facing, nonfunctional hood scoop. Advertised as delivering V-8 power with four-cylinder fuel economy, the little four was not much slower than its 5.0 counterpart, with 0 to 60 times in the 9.1-second range and an EPA rating of 28 miles per gallon in highway driving. Unfortunately, slapping a Garrett AiResearch TO-3 turbocharger onto the underperforming four also created some serious reliability problems, such as burned-out turbines and fatal oil leaks, even though boost was limited to a modest 6 psi.

The much-touted first-generation turbo motor suffered a quiet, smoky death during its two years in production, and, advertising claims aside, none were produced for 1981.

Rather primitive transmissions were limiting factors for the new Mustang, which would not see a good five-speed with overdrive until 1983. The single-rail overdrive (SROD) manual transmission that came standard on V-8 models was essentially a three-speed with an overdrive fourth gear—not exactly a road-racer's dream. The available automatic was a three-speed C-4 unit with no overdrive at all!

Despite its less-than-stellar underhood performance, the Fox Mustang (so-called by enthusiasts for its internal engineering code name) did do one thing decently—it handled corners well. Three suspension levels were engineered into the new pony: a base economy package built around bias ply tires; a handling version tuned for radials; and the top of the line TRX system, which featured high-end Michelin performance tires, unique-size alloy wheels, and special suspension components.

The only truly special model to stand out from the 1979 through 1981 crowd was the Indy 500 Pace Car replica, which was available with either the 5.0-liter V-8 or turbo motor. A total of 10,478 replicas were sold in 1979 featuring a unique front spoiler, Marchal driving lights, pewter-and-black Tu-Tone paint treatment, nonfunctional full-length hood scoop, power steering, power front disc brakes, halogen headlights, Recaro reclining front seats, and a long line of standard equipment.

Although it looks quite plain by today's standards, the design of the 1979 Mustang was ahead of its time in terms of aerodynamics and materials engineering. After the garish Cobra IIs and King Cobra of previous years, Mustangers were eager for something that didn't scream, "Look at me!" but rather had a sporty feel and adequate performance.

The new breed Mustang's taillight treatment was quite controversial in the Ford camp, as it departed from the original car's three-element theme. There was also some corporate concern that the wraparound styling would be too expensive to go into production.

1979–1981 Mustang Specifications

'79 Base price	02/66B coupe	$4,071
	02/66B V-8 coupe	$4,344
	03/61R hatchback	$4,436
	03/61R V-8 hatchback	$4,709
	04/66H Ghia coupe	$4,642
	04/66H V-8 Ghia coupe	$4,915
	05/61H Ghia hatchback	$4,824
	05/61H V-8 Ghia hatchback	$5,097
'80 Base price	02/66B coupe	$4,884
	02/66B V-6 coupe	$5,103
	03/61R hatchback	$5,194
	03/61R V-6 hatchback	$5,413
	04/66H Ghia coupe	$5,369
	04/66H V-6 Ghia coupe	$5,588
	05/61H Ghia hatchback	$5,512
	05/61H V-6 Ghia hatchback	$5,731
'81 Base price	10/66B coupe	$6,171
	10/66B V-6 coupe	$6,384
	15/61R hatchback	$6,408
	15/61R V-6 hatchback	$6,621
	12/66H Ghia coupe	$6,645
	12/66H V-6 Ghia coupe	$6,858
	13/61H Ghia hatchback	$6,729
	13/61H V-6 Ghia hatchback	$6,942
'79 Production	02/66B coupe	156,666
	03/61R hatchback	120,535
	04/66H Ghia coupe	56,351
	05/61H Ghia hatchback	36,384
'80 Production	02/66B coupe	128,893
	03/61R hatchback	98,497
	04/66H Ghia coupe	23,647
	05/61H Ghia hatchback	20,285
'81 Production	02/66B coupe	77,458
	03/61R hatchback	77,399
	04/66H Ghia coupe	13,422
	05/61H Ghia hatchback	14,273

Displacement (cubic inches/liters)		
	I-4	140/2.3
	I-4 Turbo ('79–'80)	140/2.3
	V-6 (early '79)	171/2.8
	I-6 (late '79–'81)	200/3.3
	V-8 ('79)	302/5.0
	V-8 ('80–'81)	255/4.2
Bore x stroke (inches)		
	I-4	3.78x3.13
	I-4 Turbo	3.78x3.13
	V-6	3.66x2.70
	I-6	3.68x3.13
	V-8 (302)	4.00x3.00
	V-8 (255)	3.68x3.00
VIN code/Compression ratio		
	I-4	Y 9.0:1
	I-4 Turbo	W 9.0:1
	V-6	Z 8.7:1
	I-6	T 8.6:1
	V-8 (302)	F 8.4:1
	V-8 (255)	D 8.8:1
Induction	I-4	2-bbl
	I-4 Turbo	2-bbl
	V-6	2-bbl
	I-6	1-bbl
	V-8 (302)	2-bbl
	V-8 (302 Calif.) variable venturi carb	
	V-8 (255)	2-bbl
	V-8 (255 Calif.) variable venturi carb	
Valvetrain	I-4	SOHC
	V-6	OHV
	I-6	OHV
	V-8	OHV
Horsepower	I-4	88@4,400
	I-4 Turbo	131@4,800
	V-6	109@4,800
	I-6	85@4,000
	V-8 (302)	140@3,600
	V-8 (255)	119@3,800

Transmission (std./opt.)		
	I-4	4-speed manual/3-speed auto
	I-4 Turbo (1979)	T-04 4-speed
	I-4 Turbo ('80–'81)	T-04/3-speed auto
	V-6	3-speed auto
	I-6	3-speed auto
	V-8 ('79)	SROD 4-speed/C-4 auto
	V-8 ('80–'81)	C-4 auto
	V-8 (Calif.)	C-4 auto
Rear-axle ratio	I-4, V-6, I-6	3.08:1
	I-4 Turbo	3.45:1
	V-6 4-speed ('81)	3.45:1
	V-6 auto ('81)	2.73:1
	V-8 (302), automatic	2.47:1
	V-8 (225), automatic	2.26:1
Wheelbase (inches)		100.5
Overall width (inches)		67.4
Overall height (inches)		51.6
Overall length (inches)		179.1
Track (inches)		(front) 56.6
		(rear) 56.7
Fuel capacity (gallons)		
	'79	12.25
	'80–'81	12.50
Weight (pounds)	02/66B coupe (range '79–'81)	2,431–2,524
	02/66B V-6 coupe	2,511–2,551
	03/61R hatchback	2,451–2,544
	03/61R V-6 hatchback	2,531–2,571
	04/66H Ghia coupe	2,539–2,558
	04/66H V-6 Ghia coupe	2,619–2,585
	05/61H Ghia hatchback	2,548–2,593
	05/61H V-6 Ghia hatchback	2,628–2,620
Tires		(base '79) B78x13
		(V-8 base '79) BR78x14
		(V-8 optional '79) CR78x14
		(base '80–'81) P185/80R13
		(Ghia '80–'81) P175/75R14
		(optional) Michelin TRX 190/65R390

Front suspension		modified MacPherson struts, coil springs
Rear suspension		live axle, four-link suspension system
Steering		20.03:1 to 16.05:1 variable ratio rack and pinion
Brakes	I-4, V-6, I-6	(front) 9.31-inch disc
	V-8	(front) 10.06-inch vented disc
	all models	(rear) 9.0-inch drum
Gas mileage (EPA combined est.)		
	I-4 4-speed manual ('79)	21
	I-4 4-speed manual ('80–'81)	23
	I-4 4-speed manual ('80–'81)	23
	I-4 5-speed manual ('81)	22
	I-4 3-speed auto ('79)	21
	I-4 3-speed auto ('80–'81)	22
	I-4 Turbo 4-speed manual ('79–'80)	18
	I-4 Turbo 5-speed manual ('80)	19
	I-4 Turbo 3-speed auto ('80)	19
	V-6 4-speed manual ('79)	20
	V-6 3-speed auto ('79)	18
	I-6 3-speed auto ('79)	19
	I-6 4-speed manual ('80)	21
	I-6 4-speed manual ('81)	19
	I-6 4-speed manual Calif. ('81)	20
	I-6 3-speed auto ('80)	20
	I-6 3-speed auto Calif. ('81)	20
	V-8 (302) 4-speed manual ('79)	15
	V-8 (302) 3-speed auto ('79)	16
	V-8 (255) 3-speed auto (1980)	18
	V-8 (255) 3-speed auto ('81)	19
0 to 60 (secs)	('79 coupe, 302/4-speed, 3.08:1 axle)*	8.7
	('79 302/auto)**	8.6
	('79 V-6/auto) ***	12.9
	('79 Turbo/4-speed)	9.1
Standing ¼-mile (mph/secs)	('79 coupe, 302/4-speed, 3.08:1 axle)	82@16.7
	('79 Turbo/4-speed)	82@17.4
Top speed (mph)	('79 coupe, 302/4-speed, 3.08:1 axle)	118

* *Motor Trend* August 1978

** *Road & Track* August 1978

*** Ford factory info

1979–1981 Mustang

Major Options

I-4 Turbo ('79–'80)	$542–$481
2.8-liter V-6 (later 3.3-liter I-6)	$213–$273
5.0-liter V-8 ('79)	$514
4.2-liter V-8 ('80–'81)	$263–$338
Cobra package	$1,173–$1,588
Cobra tape delete ('81)	(credit) $65
Exterior accent group ('79–'80)	$63–$72
Interior accent group	$108–$139
Light group	$25–$43
Power lock group	$93–$120
Exhaust, sport tuned (V-8 only)	$34–$38
Transmission, automatic	$307–$349
Brakes, power	$70–$76
Steering, variable ratio power	$141–$163
Suspension, handling	$33–$43
Battery, heavy-duty	$18–$20
Emissions, California	$46–$76
Emissions, high-altitude	$33–$38
Air conditioning	$484–$560
Rear defroster, electric	$84–$107
Fingertip speed control	$104–$132
Power windows ('81)	$140
Tinted glass	$59–$76
(windshield only)	$25–$29
AM radio (1979–'80)	$72–$93
AM/FM radio	$51–$120
Flip-up open-air roof	$199–$228
Full vinyl roof	$102–$115
Rocker panel moldings	$24–$30
Console	$140–$168

Recaro highback seats ('80–'81)		$531–$732
Wheels, forged metric aluminum		$259–$340
Wheels, cast aluminum		$251–$305
Styled steel wheels w/trim rings		$55–$94
Tires	B78x13 WSW ('79)	$43
	C78x14 BSW ('79)	$48
	BR78x14 BSW ('79)	$124
	CR78x14 WSW ('79)	$69–$192*
	P185/80R13 WSW ('80–'81)	$50
	P175/75R14 BSW ('80–'81)	$25
	P185/75R14 BSW ('80–'81)	$25–$49
	TRX 190/65R390 Michelin BSW ('79)	$117–$241
	TRX 190/65R390 Michelin BSW ('80–'81)	$125–$250

*With tires, first price is for Ghia model

Replacement Cost for Common Parts

Rear-wheel cylinder		$25		Vacuum canister		$25
Turbo-hood emblem		$10		Antenna kit	black	$37
Steering wheel	$100 core charge	$270		Antenna kit	stainless	$23
Hood scoop grille		$33		Antenna rod		$14
Ford emblem	rear hatch	$8		Rubber fender-to-hood bumpers		$2
Rearview mirror		$43		Hood latch assembly		$25
Power rack and pinion steering	19:1 ratio	$200		Wiper arm and blade kit		$40
Ignition coil		$60		Wiper arm		$15
Fuel pump		$30		Windshield washer nozzle		$9
Alternator		$60		Trunk lid		$170
Fan shroud	repro	$80		Floor pan		$115
Console coin tray		$37		Smog pump		$60
Arm rest pad		$65		Crankshaft pulley		$70
A/C vent registers		$20		Water pump pulley	V-8	$45
Dash pads	repro	$190		Distributor cover		$10
Side marker		$13		Smog canister		$65
Headlight retaining ring		$40		Heater core	A/C	$30
Marchal fog lamp lens		$110			exc. A/C	$35
Front-brake rotor		$40		Radiator bracket	left	$30
Master cylinder	remanufactured	$30			right	$60
Oil pressure sending unit		$20		Radiator		$110
Front fender	repro	$85		Rear-brake drum		$35
Front fender	original	$280		Power steering pump		$100
Starter		$60		Front lower control arms	pair	$200
Front seat belt buckle		$47		Pushrods	set of 16	$40
Outside door handle kit		$27		Harmonic balancer		$80
Electric window motor		$70		Radiator cap	16-pound	$6
Window crank handle		$10			13-pound	$9
Inside door handle bezel		$23		Thermostat	180-degree	$16
Door lock actuator kit		$90			195-degree	$7
Lock cylinder and key		$25		Fuel cap		$20
Hatchback quarter window molding pair		$100		Carpet		$99
Hatch weather stripping		$27		Rear-wheel cylinder		$40
Trunk weather stripping		$23		Temperature sending unit		$8
Sunroof weather stripping kit		$150		Fuel tank		$130
Door weather stripping kit		$40		Four-piece T-top weather stripping kit		$230

What They Said in 1979–1981

The Mustang has been reincarnated and sportiness has replaced luxury as its driving essence. Not since the halcyon days of the Boss 302 has any Mustang been so blatantly designed for enthusiasts. Yes, Mustangs can still be tailored to fit almost everyone's needs, but for once it's the enthusiasts who get the favored treatment: everything from trick suspensions to turbo motors is here for your driving enjoyment. *—Car and Driver, December 1978*

Ford was even less kind to the Cobra name. It appeared sporadically on various Mustang and Torino models during the late 1960s and early 1970s, and faded entirely when the Mustang II was introduced in 1974. In 1977, Ford stuck spoilers and stripes on a Mustang II and called it a Cobra. The car wasn't even a poor imitation of what the name once stood for, and those who held a deep affection for the original Mustang Cobra were greatly offended. *—Motor Trend, March 1979*

The straight, crisp linear look that has typified Ford products for so long is there, to be sure, but the overall effect is unique. Admittedly, there's a little Mercedes 450SLC in the notchback's rear deck, and you can bet that similarity wasn't an accident, but there's little else to lay off on non-Ford styling. And thankfully there's nothing of consequence left over from the Mustang II. The new breed is its own style setter. *—Car and Driver, April 1979*

I Bought a 1979–1981 Mustang

The first car I ever bought was a 1979 Mustang Ghia coupe. My boyfriend at the time (now my husband) was really into Mustangs and had a gold 1966 coupe he was always working on. I think he was surprised when I called him during summer vacation to tell him I had bought my maroon Ghia. "Bert," as it came to be known, was a four-cylinder with automatic transmission and a vinyl top that almost immediately began to crack and separate at the seams. It wasn't the best car I've ever owned, but we really enjoyed it. *—Ann Harris*

My 1979 Indianapolis 500 Pace Car replica has never been dealer-prepped or titled. I found it for sale in Wisconsin, where it had been stored all its life. It's a 5.0-liter with a sunroof and four-speed manual transmission, one of only 2,402 that were built with that powertrain. Because the Indy cars were shipped to dealers with the low-slung front spoiler unattached, my car is on display just as it rolled off the train, with the spoiler still wrapped in the box. The car only has 11 miles on the odometer. I don't plan on driving it. *—Daniel Carpenter*

1979–1981 Mustang Ratings

Base Four-Cylinder

Model Comfort/Amenities	★★
Reliability	★★★
Collectibility	★
Parts/Service Availability	★★★
Est. Annual Repair Costs	★★

3.3-Liter I-6

Model Comfort/Amenities	★★★
Reliability	★★★
Collectibility	★★★
Parts/Service Availability	★★★★★
Est. Annual Repair Costs	★

2.8-Liter V-6 (1979)

Model Comfort/Amenities	★★★
Reliability	★★★
Collectibility	★★
Parts/Service Availability	★★★
Est. Annual Repair Costs	★★

5.0-Liter V-8 (1979)

Model Comfort/Amenities	★★★
Reliability	★★★★
Collectibility	★★★
Parts/Service Availability	★★★
Est. Annual Repair Costs	★★★

Turbo Four-Cylinder (1979–1980)

Model Comfort/Amenities	★★
Reliability	★
Collectibility	★★
Parts/Service Availability	★★
Est. Annual Repair Costs	★

4.2-Liter V-8 (1980–1981)

Model Comfort/Amenities	★★★
Reliability	★★
Collectibility	★
Parts/Service Availability	★★
Est. Annual Repair Costs	★

If the 1974-1978 models are truly the Dark Times for Mustangs, then the 1979-1981 period should be known as the Poorly Lighted Years. Despite Ford's best efforts at producing a hot performance vehicle, only the unique looking Indy Pace Car replicas have any collector value whatsoever. So many of them were stored when new that they are sometimes offered for sale at less than original retail price. The turbocharged cars did not make any friends when introduced, and time has not redeemed them as collectibles.

Many 1981 Mustangs assembled during July and August had reclining seats that were built using substandard steel in the driver and passenger seat ratchet assemblies. The ratchet teeth were prone to shearing off, which allowed the seat back to unexpectedly pivot backward.

Ford first offered T-roof panels on its hatchback and coupe models in 1981. If properly maintained and lubricated, the weather stripping should give perfect service, but many of these older Mustangs experience water leakage during car washes and rain.

Ford was the first company to offer the Michelin TRX tires and unique alloy wheels on one of its models. General Motors filed a complaint with the U.S. Department of Transportation in an attempt to keep the high-performance tires off the market, claiming factory workers could be injured if they tried to mount the odd-size tire on a regular wheel.

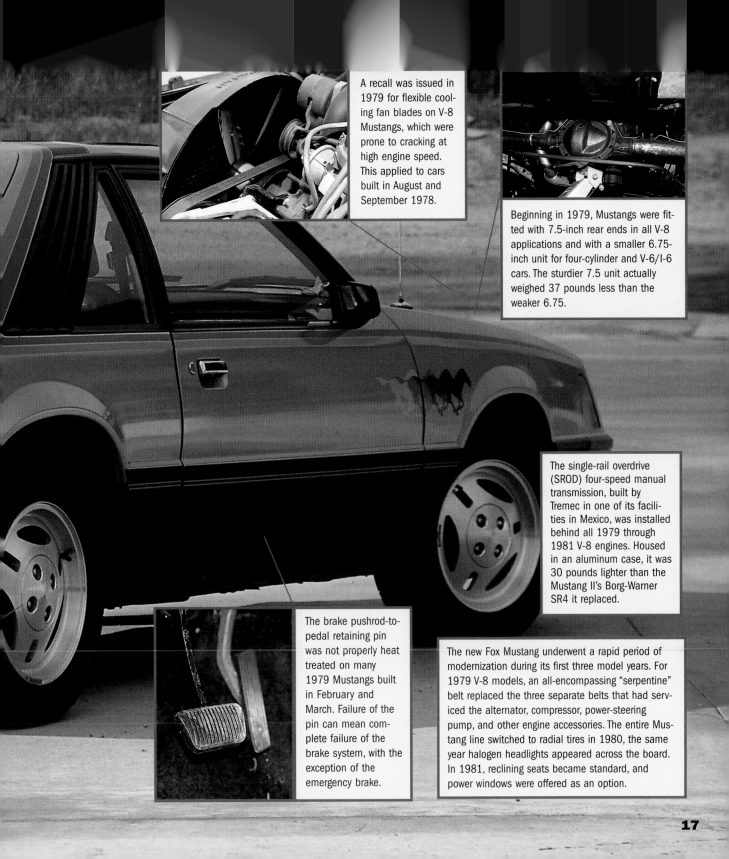

A recall was issued in 1979 for flexible cooling fan blades on V-8 Mustangs, which were prone to cracking at high engine speed. This applied to cars built in August and September 1978.

Beginning in 1979, Mustangs were fitted with 7.5-inch rear ends in all V-8 applications and with a smaller 6.75-inch unit for four-cylinder and V-6/I-6 cars. The sturdier 7.5 unit actually weighed 37 pounds less than the weaker 6.75.

The single-rail overdrive (SROD) four-speed manual transmission, built by Tremec in one of its facilities in Mexico, was installed behind all 1979 through 1981 V-8 engines. Housed in an aluminum case, it was 30 pounds lighter than the Mustang II's Borg-Warner SR4 it replaced.

The brake pushrod-to-pedal retaining pin was not properly heat treated on many 1979 Mustangs built in February and March. Failure of the pin can mean complete failure of the brake system, with the exception of the emergency brake.

The new Fox Mustang underwent a rapid period of modernization during its first three model years. For 1979 V-8 models, an all-encompassing "serpentine" belt replaced the three separate belts that had serviced the alternator, compressor, power-steering pump, and other engine accessories. The entire Mustang line switched to radial tires in 1980, the same year halogen headlights appeared across the board. In 1981, reclining seats became standard, and power windows were offered as an option.

1982 is considered to be the rebirth of Mustang performance, and it all sprang from Ford's decision to bring back the "GT" name-plate. Under the hood was a 157-horsepower version of Ford's age-old 302-cid V-8. The rest of the Mustang line could be had with a 2.3-liter four-cylinder, 3.3-liter inline-six or 4.2-liter V-8.

Chapter 2

1982 Mustang

The Fox body went into its fourth year of production with a bang thanks to the return of the 302-cid V-8 powerplant and high-performance GT model.

While it was no barnstormer, the newest iteration of the 5.0-liter ("F" code on the VIN) was an all-around stronger performer, with a new camshaft; larger capacity, dual-throat carburetor; double-roller timing chain; high-flow air cleaner; and an automatic cutoff switch for the air conditioner compressor for reduced drag at high rpm. Breathing through a Motorcraft two-barrel carburetor, it produced a healthy 157 horsepower and 240 lbs-ft of torque. Ordering the 5.0-liter mandated a 3.08:1 rear-axle ratio, SROD four-speed manual transmission, power steering, larger power front disc brakes, and a special handling package (if the TRX system was not specified).

The new 5.0 was vastly improved since its last showing in 1979. The block itself had undergone revisions and lost 15 pounds of suspension-killing fat, and the cylinder heads were treated to upgraded valves and stiffer, heat-treated springs. Cast iron exhaust manifolds don't normally spell "high-performance," but Ford tuned those on the 5.0 for maximum flow.

Base engine for all Mustangs except the GT was the 2.3-liter overhead cam four-cylinder ("A" code), rated at 87 horsepower and mated to a standard four-speed manual gearbox. The engine itself changed very little from the previous year. The three-speed automatic was still an option, as well.

Matching the four-cylinder in the horsepower department was the optional 3.3-liter inline six-cylinder ("B" code), although its greater torque made it useful for buyers who couldn't swing the cost of the 5.0 V-8 or higher insurance. The 1982 model was the last for this engine in a Mustang application.

Hanging in for one more year was the unloved 4.2-liter V-8 ("D" code), whose only selling point was a slightly better fuel efficiency than the 5.0-liter. The 4.2 was only available with a 2.73:1 rear-axle ratio and three-speed automatic.

Although the 1982 GT is most closely associated with the return of the 5.0-liter, buyers could receive a $57 credit for ordering that performance model with the low-performing 4.2. Production records suggest the idea didn't have too much appeal.

The C-4 automatic transmission became a C-5 in 1982 with the addition of a lockup torque converter and some other improvements. Standard on the six-cylinder and 4.2 V-8, the C-5 increased gas mileage and overall mechanical efficiency by eliminating the slippage that normally occurred in the torque converter's fluid coupling.

Mustang lost its 13-inch wheels in 1982, the base L model running on P175/75R14 radials and the GT making do with P185/75R14s on cast alloy wheels. Any body style or level could be ordered with the TR handling package, which continued to be based on the Michelin TRX 190/65R390 high-performance tires on alloy wheels.

Besides V-8 power, the GT also offered a Pace Car/Cobra-like front air dam with built-in driving lights, revised grille, forward-facing nonfunctional hood scoop, and kicked-up rear spoiler. The upgraded GT interior included full instrumentation, blacked-out controls and console top, and a four-spoke steering wheel. Standard lowback bucket seats could be replaced with Recaros for $834 more. A handling package that included the larger wheels and tires plus traction bars to reduce rear-suspension hop under heavy acceleration was standard with the GT. Stopping the 5.0-powered cars were 10.06-inch front disc brakes and 9.0x1.73-inch rear drums.

Its new emphasis on performance brought the 5.0-liter Mustang to the attention of the California Highway Patrol, which had been looking for a pursuit vehicle that was a match for the high-powered imports running around the West Coast. When Ford underbid its only real competitor—GM, with its Camaro—by more than $1,000 per car, it led to a lucrative relationship with law enforcement agencies all across the country that would last through the end of Fox production in 1993. These Special Service vehicles (SSV), as they came to be called, were built with many reinforced components, such as aircraft-quality hose clamps, stiffer floor pans, and stronger front-seat brackets. Otherwise, they were not substantially different from the cars Ford sold to the public. More than 15,000 SSVs were produced over the 14-year span, with most being retired through auctions with 60,000 to 100,000 miles on the odometer.

Other changes to the line for 1982 included the addition of seat belts with tension relievers, a remote-control left-hand mirror, flash-to-pass headlight switch, and a tethered gas cap. A larger gas tank was worked into the production line—up to 15.4 gallons from the previous year's 12.5.

In 1982, the Recaro Trim Package included the highback contoured seats as well as the addition of a hound's tooth pattern to other surfaces in the interior.

Although the GT's new hood scoop doesn't draw air into the engine, it serves the purpose of giving clearance for the large high-dome air cleaner.

The 1982 model year also was the first year for fresh redesigns of General Motors' Firebird and Camaro, the Mustang's fiercest competitors. Considering the Camaro only had an 8-horsepower advantage over the Mustang, the extra 400 pounds it carried made it a slug by comparison.

1982 Mustang Specifications

Base price	10/66B coupe L	$6,345
	10/66B coupe GL	$6,844
	16/61B hatchback GL	$6,979
	12/66H coupe GLX	$6,980
	13/61H hatchback GLX	$7,101
	16/61B hatchback V-8 GT	$8,308
Production	10/66B coupe	45,316
	16/61B hatchback GL (inc. GT)	69,348
	12/66H coupe GLX	5,828
	13/61H hatchback GLX	9,926
Displacement (cubic inches/liters)	I-4	140/2.3
	I-6	200/3.3
	V-8	255/4.2
	V-8	302/5.0
Bore x stroke (inches)	I-4	3.78x3.13
	I-6	3.68x3.13
	V-8 (255)	3.68x3.00
	V-8 (302)	4.00x3.00
VIN code/Compression ratio	I-4	A 9.0:1
	I-6	B 8.6:1
	V-8 (255)	D 8.2:1
	V-8 (302)	F 8.3:1
Induction	I-4	2-bbl
	I-6	1-bbl
	V-8 (255)	2-bbl
	V-8 (302)	2-bbl
Valvetrain	I-4	SOHC
	I-6	OHV
	V-8	OHV
Horsepower	I-4	86@4,400
	I-6	87@3,800
	V-8 (255)	120@3,400
	V-8 (302)	157@4,200
Transmission (std./opt.)	I-4	4-speed manual/ 3-speed auto
	I-6	3-speed auto
	V-8 (255)	C-5 3-speed auto
	V-8 (302)	SROD 4-speed
Rear-axle ratio	I-4, 4-speed	2.73:1
	I-4, 3-speed auto	3.08:1
	V-8 (225), automatic	2.73:1
	V-8 (302), 4-speed	3.08:1
Wheelbase (inches)		100.5
Overall width (inches)		67.4
Overall height (inches)		51.6
Overall length (inches)		179.1

Track (inches)		(front) 56.6
		(rear) 56.7
Fuel capacity (gallons)		15.4
Weight (pounds)	10/66B coupe L	2,511
	10/66B coupe GL	2,528
	16/61B hatchback GL	2,565
	12/66H coupe GLX	2,543
	13/61H hatchback GLX	2,579
	16/61B hatchback V-8 GT	2,629
Tires	(base)	P175/75R14
	(V-8)	P185/75R14
	(optional) Michelin TRX	190/65R390
Front suspension		modified MacPherson struts, coil springs
Rear suspension		live axle, four-link suspension system
Steering		20.03:1 to 16.05:1 variable ratio rack and pinion
Brakes	I-4, I-6, V-8 (255)	(front) 9.31-inch disc
	V-8 (302)	(front) 10.06-inch vented disc
	all models	(rear) 9-inch drum
Gas mileage (EPA est.)	I-4 4-speed manual	22
	I-4 5-speed manual	21
	I-4 3-speed auto	21
	I-6 3-speed auto	20
	V-8 (255) 3-speed auto	19
	V-8 (302) 4-speed manual	17
0 to 60 (secs)	(GT, 302/4-speed, 3.08:1 axle)*	8
Standing ¼-mile (mph/secs)	(GT, 302/4-speed, 3.08:1 axle)	84@16.3
Top speed (mph)	(GT, 302/4-speed, 3.08:1 axle)	118

* *Road & Track* June 1982

1982 Mustang

Major Options

3.3-liter I-6		$213
4.2-liter V-8		$263
	(w/GT, credit)	$57
5.0-liter V-8		$452
	(w/TR performance package)	$402
Transmission, 5-speed		$196
Transmission, 3-speed auto		$411
Differential, Traction-Lok		$76
Optional axle ratio	no	charge
Brakes, power		$93
Steering, power		$190
Appearance protection group		$48
Power lock group		$139
TRX performance suspension package		$533–$583
	(GT)	$105
Handling suspension		$50
Battery, heavy-duty		$24
Emissions, California		$46
Emissions, high altitude	no	charge
Air conditioning		$676
AM/FM radio		$76
AM/FM stereo radio		$106
	(w/8-track or cassette player)	$184
Premium sound system		$105
Dual rear speakers		$39
AM radio delete	(credit)	$61
Rear defroster, electric		$124
Fingertip speed control		$155
Power windows		$165
Leather-wrapped steering wheel		$55
Tilt steering wheel		$95
Interval wipers		$48
Rear wiper/washer		$101
Trunk light		$7
Remote right mirror		$41
T-roof		$1,021
Flip-up open-air roof		$276
Hood scoop		$38
Hatchback louvers		$165
Console		$191
Recaro highback bucket seats		$834
Cargo area cover		$51
Front floor mats, carpeted		$22
Wheels, cast aluminum		$348–$398
Wheels, styled steel w/trim rings		$72–$122

Replacement Costs for Common Parts

Steering wheel	$100 core charge	$270
Hood scoop grille		$33
Ford emblem	rear hatch	$8
Rearview mirror		$43
Ignition coil		$60
Fuel pump		$30
Alternator		$60
Fan shroud	repro	$80
Console coin tray		$37
Arm rest pad		$65
A/C vent registers		$20
Dash pads	repro	$190
Side marker		$13
Headlight retaining ring		$40
Marchal fog lamp lens		$110
Front-brake rotor		$40
Master cylinder	remanufactured	$30
Oil pressure sending unit		$20
Front fender	repro	$85
Front fender	original	$280
Starter		$60
Front seat belt buckle		$47
Outside door handle kit		$27
Electric window motor		$70
Window crank handle		$10
Inside door handle bezel		$23
Door lock actuator kit		$90
Lock cylinder and key		$25
Hatchback quarter window molding pair		$100
Hatch weather stripping		$27
Trunk weather stripping		$23
Sunroof weather stripping kit		$150
Door weather stripping kit		$40
Vacuum canister		$25
Antenna kit	black	$37
Antenna kit	stainless	$23
Antenna rod		$14
Rubber fender-to-hood bumpers		$2
Hood latch assembly		$25
Wiper arm and blade kit		$40
Wiper arm		$15
Windshield washer nozzle		$9
Trunk lid		$170
Floor pan		$115

Smog pump		$60		Front lower control arms	pair	$200
Crankshaft pulley		$70		Pushrods	set of 16	$40
Water pump pulley		$45		Harmonic balancer		$80
Distributor cover		$10		Radiator cap	16-pound	$6
Smog canister		$65			13-pound	$9
Heater core	A/C	$30		Thermostat	180-degree	$16
	exc. A/C	$35			195-degree	$7
Radiator bracket	left	$30		Fuel cap		$20
	right	$60				
Radiator		$110				
Rear-brake drum		$35				
Power steering pump		$100				

What They Said in 1982

After its introduction in 1979, the redesigned Mustang won the *Car and Driver* Readers' Choice Poll Award. The *C/D* staff called it the second-best-handling American car, behind the Pontiac Trans Am. When all is said and done, the Mustang is still a good car, but it deserves an ongoing refinement to keep it fresh. —*Car and Driver,* July 1981

The Mustang is hardly a one-dimensional quarter-mile specialist, but it clearly lacks the chassis to compete with either Porsche's finest or the latest science from GM. What the Mustang does enjoy deep within its four-year-old Fairmont-derived underpinnings is an ideal basic size. It's 10 inches shorter, 3 inches narrower, and a hefty 400 pounds lighter than the new GM kids on the block; as a result, it feels nimble and eager to get the job done. The body's comparatively blunt shape doesn't benefit from the recent intense aerodynamic-drag efforts, but there is a compensating benefit: the less-sleek Mustang offers the only real backseat in the test and the roomiest luggage compartment. —*Car and Driver,* August 1982

I Bought a 1982 Mustang

When I was finishing college in 1982, I wanted to buy a new Mazda RX-7 or Nissan Z-car but needed something with more room for passengers and luggage. I also thought it might be more fun to have an American musclecar, so I test-drove both the redesigned Camaro and Mustang GT. The Camaro felt a little faster than the Mustang, but really lost points with me when it came to the layout of the interior. I also did not like the deep well situated behind the Chevy's rear axle. Mustang, on the other hand, did everything right. The 5.0-liter had a good amount of grunt to it, although by today's standards, 157 horsepower is pretty weak. The four-speed manual transmission could be shifted quickly enough to get the pony down the road in a spirited fashion. —*David Hood*

1982 Mustang Ratings

Base Four-Cylinder

Model Comfort/Amenities	**
Reliability	***
Collectibility	*
Parts/Service Availability	***
Est. Annual Repair Costs	**

3.3-Liter I-6

Model Comfort/Amenities	***
Reliability	***
Collectibility	***
Parts/Service Availability	*****
Est. Annual Repair Costs	*

4.2-Liter V-8

Model Comfort/Amenities	***
Reliability	**
Collectibility	*
Parts/Service Availability	**
Est. Annual Repair Costs	*

5.0-Liter V-8

Model Comfort/Amenities	***
Reliability	****
Collectibility	****
Parts/Service Availability	****
Est. Annual Repair Costs	***

From a collector's standpoint, the most desirable of the 1982 Mustang line is a GT with T-tops. This was by far the coolest car on the road when it was new, and the GT is ground zero for the Fox-body late-model explosion. If performance is a priority, though, later 5.0 LX cars, especially 1987–1993 models, are vastly more powerful and offer better handling. Finding a pampered 1982 GT is extremely rare, but they do show up from time to time. The four- and six-cylinder cars make good daily drivers, but most offered for sale have suffered from 20 years of abuse and neglect.

1982 Mustang Garage Watch

As part of its new image, the Mustang's engine compartment was tidied up. Ford began painting all engines gray in 1982 and also started to pay more attention to the cosmetic appeal of the valve covers (V-8s got ribbed ones with "Powered by Ford" inscribed), wiring, hose routing, clamps, and air cleaner.

The last two-barrel carburetor in a performance Mustang application was the Motorcraft 2150A that fed the 5.0-liter V-8 in 1982. At a flow rate of 368.5 cubic feet per minute, it wasn't exactly stingy. Two-barrel versions of Ford's 429-cid V-8 used the same size carburetor.

Early Fox Mustangs with V-8s were notorious for creating wheel hop under hard acceleration. In 1982, Ford reverted to an old drag racer trick and began installing "slapper" bars on its GT and other V-8 models.

The TRX wheels and tires were on the cutting edge of performance when they were new, but locating—and paying for—the odd-size tires led many Mustang owners to swap for more conventional rubber and rims. That's why complete sets of the TRX wheels often show up at swap meets with very low prices.

The 5.0-liter V-8 was fitted with a seven-blade steel cooling fan mounted to a declutching drive hub. Some earlier 4.2-liter V-8s ordered with air conditioning also feature this setup. The steel fan replaced the plastic unit used between 1979 and 1981, which had a tendency to self-destruct under high-stress conditions.

Because of higher air quality standards in the state of California, Ford closed its San Jose plant after model year 1981. For the first time since its introduction, all 1982 Mustangs were produced at the Dearborn, Michigan, plant.

1982 marked the final year for factory hatchback louvers. This $165 option was a practical way to keep direct sunlight away from the Mustang's interior; it also was a nostalgic throwback to the Boss 302.

The Marchal driving lights that came standard on the '82 and later GTs were introduced on the 1979 Pace Car replicas. If left on long enough, most of these lights will eventually experience a switch or connection failure as the circuitry gets hot. Ford issued a technical service bulletin—number 89-17-11—explaining how to alleviate the problem.

Ford followed the GT introduction in 1983 with a convertible Mustang – the company's first such offering since 1973. Other innovations that made enthusiasts take notice included a new Borg-Warner five-speed manual transmission and an increase to 175 horsepower for the 5.0-liter V-8.

Chapter 3

1983 Mustang

The year 1983 should have given Ford reason to celebrate, with the introduction of a Fox-body convertible, the return of its new-and-improved Turbo engine, and the hottest perform-ance Mustang in more than a decade, but an industry-wide slump in new car sales limited pony production to a historic low of 120,873 units.

Base engine for all Mustangs except the convertible and GT was the 2.3-liter overhead cam four-cylinder ("A" code on VIN), rated at 90 horsepower and mated to a standard four-speed manual gearbox, optional five-speed, or automatic transmission.

In the middle of the production year, Ford attempted again to lead the way into a turbocharged future by introducing a much-improved version of its blown 2.3-liter four-cylinder ("T" code). Available only with the V-8's T-5 five-speed manual trans-mission, the 145-horsepower engine was the centerpiece of the Turbo GT hatchback. Redesigning the turbocharger for quicker response times, adding electronic fuel injection (aka EFI, its first appearance on any Mustang model), and lowering the com-pression ratio to 8.0:1 from 9.1:1 only added 5 horsepower, but with much more reliability and flexibility.

Along with EFI, this high-tech powerplant debuted something that would become a mainstay of the later Fox V-8 cars—Ford's fourth-generation electronic engine control system (EEC-IV).

Somehow, the public did not warm to the Turbo, which cost $250 more than the GT, performed slightly slower in all performance tests than the V-8, and was not available with air conditioning.

A step up the displacement ladder gave the Mustang buyer Ford's new 3.8-liter V-6 ("3" code), which benefited from light, cooler aluminum heads. The V-6 powertrain, standard equipment with the new convertible, was mated exclusively to a three-speed automatic transmission.

Adding a 600-cfm Holley carburetor to the previous year's 5.0-liter V-8 ("F" code) bumped output to 175 horse-power. Under the hood, the most obvious difference between the 1982 and 1983 5.0s was the larger (17-inch) diameter air cleaner housing with dual-snorkel intake hoses. For the first time, in 1983 the V-8 Mustang came standard with the Traction-Lok rear axle, which had been an option in 1980 and 1981. The 5.0-liter, which was only available with the T-5 five-speed transmission, could be ordered with any Mustang model except the base L.

Cars and Concepts was the Michigan-based conver-sion company that turned unfinished Mustang coupes into convertibles, answering the market's request for a good domestic droptop. The rear window was a high-quality glass pane that could be unzipped to lay flat and provide extra air circulation with the top up. Rear quarter windows on the convertibles could be raised or lowered, unlike with the coupe and hatchback bodies.

The new convertible came standard with the 3.8-liter V-6 (in GLX form) but could be upgraded to V-8 power. Later in the year, 1001 GTs were built in this new body style, featuring a long line of standard features, including power windows, AM/FM cassette stereo, air conditioning, and TRX suspension package.

To complement its more powerful engines, the 1983 Mustangs received wider tires with lower profiles. Gone were 1982's "big" P185/75R14s and Michelin P190/65HR390s; in their place were P205/70HR14 and P220/55VR390 tires mounted on 14x5.5-inch alloy wheels.

A good deal of cosmetic cleanup went into the 1983's appearance, which reduced drag by 2.5 percent over the 1979 model, its smoother nose and cleaner hood lines the result of time spent in the wind tunnel. The rear of the car received a subtle taillight design that made the turn signals amber and dedicated.

Interiors were largely carried over from the previous year, but the instrument panel was revised to include an up-shift indicator (manual transmission models only, similar to a device installed on Porsches and Volkswagens) and red background lighting. Recaro seats were no longer an option, but Ford's Sport Performance buckets became a popular add-on with GT buyers. The retractable rear-cargo cover, first introduced as an option in 1980, became standard with all Mustangs in 1983.

The GT was fitted with a non-functional hood scoop for the final year of Fox production (although some early 1984s were built with it), which was basically the 1982 scoop turned 180 degrees. Other GT cosmetic features included a blacked-out grille, window and door frames, and hood panel.

Sometime during the production year, Ford phased out its 20.03:1-16.05:1 variable-ratio rack and pinion steering for one with a constant rate of 15:1. This change and the upgrade in tire sizes greatly improved the Mustang's seat-of-the-pants driving impression, although the .75g and .76g skidpad numbers obtained through performance magazine tests at the time would be considered pretty weak by today's standards.

While not yet part of a true dual-exhaust system, the 1983 Mustang 5.0 muffler was the first of the Fox models to feature a muffler inline with the chassis, as opposed to the earlier transverse component. This straighter routing for exhaust proved less restrictive.

The new convertible required this hose for drainage, otherwise, rain would pool in the bottom of the top well. It exited under the passenger-side rear-quarter.

Many of Mustang's competitors in the convertible market—Chrysler's K-Car, for example—did not come with rear windows. The Mustang's back glass could manually be rolled up and down in 1983.

1983 Mustang Specifications

Base price	66B coupe L	$6,727
	66B coupe GL	$7,264
	61B hatchback GL	$7,439
	66B coupe GLX	$7,398
	61B hatchback GLX	$7,557
	66B V-6 convertible GLX	$9,449
	61B V-8 hatchback GT	$9,328
	66B V-8 convertible GT	$13,479
	61B Turbo hatchback GT	$9,714
Production	66B coupe	33,201
	66B convertible	23,438
	61B hatchback	64,234
Displacement (cubic inches/liters)	I-4	140/2.3
	V-6	232/3.8
	V-8	302/5.0
Bore x stroke (inches)	I-4	3.78x3.13
	V-6	3.80x3.40
	V-8	4.00x3.00
VIN code/Compression ratio	I-4	A 9.0:1
	I-4 Turbo	T 8.0:1
	V-6	3 8.7:1
	V-8	F 8.3:1
Induction	I-4	1-bbl
	I-4 Turbo	EFI
	V-6	2-bbl
	V-8	4-bbl
Valvetrain	I-4	SOHC
	V-6	OHV
	V-8	OHV
Horsepower	I-4	90@4,600
	I-4 Turbo	145@5,000
	V-6	105@4,000
	V-8	175@4,000
Transmission (std./opt.)	I-4	4-speed manual/5-speed manual/3-speed auto
	I-4 Turbo	5-speed manual
	V-6	3-speed auto
	V-8 (early)	SROD 4-speed manual
	V-8 (late)	T-5 5-speed manual
Rear-axle ratio	I-4, 4-speed	2.73:1
	I-4 and Turbo, 5-speed	3.45:1
	I-4, 3-speed auto	3.08:1
	V-8, 4-speed	3.08:1
	V-8, 5-speed	3.27:1

Wheelbase (inches)		100.5
Overall width (inches)		67.4
Overall height (inches)		51.6
Overall length (inches)		179.1
Track (inches)		(front) 56.6
		(rear) 56.7
Fuel capacity (gallons)		15.4
Weight (pounds)	66B coupe L	2,532
	66B coupe GL	2,549
	61B hatchback GL	2,584
	66B coupe GLX	2,552
	61B hatchback GLX	2,587
	66B V-6 convertible GLX	2,795
	61B V-8 hatchback GT	2,891
	66B V-8 convertible GT	N/A
	61B Turbo hatchback GT	N/A
Tires	(base)	P185/75R14
	(V-8, GT standard)	P205/70R14
	(V-8, GT TRX option)	P220/55R390
Front suspension		modified MacPherson struts, coil springs
Rear suspension		live axle, four-link suspension system
Steering	(base, early V-8)	20.03:1 to 16.05:1 variable ratio rack and pinion
	(late)	15:1 constant ratio rack and pinion
Brakes	I-4, V-6 (front)	9.31-inch disc
	V-8 (front)	10.06-inch vented disc
	all models (rear)	9.0-inch drum
Gas mileage (EPA est.)	I-4 5-speed manual	22
	I-4 3-speed auto	21
	I-4 Turbo, 5-speed manual	22
	V-6 3-speed auto	20
	V-8 4-speed manual	16
	V-8 5-speed manual	16
0 to 60 (secs)	(GT, 302/5-speed, 3.27:1 axle)*	8.2
Standing ¼ mile (mph/secs)	(GT, 302/5-speed, 3.27:1 axle)	90@15.4
Top speed (mph)	(GT, 302/5-speed, 3.27:1 axle)	125

* *Car and Driver* June 1983

1983 Mustang

Major Options

3.8-liter V-6		$309
5.0-liter V-8	(all non-GT models)	$1,467
	(GLX convertible)	$719
Transmission, 5-speed manual		$124
Transmission, automatic		$439
Differential, Traction-Lok		$95
Brakes, power		$93
Steering, power		$202
Windows, power		$180
Handling suspension		$252
Battery, heavy-duty		$26
Emissions, California		$76
Emissions, high-altitude		no charge
Sport Performance package		$196
Light group		$55
Appearance protection group		$60
Power lock group		$160
Air conditioning		$724
Rear defroster, electric		$135
Fingertip speed control		$170
Tinted glass		$105
	(windshield only)	$38
Steering wheel, leather-wrapped		$59
Steering wheel, tilt		$105
Interval wipers		$49
Remote right mirror		$44
AM/FM radio		$82
AM/FM stereo radio		$109
	(w/8-track or cassette player)	$199
Premium sound system		$117
AM radio delete		(credit) $61
T-roof		$1,055
Flip-up open-air roof		$3–10
Console		$191
Cloth/vinyl seats		$29–$57
Leather lowback bucket seats		$415
Front floor mats, carpeted		$22
Wheel covers, wire		$98–$148
Wheel covers, turbine		no charge
Wheels, cast aluminum		$354–$404
Wheels, styled steel w/trim rings		$78

Replacement Costs for Common Parts

Rearview mirror		$43
Power rack and pinion steering	19:1 ratio	$200
Ignition coil		$60
Fuel pump		$30
Fan shroud	repro	$80
Console coin tray		$37
Arm rest pad		$65
A/C vent registers		$20
Dash pads	repro	$190
Side marker		$13
Headlight retaining ring		$40
Marchal fog lamp lens		$110
Front-brake rotor		$40
Master cylinder	remanufactured	$30
Oil pressure sending unit		$20
Front fender	repro	$85
Front fender	original	$280
Starter		$60
Front seat belt buckle		$47
Outside door handle kit		$27
Electric window motor		$70
Window crank handle		$10
Inside door handle bezel		$23
Door lock actuator kit		$90
Lock cylinder and key		$25
Hatchback quarter window molding	pair	$100
Hatch weather stripping		$27
Trunk weather stripping		$23
Sunroof weather stripping kit		$150
Door weather stripping kit		$40
Vacuum canister		$25
Antenna kit	black	$37
Antenna kit	stainless	$23
Antenna rod		$14
Rubber fender-to-hood bumpers		$2
Hood latch assembly		$25
Wiper arm and blade kit		$40
Wiper arm		$15
Windshield washer nozzle		$9
Trunk lid	convertible and coupe	$170
Floor pan		$115
Smog pump		$60
Crankshaft pulley		$70
Water pump pulley	V-8	$45

Distributor cover		$10
Smog canister		$65
Heater core	A/C	$30
	exc. A/C	$35
Radiator bracket	left	$30
	right	$60
Radiator		$110
Rear-brake drum		$35
Power steering pump		$100
Front lower control arms	pair	$200
Pushrods	set of 16	$40
Harmonic balancer		$80
Radiator cap	16-pound	$6
	13-pound	$9
Thermostat	180-degree	$16
	195-degree	$7
Fuel cap		$20
Rear-wheel cylinder		$40
Temperature sending unit		$8
Fuel tank		$130
Four-piece T-top weather stripping kit		$230
Air cleaner inlet tube		$25

Clutch fork		$25
Steering wheel	$100 core charge	$270
Hood scoop grille		$55
Front-bumper cover	repro	$170
Taillamp lens		$110
Hood	repro	$170
Fuel tank sending unit		$90
Tilt wheel lever		$6
Radiator core support		$180
Convertible top boot		$80
Convertible glass rear window		$125
Convertible top		$150
Convertible top headliner		$135
Convertible sun visor	pair	$50
Convertible top motor		$200
Front inner splash shield		$90
Air check valve		$50
Motor mount	convertible	$47
Coolant temperature sensor		$30
Ignition coil		

What They Said in 1983

The most interesting thing about Ford's convertible is that it's a Mustang. Not a K-car, not a Riviera, not a J-car, but a Mustang, a car that's meant to be a driver's car. As Ford sees it, luxury convertibles like the LeBaron and Riviera miss the point of the topless phenomenon. . . . The Mustang convertible is a lot more than a nice car that we'll be able to drive in 1983. It's an indication of Ford's commitment to specialty cars in relatively small volumes. And that means a lot more drivers' cars like the Mustang convertible to come. —*Car and Driver, July 1982*

I Bought a 1983 Mustang

I was looking for a 1983 convertible to add to my collection of late-model Mustangs when I came across a GLX with the mid-year Borg-Warner five-speed manual transmission. Even though I don't intend to drive the car because of its near-zero mileage, I wanted the five-speed rather than the earlier four-speed or automatic. Because it's a GLX, mine has the plush carpet, power equipment and Premium Sound. The car's original owner was a boat dealer who used to buy Corvettes and store them away for the future. I sort of wish he had sprung for the TRX wheels. I guess he was a Chevy guy, though, and didn't really know the Ford language. —*Daniel Carpenter*

My husband, Tom, who got into late-model Mustangs in a big way around 1987, heard about a very clean, well-kept 1983 GLX convertible on an Air Force base that was being sold at a real bargain price. The red paint was a little faded, but the white top and interior were perfect. He checked it out and couldn't believe what great condition the four-year-old car was in. Tom bought it and gave it to me for our anniversary that year. Steve Johnson coated it with fresh Ford Red paint for us, including many of the trim pieces that had come from the factory in black or gray, then applied a body-length white pinstripe. Off came the TRX wheels and tires in exchange for a set of 15x6.5 Sendel five-spoke wheels and Kelly radials. The stock 5.0-liter ran great, but Tom beefed it up a bit with some 1985 headers, off-road stainless steel exhaust system with H-pipe, re-jetted carburetor, and Walker turbo mufflers. We kept the five-speed and 3.08:1 rear axle unmodified. Not only was it a great driver, but it eventually took a first-place trophy at a Mustang Club of America Grand National. —*Vicki Bader*

1983 Mustang Ratings

Base Four-Cylinder

Model Comfort/Amenities	**
Reliability	***
Collectibility	*
Parts/Service Availability	***
Est. Annual Repair Costs	***

Turbo Four-Cylinder

Model Comfort/Amenities	**
Reliability	***
Collectibility	*
Parts/Service Availability	**
Est. Annual Repair Costs	**

3.8-Liter V-6

Model Comfort/Amenities	***
Reliability	**
Collectibility	*
Parts/Service Availability	***
Est. Annual Repair Costs	***

5.0-Liter V-8

Model Comfort/Amenities	***
Reliability	****
Collectibility	****
Parts/Service Availability	****
Est. Annual Repair Costs	***

Once again, the 5.0 GT trumps everything else in the Mustang family for modern collectibility, especially in the new convertible body style. Although Ford had better engineering behind the re-introduced turbocharged four-cylinder, including its first-ever electronic fuel injection, very few Turbo models were ordered in 1983, and they haven't sparked collector interest yet. For daily driving, all but the base four-cylinder had adequate power and plenty of creature comforts.

A happy marriage of engine and transmission took place midyear 1983 when the 5.0-liter V-8 was first matched to a Borg-Warner T-5 five-speed manual transmission. Originally designed for low-torque four-cylinder applications, the 5.0-liter version featured improved metallurgy in its gears and other components to handle the V-8's output.

Ford revised its engine mounts twice during the Fox Mustang's production, with 1983 V-8 cars having a build date after April 18 receiving a re-designed engine mount appropriate to the 5.0's new power output.

Although attractive when new, the GT's blackout hood treatment quickly faded with exposure to sunlight and the elements. Other than keeping the car covered, nothing can be done to prevent this oxidation. Some owners have mistakenly applied wax over the decal, which ruins it.

Extensive bracing went into the new-for-1983 convertible's chassis, including stiffer floor pans, bars to connect the subframes, and reinforcement plates under the door sills. Some of the chassis stiffening was installed on the Ford assembly line, and Cars and Concepts applied the rest.

When the Fox Mustang chassis was designed in the mid-1970s, there was little hope it would become a performance machine with competition suspensions and torquey V-8s. Floor pans, especially, suffered with the increase in power, most notably in 1983, before Ford re-designed those components for more stiffness. The aftermarket offers many systems to reinforce all years of Fox chassis.

Due to its large hatch area, the hatchback body was the flimsiest of the Fox chassis. Early cars that were driven hard experienced stress cracks in the C-pillar. For this reason, anyone hoping to modify a 1979 through 1993 Mustang for track performance should consider starting with the stiffer coupe.

The "L" on the bottom row of the 1983 rear axle tag indicates a Traction-Lok differential. All 1983s were so equipped, and this produces smoother takeoff under hard acceleration or slippery conditions.

37

Ford commemorated the Mustang's 20th anniversary in 1984 with 5,260 Oxford White convertibles and hatchbacks decked out in faux Shelby stripes. Although based on the GT package, the "G.T. 350" was available with either 5.0-liter V-8 or turbo-four power.

Chapter 4

1984 Mustang

The top of the pony car food chain was the carryover 5.0-liter V-8 ("M" code on the VIN), which continued to churn out 175 horsepower with the help of its Holley four-barrel carburetor. This highest-output version of the 5.0 was available only with the T-5 five-speed manual transmission.

New for 1984 was a fuel-injected version of the 5.0 ("F" code), which could only be mated to the freshly introduced AOD four-speed automatic transmission. With 165 horsepower, its output was down from the manual transmission model, but the standard 3.27:1 rear-axle ratio (compared to the other engine's 3.08:1) made it seem just as powerful. Ford's fourth-generation electronic engine control management system (EEC-IV) made its V-8 debut on this powerplant, but it would become standard equipment on the 1987 Mustang line. Induction was not by way of a true fuel injection system. Instead, the central fuel injection (CFI), also known as Throttle Body Injection (TBI), was located atop the intake manifold, like a carburetor.

This TBI system was also shared with the 3.8-liter V-6 ("3" code), which was otherwise carried over unchanged from 1983. The 3.8 was only available with an automatic transmission. This combination was the standard powertrain for the Mustang convertible. Horsepower for the V-6 was rated at 120.

The standard engine for all other non-GT, non-convertible models was the 2.3-liter inline four-cylinder ("A" code), which had essentially been the "economy" powerplant since its introduction on the 1974 Mustang II. Still no spitfire, it was rated at 88 horsepower and came with a four-speed manual transmission, five-speed, or automatic.

Ford was obviously committed to the idea of small-displacement turbocharged engines, as 1984's Mustang lineup featured two very different forced-air powerplants. The T-code 2.3-liter four-cylinder turned a regular hatchback or, later in the year, convertible into a Turbo GT, a package that brought with it a five-speed manual gearbox and all the other GT equipment and identification. This 145-horsepower engine cost more than its V-8 GT counterpart but had less-impressive performance numbers. For the fourth time in six years, customers voted with their order forms to dump the expensive option, and Ford finally listened. With only 3,798 T-code packages sold in 1984, it was discontinued.

Gaining much more notoriety and acceptance among enthusiasts was the W-code version of the 2.3-liter, the heart and soul of Ford's high-tech, European-leaning SVO. The SVO's three-year run is detailed in chapter 5.

Ford doled out several running changes around midyear, most of which were part of a proposed Improved Performance 5-Liter package that never completely made it out of Dearborn. The centerpiece of the package would have been a 205-horsepower 5.0-liter V-8, but engineers questioned the durability of the piston design and operating noise levels, postponing the engine's debut. Ford repositioned the accelerator and brake pedals to give more enthusiastic drivers greater agility. A heavy-duty actuating cable was introduced to the clutch mechanism for improved reliability and smoother shifts.

Perhaps the most beneficial equipment upgrade for buyers was the Quadra-Shock rear-suspension system, which took the place of the drag-style ladder bars to reduce wheel hop under hard acceleration. Other suspension improvements included gas-pressurized struts, more sophisticated upper strut mounts, variable-rate coil springs, and a larger rear stabilizer bar. Control-arm pivot points were also lowered for a better suspension and steering geometry.

Midyear also saw the introduction of a special equipment and appearance package inspired by the 1965 and 1970 GT-350. Created to commemorate the Mustang's 20th anniversary, the package was available with all GT and Turbo GT equipment, powertrains, and platforms—the major difference being the Oxford White exterior (featuring GT-350 stripes), Canyon Red interior (with articulated sport seats), and a serial-numbered console plaque. In all, 5,260 anniversary cars were produced, only 454 of which were powered by the turbo engine.

Model designations were simplified for 1984. The base, stripper Mustang was the L, which came with the normally aspirated 2.3-liter and four-speed manual transmission, and was available only as a coupe or hatchback. The new LX could be had stripped, loaded, or anything in between, including V-8 power and convertible body style, if so desired. The GT came with V-8 or Turbo Four power, and a list of performance upgrades such as the handling suspension, V-rated or Michelin TRX tires, black hood panel, and fog lights (late 1984).

Just making a blip on the enthusiast radar in 1984 was a small shop in California that turned out three enhanced-performance Mustangs named for its designer, Steve Saleen. Modifications to the trio of V-8 hatchbacks included a Racecraft suspension system (specific-rate front and rear springs, Bilstein pressurized struts and shocks, a front G-load brace, and urethane swaybar bushings), 215/60R15 Goodyear Eagle GTs on Hayashi basket-weave wheels, and several Saleen-specific exterior and interior modifications. Ford approved these changes and allowed its franchised dealership network to sell the cars, with each vehicle individually numbered by Saleen.

Contrary to popular opinion, Saleen V-8 engines were identical to those found in Ford's regular GT and LX Mustangs from 1984 through 1989. This 1984 hatchback is the first of the three Steve Saleen built in his company's first year.

The year 1984 proved confusing to follow for Mustangers, because there were so many running changes implemented. The new Quadra-Shock rear suspension system was not even mentioned in early 1984 sales literature, but the equipment took the place of the earlier traction bars on V-8 cars in December 1983.

A rounder rear spoiler for the GT was part of the 1984½ Improved Performance program from Ford. Because of their production dates, all 20th Anniversary Mustangs received the upgrades.

1984 Mustang Specifications

Base price	66B coupe L	$7,098
	61B hatchback L	$7,269
	66B coupe LX	$7,290
	61B hatchback LX	$7,496
	66B convertible V-6 LX	$11,849
	61B hatchback GT	$9,762
	66B convertible GT	$13,245
Production	66B coupe	37,680
	66B convertible	17,600
	61B hatchback	86,200
Displacement (cubic inches/liters)		
	I-4	140/2.3
	V-6	232/3.8
	V-8	302/5.0
Bore x stroke (inches)	I-4	3.78x3.13
	V-6	3.80x3.40
	V-8	4.00x3.00
VIN code/Compression ratioI-4		A 9.0:1
	I-4 Turbo GT	T 8.0:1
	V-6	3 8.7:1
	V-8 (AOD)	F 8.3:1
	V-8	M 8.3:1
Induction	I-4	1-bbl
	I-4 Turbo	EFI
	V-6	CFI
	V-8 (AOD)	CFI
	V-8	4-bbl
Valvetrain	I-4	SOHC
	V-6	OHV
	V-8	OHV
Horsepower	I-4	88@4,000
	I-4 Turbo GT	145@4,600
	V-6	120@3,600
	V-8 (AOD)	165@3,800
	V-8	175@4,000
Transmission (std./opt.)	I-4	4-speed/5-speed/3-speed auto
	I-4 Turbo	5-speed manual
	V-6	3-speed auto
	V-8 (CFI)	AOD 4-speed auto
	V-8 (4-bbl)	T-5 5-speed manual
Rear-axle ratio	I-4, 4-speed	2.73:1
	I-4 Turbo, 5-speed	3.45:1
	I-4, 3-speed	3.08:1
	V-8, 4-speed AOD	3.27:1
	V-8, 5-speed	3.08:1
Wheelbase (inches)		100.5

Overall width (inches)		67.4
Overall height (inches)		51.6
Overall length (inches)		179.1
Track (inches)		(front) 56.6
		(rear) 56.7
Fuel capacity (gallons)		15.4
Weight (pounds)	66B coupe L	2,538
	61B hatchback L	2,584
	66B coupe LX	2,559
	61B hatchback LX	2,605
	66B convertible V-6 LX	2,873
	61B hatchback GT	2,753
	66B convertible GT	2,921
Tires	(base)	P185/75R14
	(V-8, GT standard)	P205/70R14
	(V-8, GT TRX option)	P220/55R390
Front suspension		modified MacPherson struts, coil springs
Rear suspension		live axle, four-link suspension system, Quadra-Shock (late)
Steering	(base)	20.0:1 to 15.97:1 variable ratio rack and pinion
	(V-8)	15:1 constant ratio rack and pinion
Brakes	I-4, V-6	(front) 9.31-inch disc
	V-8	(front) 10.06-inch vented disc
	all models	(rear) 9.0-inch drum
Gas mileage (EPA est.)	I-4 4-speed manual	24
	I-4 3-speed auto	23
	I-4 Turbo, 5-speed manual	21
	V-6 3-speed auto	21
	V-8 4-speed AOD	16
	V-8 5-speed manual	16
0 to 60 (secs)	(GT, 302/5-speed, 3.27:1 axle)**	6.86
Standing ¼-mile (mph/secs)	(GT, 302/5-speed, 3.27:1 axle)	91.8@15.33
Top speed (mph)	(GT, 302/5-speed, 3.27:1 axle)	129.6

* See chapter 5 for SVO specifications.
** *Motor Trend*, August 1984

1984 Mustang

Major Options

3.8-liter V-6	$409
5.0-liter V-8 package	$1,574
(LX convertible)	$727
Transmission, 5-speed manual	no charge
Transmission, 3-speed automatic	$439
Transmission, 4-speed AOD	$551
Differential, Traction-Lok	$95
Optional axle ratio	no charge
SVO competition package (delete air, power locks/windows, AM/FM/cassette)	credit $1,253
VIP package, L/LX with AM/FM stereo or tilt wheel	$93
(both)	$196
VIP package, GT	$110
VIP package, 20th Anniversary	$25–$144
Brakes, power	$93
Steering, power	$202
Handling suspension	$252
(w/VIP package)	$50
Battery, heavy-duty	$27
Emissions, California	$99
Emissions, high-altitude	no charge
Power lock group	$177
Air conditioning	$743
Rear defroster, electric	$140
Fingertip speed control	$176
Power windows	$198
Tinted glass	$110
Tilt steering wheel	$110
AM/FM stereo radio	$109
(w/cassette player)	$222
(SVO or w/VIP package)	$113
Premium sound system	$151
AM radio delete	credit $39
T-roof	$1,074
(w/VIP package)	$760
Flip-up open-air roof	$315
Console	$191
Seats, articulated sport	$196
Seats, highback bucket vinyl (L)	$29
(lowback, LX/GT)	$29
Seats, leather bucket	$189
Front floor mats, carpeted	$22
Wire wheel covers	$98
Wheels, cast aluminum	$354
Wheels, styled steel with trim rings	$78
Tires, TRX P220/55R390 BSW	$327–$551
(GT)	credit $27

Replacement Costs for Common Parts

Power rack and pinion steering	19:1 ratio	$200
Ignition coil		$60
Fuel pump	exc. EFI	$30
Alternator		$60
Fan shroud	repro	$80
Console coin tray		$37
Arm rest pad		$65
A/C vent registers		$20
Dash pads	repro	$190
Side marker		$13
Headlight retaining ring	exc. SVO	$40
Marchal fog lamp lens		$110
Front-brake rotor		$40
Master cylinder	remanufactured	$30
Oil pressure sending unit		$20
Front fender	repro	$85
Front fender	original	$280
Starter		$60
Front seat belt buckle		$47
Outside door handle kit		$27
Electric window motor		$70
Window crank handle		$10
Inside door handle bezel		$23
Door lock actuator kit		$90
Lock cylinder and key		$25
Hatchback quarter window molding pair		$100
Hatch weather stripping		$27
Trunk weather stripping		$23
Sunroof weather stripping kit		$150
Door weather stripping kit		$40
Vacuum canister		$25
Antenna kit	black	$37
Antenna kit	stainless	$23
Antenna rod		$14
Rubber fender-to-hood bumpers		$2
Hood latch assembly		$25
Wiper arm and blade kit		$40
Wiper arm		$15
Windshield washer nozzle		$9
Trunk lid	convertible and coupe	$170
Floor pan		$115
Smog pump		$60
Crankshaft pulley		$70
Water pump pulley	GT/LX	$45
Distributor cover		$10

Replacement Costs for Common Parts

Part	Spec	Price
Smog canister		$65
Heater core	A/C	$30
	exc. A/C	$35
Radiator bracket	left	$30
	right	$60
Radiator		$110
Rear-brake drum		$35
Power steering pump		$100
Front lower control arms	pair	$200
Pushrods	set of 16	$40
Harmonic balancer		$80
Radiator cap	16-pound	$6
	13-pound	$9
Thermostat	180-degree	$16
	195-degree	$7
Fuel cap		$20
Carpet		$99
Temperature sending unit		$8
Fuel tank	exc. EFI	$130
Four-piece T-top weather stripping kit		$230
Air cleaner inlet tube		$25
Clutch fork		$25
Front-bumper cover	LX repro	$170
Taillamp lens		$110
Hood	repro	$170
Fuel tank sending unit		$90
Tilt wheel lever		$6
Radiator core support		$180
Convertible top boot		$80
Convertible glass rear window		$125
Convertible top		$150
Convertible top headliner		$135
Convertible sun visor	pair	$50
Convertible top motor		$200
Front inner splash shield		$90
Air check valve		$50
Motor mount	convertible	$47
Coolant temperature sensor		$30
Ignition coil		$55
Front-bumper cover	GT repro	$400
Rearview mirror		$38
LX decklid emblem		$11
Fuel tank	EFI	$140

I Bought a 1984 Mustang

The first Saleen I bought turned out to be the first one ever made, although it wasn't what I wanted at the time. A local car collector had bought several cars from Steve Saleen in the early 1990s and was selling them off as he found buyers. I had gotten all excited about the 1987 model he had, because it was numbered 0001 and had been the test mule for Saleen's SSC engine during the certification process. I knew that would be a historically significant car in years to come, but somehow we couldn't come to terms on a trade. He did, however, have the 84-0032 Saleen, which I knew to be a rare car from the first year of production but did not realize it was the very first one ever made. There must have been something special about that first Saleen, because it led me to build a collection of more than a dozen cars that now includes all three Mustangs that Steve built in 1984. *—Stu Akers*

I'm a paint and body man, so when I got my 1984 Mustang GT hatchback with T-tops, I had in mind a few changes that would take the performance and looks to an all-new level. Essentially, I turned it into a Pro Street car. Its new engine was a 1970 302 V-8 with a Boss 302 crankshaft and connecting rods, TRW 12:1 pistons and rings, Motorsports camshaft, Boss 302 heads, Manley stainless steel valves, and several other custom and modified pieces. A Mallory dual-point distributor, coil, and wires handled ignition upgrades, and the exhaust flowed freely through a set of Kaufmann-built headers and twin turbo mufflers. I knew the stock transmission couldn't handle the new power level, so I installed a 1985 T-5 and a 10.5-inch heavy-duty rear axle with 5.14:1 Detroit Locker gears and Mark Williams–built custom axles. Wheel tubs had to be welded into the rear of the car to fit the drag-style tires, and I installed a six-point rollcage. There's also a custom-made 22-gallon fuel cell tucked out of sight. *—Randy Meek*

1984 Mustang Ratings

Base Four-Cylinder

Model Comfort/Amenities	**
Reliability	***
Collectibility	*
Parts/Service Availability	***
Est. Annual Repair Costs	***

Turbo Four-Cylinder

Model Comfort/Amenities	**
Reliability	***
Collectibility	*
Parts/Service Availability	**
Est. Annual Repair Costs	**

3.8-Liter V-6

Model Comfort/Amenities	***
Reliability	**
Collectibility	*
Parts/Service Availability	***
Est. Annual Repair Costs	***

5.0-Liter V-8, 5-Speed

Model Comfort/Amenities	***
Reliability	****
Collectibility	****
Parts/Service Availability	****
Est. Annual Repair Costs	***

5.0-Liter V-8, Automatic

Model Comfort/Amenities	***
Reliability	****
Collectibility	***
Parts/Service Availability	****
Est. Annual Repair Costs	***

5.0-Liter V-8 Saleen

Model Comfort/Amenities	***
Reliability	****
Collectibility	*****
Parts/Service Availability	****
Est. Annual Repair Costs	***

In terms of everyday drivability and comfort, the Mustang line continued to improve for 1984. Although enthusiasts of the time were reluctant, Ford's gradual adoption of EEC-IV and EFI produced better running, better performing cars. GTs still command top dollar when in good shape, especially in convertible or T-top form. The 20th Anniversary cars, with a V-8, 5-speed, and ample options, can be readily found in good condition because so many of them were pampered by their original owners as future collectibles. The three Saleen Mustangs built in 1984 are so rare that it would be difficult to place a value on them.

The secondary throttle shafts of five-liter V-8s built between August 1983 and March 1984 were prone to outside contamination, which could result in a stuck throttle. Ford offered to replace for free the primary to secondary throttle closure link on the affected four-barrel carburetors.

V-8 Mustangs received a smaller trimline power brake booster for 1984. The four- and six-cylinder cars (other than the SVO) were built with the older, larger design assembly through 1993.

The 1984 model year featured a few holdover items. Some early GTs came with the 1983 hood scoop, for example, and were built without the later cars' air dam–mounted fog lights.

Ford installed a clutch-operated starter motor bypass switch on all Mustangs starting in 1984, which effectively prevents a driver from starting the car while in gear. If the switch goes bad or if a floor mat or other obstruction keeps the pedal from being depressed all the way, the car may not start.

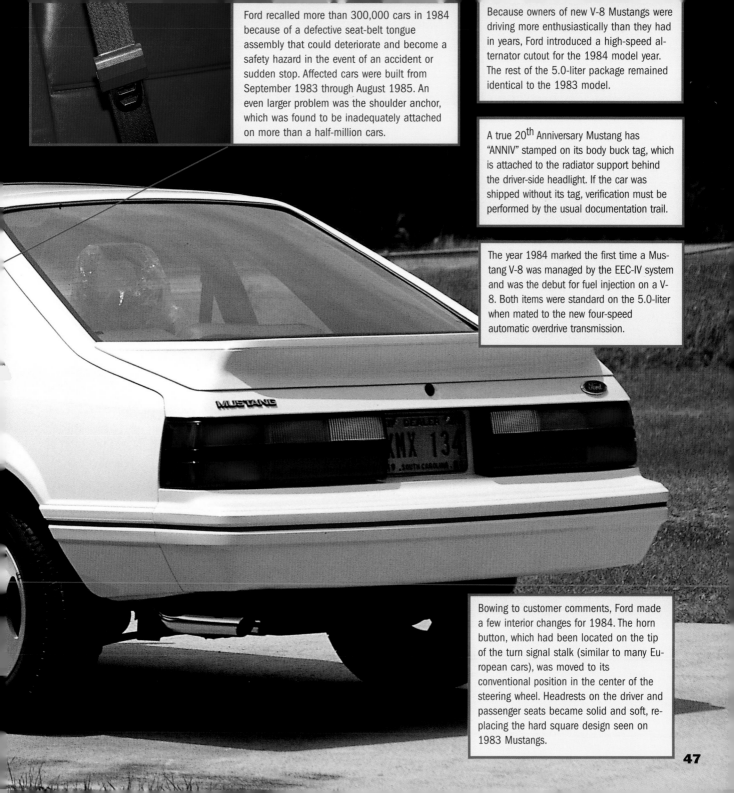

Ford recalled more than 300,000 cars in 1984 because of a defective seat-belt tongue assembly that could deteriorate and become a safety hazard in the event of an accident or sudden stop. Affected cars were built from September 1983 through August 1985. An even larger problem was the shoulder anchor, which was found to be inadequately attached on more than a half-million cars.

Because owners of new V-8 Mustangs were driving more enthusiastically than they had in years, Ford introduced a high-speed alternator cutout for the 1984 model year. The rest of the 5.0-liter package remained identical to the 1983 model.

A true 20th Anniversary Mustang has "ANNIV" stamped on its body buck tag, which is attached to the radiator support behind the driver-side headlight. If the car was shipped without its tag, verification must be performed by the usual documentation trail.

The year 1984 marked the first time a Mustang V-8 was managed by the EEC-IV system and was the debut for fuel injection on a V-8. Both items were standard on the 5.0-liter when mated to the new four-speed automatic overdrive transmission.

Bowing to customer comments, Ford made a few interior changes for 1984. The horn button, which had been located on the tip of the turn signal stalk (similar to many European cars), was moved to its conventional position in the center of the steering wheel. Headrests on the driver and passenger seats became solid and soft, replacing the hard square design seen on 1983 Mustangs.

If the Mustang II was Ford's "right car at the right time," the SVO will be remembered as the "right car at the wrong time." With enough go-fast hardware to make any enthusiast drool – a 175-horse turbo motor, four-wheel disc brakes, 16-inch high-performance tires on alloy wheels and Koni gas-filled shocks to name but a few features – its high price doomed it to historical footnote status.

Chapter 5

1984–1986 Mustang SVO

1984 ½ to 1985 ½

In 1981, Ford formed the Special Vehicle Operations (SVO) department to nurture its renewed motorsports involvement and to develop a line of special limited edition, high-performance vehicles.

Its self-named SVO Mustang, which *Motor Trend* declared "the best-driving street Mustang the factory has ever produced," was the first to be offered to a hungry public. Other magazines compared it favorably to the Datsun ZX, Ferrari 308, and Porsche 944, touting its lower price tag as further proof of its superior engineering.

Introduced in midyear 1984, Ford's new SVO Mustang offered as much performance as the V-8 GT model but with a four-cylinder engine. Developed by the high-performance development arm of Ford, the SVO was a giant leap in turbo technology, with an air-to-air intercooler on its 2.3-liter turbocharged, fuel-injected four-cylinder engine, a package that produced 175 horsepower with better low-end grunt than the company's earlier turbo models. Part of the increase came from the addition of the intercooler, essentially an air cooler that allowed for more compressed air to enter the combustion chamber. Ford's EEC-IV system made it possible to safely increase turbo boost to 14 psi (from the earlier engine's 6-psi limit).

A Borg-Warner T-5 five-speed manual gearbox with Hurst linkage; four-wheel disc brakes; performance suspension with adjustable Koni gas-filled shocks and the Mustang's new Quadra-Shock rear-axle damper; P225/50VR-16 Goodyear NCT tires on cast aluminum 16x7-inch wheels; and a functional hood scoop were all standard equipment for the SVO. The rear-axle ratio on the first generation SVO (introduction through mid-1985) was 3.45:1.

According to Ford, the hyper four-banger had a top speed of 134 miles per hour and a 0 to 60 time of just 7.5 seconds. Creature comforts were addressed through the use of multi-adjustable articulated leather bucket seats, and shock absorbers and struts with three settings: cross-country, GT, and competition. For the first time ever on a production Mustang, four-wheel disc brakes were standard.

Although built on the same Fox body as the regular Mustang, the SVO had a different, more streamlined look, with a grilleless fascia and integrated fog lamps. A Ford oval was perched above the single air-intake slot. Large wrap-around lenses flanked deeply recessed single rectangular headlamps. The SVO's polycarbonate, dual-wing rear spoiler was the wildest thing to sit on a trunk lid or hatchback since Dodge's 1969 Daytona. It was meant to increase downforce on the car at speed for better handling, while rear-wheel "spats" directed airflow around the wheel wells.

Ford never intended to produce the SVO in numbers equal to its V-8 models—it was priced more than double a base four-cylinder Mustang and around $5,600 more than the GT. It was, instead, Ford's technology leader, with more of a following among the European performance-car crowd than with the traditional hot rod establishment.

In its first year, the hatchback-only SVO was available in black, silver metallic, dark charcoal metallic or red metallic, with charcoal interiors.

An 8,000-rpm tachometer; unique instrument panel appliqués; narrow body side moldings; unique C-pillar and tail-lamp treatments; quick-ratio power steering; Traction-Lok rear axle; and leather-wrapped steering wheel, shift knob, and brake handle were all standard equipment on the SVO. Unusual for any car at the time (or now) was a console-mounted switch that calibrated the ignition instantly for regular or premium unleaded gasoline. SVO's engineers, who prided themselves on their automotive enthusiasm, revised the car's brake and accelerator pedal positions to allow drivers to use the heel-and-toe method for spirited driving. Another uniquely European-style accessory, the driver footrest, was installed on all SVOs to improve the pilot's position during hard cornering.

1985 ½ to 1986

Although barely a year old, the SVO received a fresh look in the middle of 1985 when Ford got approval to install a set of cutting-edge flush headlights. Under the hood, it also gained an impressive 30 horsepower (to 205) with the addition of a higher-performance camshaft, higher-flow exhaust system, reconfigured turbocharger, larger fuel injectors, and a higher boost limit (15 psi). The rear-axle ratio was changed to 3.73:1, which made the boost in horsepower feel even stronger.

All that power required modified engine mounts and brackets to keep powertrain noise from increasing. Stiffer shocks and Teflon-lined stabilizer bar bushings improved the already impressive handling, and Goodyear replaced its NCT radials with Eagles.

For its final year of production, 1986, the SVO received more conservative programming of its EEC-IV, which dropped the horsepower rating to 200 at 5,000 rpm.

In all, Ford sold 9,844 SVOs.

The SVO's four-cylinder was even more crowded in its engine compartment than the 5.0-liter. Changing spark plugs requires removal of the air box and other assorted components.

SVOs were available in black, silver metallic, dark charcoal metallic, or red metallic, but interiors only came in charcoal.

To reflect its true performance, SVO engineers installed a 140 mile-per-hour speedometer, but Ford mandated a gauge limit of 85 miles per hour. The loophole was to have the numbers stop at 85 but let the 10 miles per hour increments continue to 140 unmarked.

1984–1986 SVO Specifications

Base price	61B hatchback SVO ('84)	$15,596
	61B hatchback SVO ('85)	$14,521
	61B hatchback SVO ('86)	$15,272
Production	61B hatchback SVO ('84)	$4,508
	61B hatchback SVO ('85)	$1,954
	61B hatchback SVO ('86)	$3,382
Displacement (cubic inches/liters)		I-4 140/2.3
Bore x stroke (inches)		3.78x3.13
VIN code/Compression ratio		W 8.0:1
Induction		EFI
Valvetrain		SOHC
Horsepower	('84)	175@4,400
	(late '85)	205@5,000
	('86)	200@5,000
Transmission		5-speed manual
Rear-axle ratio	('84)	3.45:1
	(early '85–'86)	3.73:1
Wheelbase (inches)		100.4
Overall width (inches)		68.0
Overall height (inches)		50.5
Overall length (inches)		181.4
Track (inches)		(front) 57.8
		(rear) 58.3
Fuel capacity (gallons)		15.4
Weight (pounds)		2,987
Tires		Goodyear P225/50VR16
Front suspension		MacPherson struts, adjustable gas-pressurized Koni shocks, coil springs, stabilizer bar
Rear suspension		four-bar link, coil springs, stabilizer bar, adjustable gas-pressurized Koni shocks, longitudinally mounted hydraulic shocks
Steering		20:1 variable ratio rack and pinion
Brakes	(front)	11.08-inch vented disc
	(rear)	11.6-inch vented disc
Gas mileage (EPA est.)		25
0 to 60 (secs)	('84)*	7.5
Standing ¼-mile (secs)	('84)	15.2
Top speed (mph)	('84)	134

* Ford factory info

1984–1986 Mustang SVO

Major Options

SVO competition package	
(delete air, power locks/windows, AM/FM/cassette) credit	$1,253
Battery, heavy-duty	$27
Emissions, California	$99
Emissions, high-altitude	no charge
Power lock group	$177
Air conditioning	$743
Power windows	$198
Tinted glass	$110
Flip-up open-air roof	$315
AM/FM stereo radio (w/cassette player)	$113

Replacement Cost for Common Parts

Headlight retaining ring		$8
Steering wheel	$100 core charge	$300
Intercooler-to-hood seal		$40
SVO emblem		$8
Master cylinder		$90
Rearview mirror		$38
Fuel tank	EFI	$140
Front-bumper cover	repro	$400
Rear-bumper cover		$120
Taillamp lens		$80
Belt tensioner		$73
Fuel tank shield		$130
EFI distributor		$210
Battery tray		$44
Alternator		$150
H-pipe smog tube		$100
Fan shroud	repro	$90
Fan shroud	original	$110
PCV valve grommet		$4
Console coin tray		$37
Arm rest pad		$65
A/C vent registers		$20
Side marker		$13
Marchal fog lamp lens		$110
Oil pressure sending unit		$20

Front fender	repro	$85
Front fender	original	$280
Starter		$60
Front seat belt buckle		$47
Outside door handle kit		$27
Electric window motor		$70
Window crank handle		$10
Inside door handle bezel		$23
Door lock actuator kit		$90
Lock cylinder and key		$25
Hatchback quarter window molding	pair	$100
Hatch weather stripping		$27
Sunroof weather stripping kit		$150
Door weather stripping kit		$40
Vacuum canister		$25
Antenna kit	black	$37
Antenna kit	stainless	$23
Antenna rod		$14
Rubber fender-to-hood bumpers		$2
Hood latch assembly		$25
Wiper arm and blade kit		$40
Wiper arm		$15
Windshield washer nozzle		$9
Floor pan		$115
Smog canister		$65
Heater core	A/C	$30
	exc. A/C	$35
Radiator bracket	left	$30
	right	$60
Radiator		$110
Power steering pump		$100
Front lower control arms	pair	$200
Radiator cap	16-pound	$6
	13-pound	$9
Thermostat	180-degree	$16
	195-degree	$7
Fuel cap		$20
Temperature sending unit		$8
Fuel tank sending unit		$90
Tilt wheel lever		$6
Radiator core support		$180
Front inner splash shield		$90
Coolant temperature sensor		$30

What They Said in 1984–1986

The SVO is Ford's Porsche 930 Turbo, an old design that's kept vital with large doses of technology administered by dedicated engineer/racers. This strategy works well for the German firm, but it's a double-edge sword for Ford, where the engineers have had their hands full trying to make an old car act new. Ford has certainly gotten the SVO's looks right, and its performance is truly potent. It's the hottest car in this test by far. Fire it down a test track and you'll see 60 miles per hour in 6.8 seconds, a top speed of 129 miles per hour, and a 0.79-g cornering limit. . . . Keeping the turbo on the boil means keeping the revs up, and that translates into a ton of engine noise—all of it the wrong kind. Between the lack of power at low revs and the high-rpm assault on your ears, the SVO is never really happy. It's enough to make you wish for the 4.9-liter V-8 from the GT. —*Car and Driver,* **May 1985**

For 1985½, Ford's SVO has had a number of evolutionary changes aimed specifically at refining the breed, first introduced in late 1983. Without question the most important improvements, from a potential buyer's standpoint, are the improved engine characteristics. Probably the most common complaint heard about the earlier SVOs was the "buzzy" nature of the engine. The motor transmitted all manner of vibrations to the driver. When the engine was being used hard, the steering wheel, gear lever, pedals, mirrors—seemingly everything—vibrated in a concert of resonating frequencies. . . . The 1985 ½ edition of this Ford engine is a night-to-day improvement. It develops more power, more torque, is an order of magnitude smoother, and is great fun to drive. —*Motor Trend,* **July 1985**

I Bought a 1985½ Mustang SVO

My 1985½ SVO is a super-clean car from Massachusetts. The guy who ordered it was very wealthy and had a 10-car garage that kept everything nice and dry. It was one of 11 ordered with the Competition Prep package, and it only has 380 miles on the odometer. He specified he did not want the dual-plane rear wing, which was an option, but when the car showed up at the dealership it had the wing—even though the window sticker says it was deleted. —*Daniel Carpenter*

1984–1986 Mustang SVO Ratings

Model Comfort/Amenities	****
Reliability	****
Collectibility	****
Parts/Service Availability	**
Est. Annual Repair Costs	***

The SVOs were, in many ways, superior to the V-8 Mustangs, but collector interest still lies with the 5.0-liters. Locating parts for the SVO is not too difficult, despite its limited three-year run. The major body components are standard Fox Mustang, and the powertrain was shared with Ford's Thunderbird, Cougar, and Merkur.

1984–1986 Mustang SVO Garage Watch

Ordering an SVO Mustang with the Competition Prep package saved the buyer more than $1,200, but it meant doing without air conditioning and other creature comforts. Today, such models are very rare, as only 11 were ordered that way.

The dual-plane rear spoiler was an SVO-specific piece, but buyers could order the car with a simpler, GT-like single-stage piece. The spoiler's second tier limits vision to the rear of the car.

Articulated sport seats featured adjustable side bolsters and inflatable lumbar support. The lumbar was adjusted by squeezing a rubber bulb that lay to the left of the driver's seat.

The SVO's 16-inch wheels were cast in a low-pressure mold to minimize porosity (engineer talk for "getting rid of bubbles") and give a smooth appearance.

No expense was spared to build this driving enthusiast's machine. For example, the stock 5.0-liter shifter was replaced with a shorter-throw Hurst unit in the SVO.

The 1984 SVO featured the first functional Mustang hood scoop since the 1973 Dual Ram Induction option. The slightly off-center scoop sat square atop the 2.3-liter Turbo's intercooler— a small radiator-like device that boosted the engine's horsepower output by cooling and condensing the air before it was fed into the cylinders.

Perhaps to show off the flexibility of the new EEC-IV engine management system, a switch was installed to allow the use of low- or high-octane fuels. This recalibration switch sits to the left of the shifter.

The Mustang body became smoother in 1985, thanks largely to a redesigned front cap that owed plenty to the SVO model. Pony power cracked the 200 mark for the first time in a dozen years when the 5.0-liter turned out a reported 210 horsepower and the SVO had a mid-year performance increase to 205.

Chapter 6

1985 Mustang

If anything proved to the American public that Ford was on the right track in the 1980s to returning the Mustang to its musclecar roots, it was the 210-horsepower 5.0-liter V-8 ("M" code in the VIN) that debuted in its 1985 GT and LX models. This is the engine that had been anticipated as a midyear 1984 offering, but developmental difficulties postponed its introduction. The engineers must have felt the more powerful 5.0 was jinxed, because further trouble with the new pistons and clearance issues concerning the new-for-1985 header exhaust caused yet another delay, pushing first deliveries of V-8 Mustangs into January.

Upon arrival, the four-barrel 5.0-liter had gained 35 horsepower from a number of modifications, including a hydraulic roller camshaft setup, the tricky stainless steel headers, and a low-restriction exhaust system. Plans had been announced for a two-speed accessory drive that would have perhaps freed up some horsepower by reducing engine drag above idle, but it was not put into production.

The 210-horsepower motor was only available with the T-5 five-speed manual transmission, which benefited from shorter ratios and an improved shifter. Ordering a GT or 5.0 LX with the AOD automatic delivered a reduced-performance version of the V-8 that featured central fuel injection (CFI) and initially put out 165 horsepower. Midyear saw an improved version of the 5.0/AOD combination, when Ford applied the 210-horse engine's headers and exhaust system to free up an additional 15 ponies. Neither of the 5.0/AOD powerplants received the 5.0/T-5's roller camshaft arrangement, but both were fitted with aluminum intake manifolds.

Rear-axle ratios for the V-8s shifted toward numerically lower setups in 1985. The 5.0/T-5 came standard with a very long-legged 2.73:1 gear with a 3.08:1 ratio optional. On the 5.0/AOD, only the stock 3.27:1 could be ordered.

For the first time in Mustang history, all V-8 cars came standard with power-assisted rack-and-pinion steering, which had previously been considered a "mandatory option." Central fuel injection also continued to feed the 3.8-liter V-6 ("3" code), which was still only available with the three-speed automatic transmission. The standard engine for all other non-GT, non-convertible models was still the 2.3-liter inline four-cylinder ("A" code), which was rated at 88 horsepower and came with a four-speed manual transmission, five-speed, or optional three-speed automatic.

Ford dropped the base L model before going into the 1985 production year, leaving a very simple lineup of LX and GT Mustangs for buyers to choose from. The LX, available in coupe, hatchback, or convertible body styles, came standard with power brakes and steering, remote-control right-side mirror, dual-note horn, interval windshield wipers, and an AM/FM stereo radio. New interior features included a console, lowback bucket seats (on LX), articulated sport seats (on GT), luxury door-trim panels, and covered visor mirrors. On the convertible, quarter-trim panels were revised for an improved seat belt system. An electronic AM/FM stereo radio with cassette player found its way onto the options list, while standard mechanical radio faces assumed a flat design.

On the outside, the Mustang LX and GT were slowly evolving in the direction of their European-styled SVO stablemate, with a four-hole integral air dam below the bumper and flanked by low rectangular parking lamps (integral fog lamps returned on GTs). Even the grille seemed to mimic that of the SVO, with one wide slot in the center of a sloping front panel. At the rear, taillight lenses seemed to reach from one side of the car to the other, interrupted only by the license plate mount, with backup lenses positioned at the upper inboard portion.

The blacked-out treatment of earlier GTs and Cobras gave way to a more subtle charcoal gray shade, which completely bisected the top half of the car from its bottom in the form of a horizontal rub strip.

All Mustangs benefited from wider tires in 1985, with base LXs receiving P195/75R14s. The GT's unidirectional Goodyear Gatorbacks, which measured P225/60VR15 and were mounted on all-new 15-inch alloy wheels, were developed through the company's involvement in Formula 1 racing. Suspension components for the V-8 cars, including the Quadra-Shock setup, variable-rate coil springs, and front and rear stabilizer bars, carried over from the improvements introduced in mid-1984. Starting in 1985, Teflon lined the front stabilizer bar's main bushings, and urethane replaced the softer rubber end-link bushings. All LX Mustangs could be ordered with the Special Handling package (essentially the stock GT system), whether four-cylinder, V-6, or V-8.

The 1985 model year brought with it a new dash design with improved heating and ventilation for Mustang passengers, with four air registers. GT dashes were outfitted in gray and black, while those on LX models were color-keyed to the rest of the interior.

It was a little optimistic in terms of top speed, but the 1985 Mustang's speedometer finally hinted at the GT's true performance. Previous models had been strapped with a ridiculous speedometer that stopped at 85 miles per hour.

Only 90 GT-based Twister II Mustangs were sold in the Midwest in 1985. A throwback to the 1970 Twister Special, the 1985 version sported special side decals and rear hatch louvers. This example also was equipped with T-tops.

1985 Mustang Specifications

Base price	66B coupe LX	$6,885
	61B hatchback LX	$7,345
	66B convertible V-6 LX	$11,985
	61B hatchback GT	$9,885
	66B convertible GT	$13,585
Production	66B coupe	56,781
	66B convertible	15,110
	61B hatchback	84,623
Displacement (cubic inches/liters)	I-4	140/2.3
	V-6	232/3.8
	V-8	302/5.0
Bore x stroke (inches)	I-4	3.78x3.13
	V-6	3.80x3.40
	V-8	4.00x3.00
VIN code/Compression ratio	I-4	A 9.0:1
	V-6	3 8.7:1
	V-8	M 8.3:1
Induction	I-4	1-bbl
	V-6	CFI
	V-8 (AOD)	CFI
	V-8	4-bbl
Valvetrain	I-4	SOHC
	V-6	OHV
	V-8	OHV
Horsepower	I-4	88@4,000
	V-6	120@3,600
	V-8 (AOD, early '85)	165@3,800
	V-8 (AOD, late '85)	180@4,200
	V-8	210@4,400
Transmission (std./opt.)	I-4	4-speed/5-speed/3-speed auto
	V-6	3-speed auto
	V-8 (CFI)	AOD 4-speed auto
	V-8 (4-bbl)	T-5 5-speed manual
Rear-axle ratio	I-4, 4-speed	2.73:1
	I-4, 3-speed	3.08:1
	V-8, 4-speed AOD	3.27:1
	V-8, 5-speed	2.73:1
Wheelbase (inches)		100.5
Overall width (inches)		69.1
Overall height (inches)		52.1
Overall length (inches)		179.3
Track (inches)		(front) 56.6
		(rear) 57.0
Fuel capacity (gallons)		15.4
Weight (pounds)	66B coupe LX	2,559
	61B hatchback LX	2,605
	66B convertible V-6 LX	2,873
	61B hatchback GT	2,899
	66B convertible GT	3,043
Tires	(base)	P195/75R14
	(V-8, early '85 LX)	P205/70R14
	(V-8, GT and late '85 LX)	P225/60VR15
Front suspension		modified MacPherson struts, coil springs
Rear suspension		live axle, four-link suspension system, Quadra-Shock
Steering	(base)	20.0:1 to 15.97:1 variable ratio rack and pinion
	(V-8)	15:1 constant ratio rack and pinion
Brakes	I-4, V-6	(front) 9.31-inch disc
	V-8	(front) 10.06-inch vented disc
	all models	(rear) 9.0-inch drum
Gas mileage (EPA city/hwy.)	I-4 4-speed manual	23/29
	I-4 3-speed auto	21/25
	V-6 3-speed auto	19/22
	V-8 4-speed AOD	16/24
	V-8 5-speed manual	16/24
0 to 60 (secs)	(GT, 302/5-speed, 3.08:1 axle)**	7.2
	(302/5-speed, 3.08:1 axle) ***	6.4
Standing ¼-mile (mph/secs)	(GT, 302/5-speed, 3.08:1 axle)	89.7@15.51
	(302/5-speed, 3.08:1 axle)	91@14.9
Top speed (mph)	(GT, 302/5-speed, 3.08:1 axle)	131.3
	(302/5-speed, 3.08:1 axle)	135

* See chapter 5 for 1985 SVO specifications.
** *Road & Track* September 1985
*** *Car and Driver* January 1985

1985 Mustang

Major Options

3.8-liter V-6	(LX)	$439
5.0-liter V-8 package		$1,000
	(LX convertible)	$152
Transmission, 5-speed	(LX)	$124
Transmission, 3-speed automatic	(LX)	$439
Transmission, 4-speed AOD	(LX)	$676
	(GT)	$551
Differential, Traction-Lok		$95
Optional axle ratio		no charge
Handling suspension	(LX)	$258
Emissions, California		$99
Emissions, high-altitude		no charge
Light/convenience group		$55
Power lock group		$177–$210
Air conditioning		$743
Rear defroster, electric		$140
Fingertip speed control		$176
Windows, power		$198
	(convertible)	$272
Tinted glass		$110
Wheel, tilt steering	(LX)	$110
AM/FM stereo radio	(LX/GT)	$148
w/cassette player		
Electronic AM/FM stereo	(LX/GT)	$300
w/cassette		
Premium sound system	(LX/GT)	$138
Radio delete		credit $148
T-roof	(hatchback)	$1,074
Flip-up open-air roof	(hatchback)	$315
Console		$191
Seats, lowback vinyl bucket	(LX)	$29
Seats, leather sport bucket	(LX convertible)	$780
	(GT convertible)	$415
Wheel covers, wire	(LX)	$98
Wheels, styled steel		$178

Replacement Costs for Common Parts

Ignition coil		$60
Fuel pump	exc. EFI	$30
Alternator		$60
Fan shroud	repro	$80
Console coin tray		$37
Arm rest pad		$65
A/C vent registers		$20
Dash pad	repro	$190
Side marker		$13
Headlight retaining ring	exc. SVO	$40
Marchal fog lamp lens		$110
Front-brake rotor		$40
Master cylinder	remanufactured	$30
Oil pressure sending unit		$20
Front fender	repro	$85
Front fender	original	$280
Starter		$60
Front seat belt buckle		$47
Outside door handle kit		$27
Electric window motor		$70
Window crank handle		$10
Inside door handle bezel		$23
Door lock actuator kit		$90
Lock cylinder and key		$25
Hatchback quarter window molding	pair	$100
Hatch weather stripping		$27
Trunk weather stripping		$23
Sunroof weather stripping kit		$150
Door weather stripping kit		$40
Vacuum canister		$25
Antenna kit	black	$37
Antenna kit	stainless	$23
Antenna rod		$14
Rubber fender-to-hood bumpers		$2
Hood latch assembly		$25
Wiper arm and blade kit		$40
Wiper arm		$15
Windshield washer nozzle		$9
Trunk lid	convertible and coupe	$170
Floor pan		$115
Smog pump		$60
Crankshaft pulley		$70
Water pump pulley	GT/LX	$45
Distributor cover		$10
Smog canister		$65

Heater core	A/C	$30
	exc. A/C	$35
Radiator bracket	left	$30
	right	$60
Radiator		$110
Rear-brake drum		$35
Power steering pump		$100
Front lower control arms	pair	$200
Pushrods	set of 16	$40
Harmonic balancer		$80
Radiator cap	16-pound	$6
	13-pound	$9
Thermostat	180-degree	$16
	195-degree	$7
Fuel cap		$20
Carpet		$99
Rear-wheel cylinder		$40
Temperature sending unit		$8
Fuel tank	exc. EFI	$130
Four-piece T-top weather stripping kit		$230
Air cleaner inlet tube		$25
Clutch fork		$25
Hood	repro	$170
Fuel tank sending unit		$90
Tilt wheel lever		$6
Radiator core support		$180
Convertible top boot		$80
Convertible glass rear window		$125
Convertible top		$150
Convertible top headliner		$135
Convertible sun visor	pair	$50
Convertible top motor		$200
Front inner splash shield		$90
Air check valve		$50
Motor mount	convertible	$47
Coolant temperature sensor		$30
Ignition coil		$55
Front-bumper cover	GT repro	$400
Rearview mirror		$38
LX decklid emblem		$11
Fuel tank	EFI	$140
Front-bumper cover	LX repro	$170
Rear-bumper cover		$120
Taillamp lens		$80
Belt tensioner		$73
Fuel tank shield		$130
Power rack and pinion steering	15:1 ratio	$200
Hydraulic roller lifters	set of 16	$130

What They Said in 1985

Every bit as much effort was put into improving the GT's road manners, which is nothing if not good news. Mustangs have always been front-line power cars; it's their handling that's been gimpy. For 1985, variable-rate springs have been fitted all around and the gas-filled front struts and rear shocks are valved about 50 percent tighter. The quad-shock rear suspension layout introduced in the middle of last season for the SVO has been added, and the rear anti-sway bar is larger. . . . Everything Ford has changed, however, seems to work like a charm—at least as far as we could tell during our short proving-grounds session. . . . We predict this will be a strong year for the Mustang GT. The timing couldn't be better for a car at the zenith of its zoom. —*Car and Driver,* October 1984

I Bought a 1985 Mustang

I got my black 1985 GT for Father's Day in 1987. The five-speed hatchback was my daily driver and was shown on the weekends at Mustang Club of America shows throughout the Southeast. When it was still stock, it was the first late-model Mustang to ever appear on the cover of MCA's monthly magazine. Once I started modifying it for performance and appearance, it underwent a radical change. The 5.0-liter received every part upgrade available, including underdrive pulleys, an Edelbrock dual-plane intake manifold, SVO nickel-plated headers, and a Kaufmann three-core radiator. I installed most of the Saleen body pieces and had the local body shop integrate them onto the car so they showed almost no break line and had the entire car repainted black. To make it sit right, I put Saleen's Race-craft suspension parts at all four corners and changed the car from a four-lug to a five-lug setup so it would accept a set of 1968 Shelby 10-spoke wheels and Yokohama 008 tires. I threw out the stock 85 miles per hour speedometer and replaced it with a unit that measured to 140. When finished, it won a first-place trophy in its debut show and competed for many years afterwards. It now prowls the streets of San Antonio, where it still looks and runs great for its new owner. —*Tom Bader*

1985 Mustang Ratings

Base Four-Cylinder

Model Comfort/Amenities	**
Reliability	***
Collectibility	*
Parts/Service Availability	***
Est. Annual Repair Costs	***

3.8-Liter V-6

Model Comfort/Amenities	***
Reliability	**
Collectibility	*
Parts/Service Availability	***
Est. Annual Repair Costs	***

5.0-Liter V-8, 5-Speed

Model Comfort/Amenities	***
Reliability	****
Collectibility	****
Parts/Service Availability	****
Est. Annual Repair Costs	***

5.0-Liter V-8, Automatic

Model Comfort/Amenities	***
Reliability	****
Collectibility	***
Parts/Service Availability	****
Est. Annual Repair Costs	***

5.0-Liter V-8 Saleen

Model Comfort/Amenities	***
Reliability	****
Collectibility	****
Parts/Service Availability	****
Est. Annual Repair Costs	***

If it's collectibility you seek, buy a 1985 GT five-speed convertible with the last of the four-barrel carburetors. If burning up a road course is your favorite form of relaxation, buy a late 1985 SVO (reviewed in chapter 5). Very few were made, and they came from the factory with everything a road racer might want, including a better-balanced chassis than the heavier 5.0-liter cars. Look hard enough and you might find one of the lighter SVOs with Competition Prep packages that deleted several non-essentials.

1985 Mustang Garage Watch

For the first time, Saleen Mustangs were offered with either standard five-speeds or optional AOD transmissions. Production for the year included 130 hatchback models and two convertibles.

The Mustang's new headers could more accurately be called "steel-tube manifolds," as many compromises had to be made in the interest of fitment and reliability. Still, they were a vast improvement over the previous year's cast iron manifold in terms of scavenging exhaust gases and reducing back pressure.

Ford recalled Mustangs built during April with 3.8- and 5.0-liter engines because of concerns that the power brake boosters could fail due to inadequate shell thickness.

The 5.0-liter block received a slight revision for the 1985 model year to accommodate the new roller tappets. Midyear CFI 5.0-liters received a 15-horsepower boost from the addition of the carbureted version's headers, a less-restrictive exhaust system, and an automatic air conditioning cutoff switch for more high-rpm power.

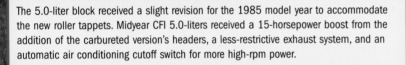

In the interest of stiffening the rather flexible Fox chassis, in 1985 Ford engineers began reinforcing its pinch-welded sheet metal joints with an industrial-strength adhesive.

The 210-horsepower 5.0-liter V-8 for 1985 featured forged-aluminum pistons. This design created greater strength and improved heat transfer to the cylinder walls. Ford had planned to introduce this modification with the Improved Performance package of equipment for 1984½.

Despite the tremendous increase in power, the 1985 Mustang was equipped with essentially the same 7.5-inch rear end ring gear that handled the 1979 V-8's 140 horsepower. This would be the last model year for the 7.5-inch unit.

After six years of production, Ford dropped the odd-sized Michelin TRX high-performance wheel and tire option. The 1985 GT came standard with 15x7-inch 10-hole alloy wheels and P225/60VR15 tires. The V-8 LX models produced early in the year were built with 14x5.5-inch wheels but in midyear were switched to the GT's 10-hole rims and bigger tires.

1986 brought Mustang performance into the fuel-injected age. Only the base four-cylinder engine still got its fuel through a carburetor –
in this case, a single-barrel Carter unit.

Chapter 7

1986 Mustang

The year 1986 was a transitional one for the Fox Mustang. The body was clearly a holdover from the 1979 model—albeit with many improvements—while the V-8 engine it held would soon turn a generation of hot rodders into Mustang fans.

The flagship of the Mustang line was again the 5.0-liter V-8 ("M" code in the VIN), this time available in only one version. Mating a new sequential multipoint electronic fuel injection (SEFI) system and sophisticated EEC-IV electronics to the low-friction pistons and roller camshaft designs introduced in 1985 created a high-tech powerplant that produced 10 horsepower *less* than the previous model (200) but 15 *more* lbs-ft of torque (285). Ford engineers pointed the blame for the horsepower loss on a unique masked-valve cylinder-head design that had been put into production to meet rising Corporate Average Fuel Economy (CAFE) standards. Despite the deficit on paper, the new Mustang felt more powerful on the street and turned in improved acceleration figures due to the torque increase. The E6AE (or "vanilla") heads would be used in Mustangs for 1986 only, as it was determined they limited future horsepower potential.

The 5.0 breathed through an inlet tract monitored by a speed density meter. Air was drawn in through a new passenger-side airbox (which relocated the battery to the driver side), a 58-mm throttle body, and individual fuel injector nozzles (one per cylinder). Supporting the greater fuel pressure needs was a 23.3-gph pump mounted inside the 15.4-gallon gas tank.

Other changes went into the 1986 motor in the interest of reliability and driveability. The iron block was cast in a semi-Siamese arrangement, which provided greater strength against flexing and more consistent cooling of the cylinder walls. The V-8's forged-aluminum flattop pistons were re-designed for a bump in compression and seats that accommodated new low-friction rings.

The 5.0-liter came standard in the GT model or at extra cost in any LX body style, with a T-5 five-speed manual transmission or optional AOD automatic. For the first time since its introduction in 1982, a High-Output 5.0 could be combined with an automatic without a reduction in crank horsepower. Welcome additions to the powertrain family were a stronger 8.8-inch rear axle (up from 7.5) and a slightly larger clutch disc (from 10.0 to 10.5 inches in diameter).

Rear-axle ratios among the V-8 powerplants remained the same. The 5.0/T-5 came standard with a very long-legged 2.73:1 gear with a 3.08:1 ratio optional. On the 5.0/AOD, only the stock 3.27:1 could be ordered.

It may be difficult to realize now, but in 1986, several automotive magazines predicted the addition of SEFI to the 5.0-liter would be the beginning of the end for Ford's pony car. There was also concern that the EEC-IV engine-management system accompanying the SEFI would effectively thwart any attempts to modify the V-8 for more power, thereby killing the fledgling aftermarket industry for late-model Mustangs. Comparisons to the failed New Coke product were common in the buff books.

Central fuel injection continued to feed the 3.8-liter V-6 ("3" code), which was still only available with the three-speed automatic transmission. Both the V-6 and V-8 engines switched to viscous engine mounts for 1986 to further reduce powertrain noise and vibration, part of an ongoing program to make the Mustangs feel like more expensive models that included additional sound-deadening material throughout the cabin.

Standard engine for all other non-GT, non-convertible models was still the 2.3-liter inline four-cylinder ("A" code), which was rated at 88 horsepower and came with a four-speed manual transmission, five-speed, or optional three-speed automatic.

The GT/Handling suspension components could be ordered with four- or six-cylinder LXs. The package included the GT-unique parts plus standard P205/70VR14 tires on stamped-steel wheels or an optional set of 15-inch wheels and tires.

Considering how much engineering work went into the Mustang's new powertrain, it's no surprise the rest of the car received so few changes. Other than some slight exterior/interior color changes, the only differences from 1985 included a more thorough anti-corrosion warranty and single-key operation.

In order to keep ahead of the production Mustang, Saleen Autosport stepped up the standard equipment list for its car in 1986. For improved street performance, Saleen added P225/50VR-16 Fulda radials on Riken alloy rims, specific rate front and rear coil springs, Saleen-specific strut mounting bearings, Koni quad shocks, urethane swaybar pivot bushings, urethane aerodynamic body pieces, Lexan headlight covers, 170 miles per hour speedometer, leather-covered shift knob, and an Escort radar detector. Coddling the enthusiast driver was an articulated sport seat, SVO-style "dead pedal," short-throw Hurst shifter, and three-spoke, leather-covered Momo steering wheel.

A total of 201 Saleen Mustangs were built for the public in 1986—190 hatchbacks and 11 convertibles. Three competition, or "R" models, were also produced. This white hatchback is a five-speed car with Saleen serial number 0072.

This Special Service Vehicle (SSV) Mustang once served the California Highway Patrol. It is difficult, but not impossible, to locate such clean examples still outfitted with proper badges, radios, gun mounts, and lights. It was policy to convert the cars to non-police equipment before selling them to the public. This example belongs to a collector in Virginia.

Ford's own convertible sales cut into demand for the once-popular T-top option. Because the Fox hatchback's chassis was very flexible to start with, cutting big squares out of the roof only made matters worse. The more the body flexed, the more the panels rattled and leaked. They saw production for only another full year.

1986 Mustang Specifications

Base price	66B coupe LX	$7,189
	61B hatchback LX	$7,744
	66B convertible V-6 LX	$12,821
	61B hatchback GT	$10,691
	66B convertible GT	$14,523
Production	66B coupe	84,774
	66B convertible	22,946
	61B hatchback	117,690
Displacement (cubic inches/liters)		
	I-4	140/2.3
	V-6	232/3.8
	V-8	302/5.0
Bore x stroke (inches)	I-4	3.78x3.13
	V-6	3.80x3.40
	V-8	4.00x3.00
VIN code/Compression ratio	I-4	A 9.5:1
	V-6	3 8.7:1
	V-8	M 9.2:1
Induction	I-4	1-bbl
	V-6	CFI
	V-8	SEFI
Valvetrain	I-4	SOHC
	V-6	OHV
	V-8	OHV
Horsepower	I-4	88@4,200
	V-6	120@3,600
	V-8	200@4,000
Transmission (std./opt.)	I-4	4-speed/5-speed/3-speed auto
	V-6	3-speed auto
	V-8	T-5 5-speed manual/4-speed AOD
Rear-axle ratio	I-4, 4-speed	2.73:1
	I-4, 3-speed	3.08:1
	V-8, 4-speed AOD	3.27:1
	V-8, 5-speed	2.73:1
Wheelbase (inches)		100.5
Overall width (inches)		69.1
Overall height (inches)		52.1
Overall length (inches)		179.3
Track (inches)		(front) 56.6
		(rear) 57.0
Fuel capacity (gallons)		15.4
Weight (pounds)	66B coupe LX	2,601
	61B hatchback LX	2,661
	66B convertible V-6 LX	2,908
	61B hatchback GT	2,976
	66B convertible GT	3,103

Tires	(base)	P195/75R14
	(V-8, GT and LX)	P225/60VR15
Front suspension		modified MacPherson struts, coil springs
Rear suspension		live axle, four-link suspension system, Quadra-Shock
Steering	(base)	20.0:1 to 15.97:1 variable ratio rack and pinion
	(V-8)	15:1 constant ratio rack and pinion
Brakes	I-4, V-6	(front) 9.31-inch disc
	V-8	(front) 10.06-inch vented disc
	all models	(rear) 9.0-inch drum
Gas mileage (EPA city/hwy.)	I-4 4-speed manual	23/28
	I-4 3-speed auto	21/25
	V-6 3-speed auto	19/23
	V-8 4-speed AOD	17/26
	V-8 5-speed manual	17/25
0 to 60 (secs)(LX, 302/5-speed, 3.08:1 axle)**		6.2
Standing ¼-mile (mph/secs)(LX, 302/5-speed, 3.08:1 axle)		95@14.9
Top speed (mph)(LX, 302/5-speed, 3.08:1 axle)		132

* See chapter 5 for 1986 SVO specifications.
** *Car and Driver*, June 1986

1986 Mustang

Major Options

3.8-liter V-6	(LX)	$454
5.0-liter V-8 package		$1,120
	(LX convertible)	$106
Transmission, 5-speed manual	(LX four-cylinder)	$124
Transmission, 3-speed automatic	(LX, standard on convertible)	
		$510
Transmission, 4-speed AOD	(LX)	$746
	(GT)	$622
Battery, heavy-duty		$27
Emission system, California		$102
Emission system, high-altitude	no	charge
Air conditioning		$762
Rear defroster, electric		$145
Fingertip speed control		$176
Power windows		$207
	(LX and GT convertible)	$282
Tinted glass	(standard convertible)	$115
Tilt steering wheel	(LX)	$115
Radio, AM/FM w/cassette player	(LX/GT)	$148
Radio, electronic AM/FM w/cassette	(LX/GT)	$300
Premium sound system		$138
T-roof	(hatchback only)	$1,100
Flip-up open-air roof	(hatchback only)	$315
Lower charcoal accent paint		$116
Console w/clock and systems monitor		$191
Vinyl bucket seats	(LX)	$29
Articulated leather sport bucket seats	(LX convertible)	$807
	(GT convertible)	$429
Wheel covers, wire	(LX)	$98
Wheels, styled steel		$178
Tires, P205/75R-14 WSW		$109
Tires, P225/60VR-15 on cast aluminum wheels		$665

Replacement Costs for Common Parts

Console coin tray		$37
Arm rest pad		$65
A/C vent registers		$20
Dash pads	repro	$190
Side marker		$13
Headlight retaining ring	exc. SVO	$40
Marchal fog lamp lens		$110
Front-brake rotor		$40
Master cylinder	remanufactured	$30
Oil pressure sending unit		$20
Front fender	repro	$85
Front fender	original	$280
Starter		$60
Front seat belt buckle		$47
Outside door handle kit		$27
Electric window motor		$70
Window crank handle		$10
Inside door handle bezel		$23
Door lock actuator kit		$90
Lock cylinder and key		$25
Hatchback quarter window molding	pair	$100
Hatch weather stripping		$27
Trunk weather stripping		$23
Sunroof weather stripping kit		$150
Door weather stripping kit		$40
Vacuum canister		$25
Antenna kit	black	$37
Antenna kit	stainless	$23
Antenna rod		$14
Rubber fender-to-hood bumpers		$2
Hood latch assembly		$25
Wiper arm and blade kit		$40
Wiper arm		$15
Windshield washer nozzle		$9
Trunk lid	convertible and coupe	$170
Floor pan		$115
Smog pump		$60
Crankshaft pulley		$70
Water pump pulley	GT/LX	$45
Distributor cover		$10
Smog canister		$65
Heater core	A/C	$30
	exc. A/C	$35

Radiator bracket	left	$30	Front inner splash shield			$90
	right	$60	Air check valve			$50
Radiator		$110	Motor mount	convertible		$47
Rear-brake drum		$35	Coolant temperature sensor			$30
Power steering pump		$100	Ignition coil			$55
Front lower control arms	pair	$200	Front-bumper cover	GT repro		$400
Pushrods	set of 16	$40	Rearview mirror			$38
Harmonic balancer		$80	LX decklid emblem			$11
Radiator cap	16-pound	$6	Fuel tank			$140
	13-pound	$9	Front-bumper cover	LX repro		$170
Thermostat	180-degree	$16	Front-bumper cover	SVO repro		$400
	195-degree	$7	Rear-bumper cover			$120
Fuel cap		$20	Taillamp lens			$80
Carpet		$99	Belt tensioner			$73
Rear-wheel cylinder		$40	Fuel tank shield			$130
Temperature sending unit		$8	Power rack and pinion steering		15:1 ratio	$200
Fuel tank	exc. EFI	$130	Hydraulic roller lifters	set of 16		$130
Four-piece T-top weather stripping kit		$230	Airbox-to-throttle body inlet tube			$35
Clutch fork		$25	5.0 upper intake plaque			$60
Front-bumper cover	LX repro	$170	PCV adapter tube			$20
Taillamp lens		$110	PCV hose			$9
Hood	repro	$170	Heater tube assembly			$70
Fuel tank sending unit		$90	EFI distributor			$210
Tilt wheel lever		$6	Battery tray			$44
Radiator core support		$180	Alternator			$150
Convertible top boot		$80	Mass air meter boot			$63
Convertible glass rear window		$125	H-pipe smog tube			$100
Convertible top		$150	Vacuum tree			$30
Convertible top headliner		$135	Fan shroud	repro		$90
Convertible sun visor	pair	$50	Fan shroud	original		$110
Convertible top motor		$200	PCV valve grommet			$4

What They Said in 1986

Lest you think nothing has happened in the last eight seasons . . . witness the change under the hood. Sure, the engine is the same basic 302-cid V-8 that powered our 1979 Mustang Cobra test vehicle, but instead of the minimal 152 horsepower pumped out by the 1979 motor, the 1986 HO V-8 cranks out a solid 200 horsepower. . . . Of course, all the development in the world is meaningless if the car doesn't work on the road. This car does. Convertibles, particularly the chopped sedan variety, have a distinct tendency to rattle and moan when pushed. Our Mustang GT tester isn't going to be mistaken for a Rolls in a quiet contest, but you never get the impression that its four wheels are going in four different directions at once. Understeer is a bit heavy; even with all the torque on tape it's hard to kick the tail out, but the GT is always predictable and taut. . . . The Mustang convertible's only real weakness is its long-in-the-tooth styling, inside and out. —*Motor Trend*, June 1986

Sometimes one can easily predict the relative performance of two cars by examining their vital statistics. For example, the Camaro's sleeker bodywork and higher power output strongly suggest that it will outrun the Mustang on the top end; and so it did in our tests, by a 10 miles per hour margin over the Mustang's 132 miles per hour maximum. However, in acceleration, cornering, and braking, the Mustang's lighter weight appears to be a tremendous advantage, partially offsetting the Camaro's edge in both traction and power. In the end, the only way to find the better performer is to set aside the bench racing and conduct careful, head-to-head testing. —*Car and Driver*, June 1986

I Bought a 1986 Mustang

One of my first cars was a mid-1980s Mustang GT, which I made the mistake of selling. After my Mustang parts reproduction business took off, I decided to locate a low-mileage 1985 or 1986 GT to put up and maybe drive occasionally. What I found turned out to be the beginning of my car collection—a white 1986 GT with only 37 miles on the odometer. It's a T-top car that has never been prepped by the dealer, so the original factory markings and labels are still in place. Everything is still wrapped in plastic. I was so excited about the prospect of turning up more low- and no-mile cars that I started asking my friends and customers if they knew of any. Right away, some folks I know in Ohio told me about a red 1986 GT T-top car in Massachusetts with only 325 miles on it. The original owner had worked for Ford his entire life and loved the car, but a divorce forced him to sell it and some other things. The red car was built to the first owner's specifications, which included deletion of the GT hood stripe and manual door locks. Most of its 325 miles were accumulated driving it to and from the Ford dealer for various recall work. *—Daniel Carpenter*

When Saleen 86-0123 first was available on the used car market, I had just bought a Mustang GT and couldn't justify buying the 1986, too. The Saleen was white with the gray GT interior, white basket-weave wheels, blue graphics, and it was all original. In 1990, the car's second owner, G.A. Redding, had it at a car show that was hosted by Saleen Locators and the Saleen Owners and Enthusiasts Club. Redding said he was considering selling the 1986 and asked if I would help him with the process. When my wife, Laura, and I drove it, we knew we had to have it, so Redding agreed to hold it until we could sell our 1985 GT and 1984 SVO. Once it was ours, we subjected 86-0123 to a thorough cleaning inside and out. It's been fun owning such an early car from Saleen's history, because so few people seem to know about anything before 1994. It's got the power of a GT, the handling of the SVO, and the prestige of a name that every Mustang enthusiast reveres. We've kept the car completely original—any replacement parts have been OEM.
—Greg Wackett

1986 Mustang Ratings

Base Four-Cylinder

Model Comfort/Amenities	**
Reliability	***
Collectibility	*
Parts/Service Availability	***
Est. Annual Repair Costs	***

3.8-Liter V-6

Model Comfort/Amenities	***
Reliability	**
Collectibility	*
Parts/Service Availability	***
Est. Annual Repair Costs	***

5.0-Liter V-8

Model Comfort/Amenities	***
Reliability	****
Collectibility	***
Parts/Service Availability	****
Est. Annual Repair Costs	***

5.0-Liter V-8

Model Comfort/Amenities	***
Reliability	****
Collectibility	****
Parts/Service Availability	****
Est. Annual Repair Costs	***

For a long time, the 1986 5.0-liter V-8 suffered by comparison to the previous year's four-barrel version. Ford's abandonment of the 1986-only head design gave the public the impression it had been flawed in some way. Now that all the Fox years can be reviewed at once, the 1986 seems more like a groundbreaker and a precursor of great cars to come, with its EFI, EEC-IV, and 8.8-inch rear axle. From a collector standpoint, the hot ticket for 1986 is a GT or Saleen convertible, and nostalgia buffs get excited over the somewhat troublesome T-top models.

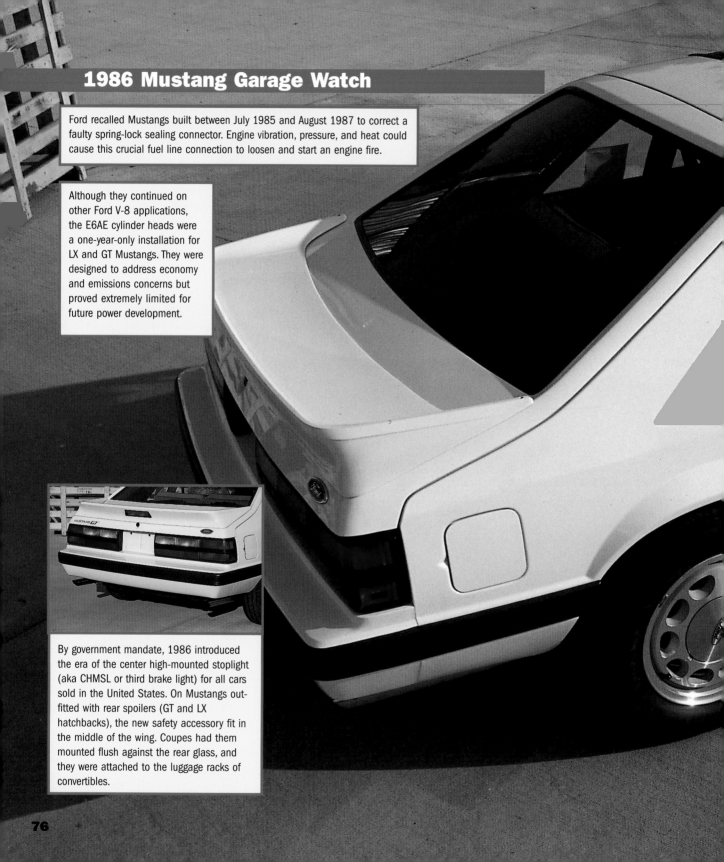

1986 Mustang Garage Watch

Ford recalled Mustangs built between July 1985 and August 1987 to correct a faulty spring-lock sealing connector. Engine vibration, pressure, and heat could cause this crucial fuel line connection to loosen and start an engine fire.

Although they continued on other Ford V-8 applications, the E6AE cylinder heads were a one-year-only installation for LX and GT Mustangs. They were designed to address economy and emissions concerns but proved extremely limited for future power development.

By government mandate, 1986 introduced the era of the center high-mounted stoplight (aka CHMSL or third brake light) for all cars sold in the United States. On Mustangs outfitted with rear spoilers (GT and LX hatchbacks), the new safety accessory fit in the middle of the wing. Coupes had them mounted flush against the rear glass, and they were attached to the luggage racks of convertibles.

In 1986, Ford let buyers choose whether they wanted the large GT blackout panel installed on their hoods. More than a few Mustangers chose to delete the large decal, probably aware of the long-term negative effect sunlight has on the panel.

Although much was made of the 1985 free-flowing system, the Mustang did not have a true dual-exhaust setup until 1986. Unlike the single-cat 1985, the 1986 featured one header, an oxygen sensor, two catalytic converters, a muffler, and tailpipe for each of the V-8's two cylinder banks.

The 1986 model year marked the first in Mustang history to include a remote air filtration system on V-8 models. This airbox contains a baffle resonator to quiet the induction noise, but Mustang owners quickly learned how to remove it with a couple of wrenches for more horsepower.

Aware that more power would be forthcoming in its V-8, Ford upgraded the GT and 5.0 LX rear axle from the 7.5-inch unit that had served since 1979 to a heftier 8.8-inch piece. This single component greatly increased the reliability record of the Mustang's high-performance powertrain.

Ford bought itself another seven years of Fox-body Mustang production with its aerodynamic and much-improved 1987 model. The entire line benefited from flush headlamps, a stiffer body and all-around improved performance. The new look worked great in the wind tunnel, too, with the base hatchback registering a 0.36 coefficient of drag and the GT slicing through the wind with a 0.38 reading.

Chapter 8

1987–1989 Mustang and Saleen

The ongoing refinement that was a hallmark of the 1979 through 1993 Fox-body Mustang made a major leap forward with the introduction of the 1987 model. In terms of engineering, power, comfort, and noise/vibration/harshness levels, the 1979 Mustang could be compared to the Wright brothers' Kitty Hawk flyer, and the 1987, by comparison, to an F-15 fighter jet.

The year 1987 brought an end to the myriad powertrain, trim level, and body style combinations that had earlier been a source of confusion for Mustang buyers. Gone were the SVO, Turbo GT, and V-6. Remaining were the 5.0-liter V-8 and 2.3-liter I-4, which could be had in either the coupe, hatchback, or convertible body styles with a four-speed AOD transmission or a five-speed manual. LX models in all three body styles were the plain trim level; GTs were the fancy version, only available as convertibles or hatchbacks.

The 5.0-liter ("M" code in the VIN) was rated at 225 horsepower and 300 lbs-ft of torque for the 1987 model year, having benefited from a return to pre-1986 head designs, deep-dish forged aluminum pistons with built-in valve-clearance indentions, lower compression ratio (dropped from 9.2:1 to 9.0:1), 60-mm throttle body, and a slightly reshaped exhaust system for better flow. Power, reasonable emissions output, and respectable gas mileage were finally achieved in the Mustang family thanks to the computerized benefits of sequential electronic fuel injection (SEFI) and Ford's fourth-generation electronic engine control (EEC-IV).

The 2.3-liter four-cylinder ("A" code) received the first real improvement since its 1974 introduction in the Mustang II line with the replacement of the two-barrel carburetor with electronic fuel injection. On paper, the mechanical upgrade only reflected a two-horsepower increase (to 90 at 3,800 rpm), but drivability, reliability, and gas mileage all improved, making the 1987 and later four-cylinders all-around better powerplants.

Ford gave the Fox Mustang the same aerodynamic features it was designing into the entire corporate line in the late 1980s, including single rectangular headlamps (similar to what first appeared on the defunct SVO), a smoother front fascia, revised rain channels and drip rails, and rear quarter windows that fit flush against the body. The wind tunnel loved the new model, which registered a 0.36 drag coefficient in LX form and 0.38 as a GT. This compares very favorably to the once-impressive 1979 Mustang's 0.44 rating.

For the first time in Mustang history, the GT was substantially different in appearance from the less-expensive models in the line. Perhaps the most striking aspect of the GT package (which was otherwise mechanically identical to an LX with the 5.0-liter V-8) was the closed-off grille between the headlights. With engineering turning out more efficient and easier-to-cool powerplants, and aerodynamics favoring smooth surfaces, large, radiator-exposing grilles on cars were going the way of wire wheels and vinyl tops. The GT's air intake was moved to below the bumper, where a wide slot situated between two round fog lamps gave the car a distinctive smiling demeanor. LX models, on the other hand, retained two small mail-slot intakes between the headlamps but also featured a wide mouth under the bumper.

In back, the LX received very clean SVO-like taillight lenses, while the GT featured a hot rod–style louvered treatment that some enthusiasts considered too busy to be attractive. A 16-spoke, 15-inch alloy wheel was standard on the GT, while the 5.0-liter LX came standard with the previous year's 10-hole rim. Tire technology had caught up to the V-8's performance, and an improved version of Goodyear's Gatorbacks became standard equipment with the big-motor option.

With a few exceptions, the specifications for 1987 were essentially frozen in place for the next seven model years as Ford concentrated on an all-new 1994 Mustang. The 1988 Mustangs were upgraded with heavy-duty batteries as standard equipment in all V-8 cars. The speed-density management system introduced on the 1986 V-8 was replaced by a Mass Airflow Sensor (MAS) metering system on California-bound cars in 1988 and on all cars sold in the United States in 1989. Also in 1989, Ford established the LX 5.0L Sport to be its own model. This made ordering the extremely popular LX with V-8 mechanicals much simpler for buyers but did not substantially alter the equipment in any way.

The years 1987 through 1989 saw tremendous growth and diversification for Saleen Autosport, whose modified Mustangs benefited from the Ford's new power and styling plus four-wheel disc brakes, 16-inch wheels and tires, a lowered stance, chassis bracing, FloFit articulated seats, and optional 3.55:1 rear-axle ratio.

One hundred and sixty-one copies of Saleen's all-white 1989½ SSC were sold at an unheard of $36,500 each. These historic cars featured the company's first 50-states emission-certified modified 5.0-liter V-8s, rated at 292 horsepower, and a raft of other stylish and high-tech goodies, such as cockpit-adjustable Koni shocks, a four-point interior chassis stiffener (which some have erroneously called a rollbar) and a heavy-duty Auburn rear axle.

The SSC was a one-year-only model, but a similar SC package was offered from 1990 through 1993.

Realizing that a flexible chassis could not be the basis for a race car-like suspension, Saleen stiffened the Fox Mustang's chassis through several braces, such as this triangulated strut tower brace.

Since the very first Saleen Mustang was built in 1984, each car was given a specific serial number in addition to the Ford factory VIN. The number appears in several locations around the vehicle, including the driver-side front bumper, console, and engine compartment. In 1987, Saleen sold 246 hatchbacks, 33 convertibles, and 1 coupe. For 1988, it built 546 hatchbacks, 137 convertibles, and 25 coupes. Still more Saleens were sold in 1989—549 hatchbacks, 165 convertibles, 20 coupes, and 161 SSCs.

Here you see why the Mustang hatchback chassis was not as stiff as the coupe. That hatch is quite a large piece of sheet metal to chop out of the car. Just imagine how flexible the T-top hatchbacks were! Such inherent Fox chassis problems created a segment of the Mustang aftermarket devoted to stiffeners and subframe connectors.

1987–1989 Mustang Specifications

Base price ('87–'89)	66B coupe LX	$8,043–$9,050
	61B hatchback LX	8,474–$9,556
	66B convertible LX	12,840–$14,140
	61B hatchback GT	11,835–$13,272
	66B convertible GT	15,724–$17,512
Production ('87/'88/'89)	66B coupe	43,257/53,221/50,560
	66B convertible	21,447/32,074/42,244
	61B hatchback	94,441/125,930/116,965
Displacement (cubic inches/liters)	I-4	140/2.3
	V-8	302/5.0
Bore x stroke (inches)	I-4	3.78x3.13
	V-8	4.00x3.00
VIN code/Compression ratio	I-4	A 9.5:1
	V-8	M 9.0:1
Induction	I-4	SEFI
	V-8	SEFI
Valvetrain	I-4	SOHC
	V-8	OHV
Horsepower	I-4	90@3,800
	V-8	225@4,200
Transmission (std./opt.)	I-4	5-speed manual/4-speed AOD
	V-8	T-5 5-speed manual/4-speed AOD
Rear-axle ratio	I-4, 5-speed	2.73:1
	I-4, 4-speed AOD	3.08:1
	V-8, 5-speed	2.73:1
	V-8, 4-speed AOD	3.08:1
Wheelbase (inches)		100.5
Overall width (inches)		69.1
Overall height (inches)		52.1
Overall length (inches)		179.3
Track (inches)		(front) 56.6
		(rear) 57.0
Fuel capacity (gallons)		15.4
Weight (pounds)	66B coupe LX	2,724–2,754
	61B hatchback LX	2,782–2,819
	66B convertible LX	2,921–2,966
	61B hatchback GT	3,080–3,194
	66B convertible GT	3,214–3,333
Tires	(base)	P195/75R14
	(V-8, GT and LX)	P225/60VR15
Front suspension		modified MacPherson struts, coil springs
Rear suspension		live axle, four-link suspension system, Quadra-Shock
Steering	(base)	20.0:1 to 15.97:1 variable ratio rack and pinion

	(V-8)	15:1 constant ratio rack and pinion
Brakes	I-4	(front) 9.31-inch disc
	V-8	(front) 10.84-inch vented disc
	all models	(rear) 9.0-inch drum
Gas mileage (EPA city/hwy.)	I-4 5-speed manual	25/31, 25/30, 23/29
	I-4 4-speed AOD	22/28, 21/27, 21/27
	V-8 5-speed manual	18/27, 18/27, 17/24
	V-8 4-speed AOD	16/24, 16/24, 17/25
0 to 60 (secs)	('87 302/5-speed, 3.08:1 axle)*	6.3
	('89 302/5-speed, 2.73:1 axle)**	6.2
Standing ¼-mile (mph/secs)	('87 302/5-speed, 3.08:1 axle)	94@14.7
	('89 302/5-speed, 2.73:1 axle)	95@14.8
Top speed (mph)	('87 302/5-speed, 3.08:1 axle)	137
	('89 302/5-speed, 2.73:1 axle)	141

* Car and Driver, June 1987
** P, July 1989

1987–1989 Mustang

Major Options

5.0-liter V-8 package	(LX)	$1,885
Transmission, 4-speed AOD		$515
Climate Control Group ('87)	(LX coupe)	$1,005
	(LX coupe w/V-8)	$978
	(LX convertible)	$740
	(LX coupe w/V-8)	$713
	(GT hatchback)	$858
	(GT convertible)	$713
Air conditioning		$788–$807
Rear defogger		$145
Tinted glass		$120
Custom Equipment Group ('87)	(LX coupe)	$624
	(LX convertible)	$538
	(GT hatchback)	$500
	(GT convertible)	$414
Graphic Equalizer		$218
Dual power mirrors		$60
Lighted visor mirrors		$100
Tilt steering column	(LX)	$124
Power windows	(coupe)	$22
	(convertible)	$296
Power Lock Group ('87)	(LX w/V-8)	$735
	(GT)	$519
	(LX)	$244
	(GT)	$206
Power Lock Group ('89)		$246
Radio, AM/FM w/cassette		$137
Premium Sound System		$168
Speed control		$176
Bodyside molding insert stripe		$49–$61
Sunroof, flip-up		$355
T-roof ('87)	(LX)	$1,737
	(LX w/Climate Control Group)	$1,667
	(LX w/Special Value Group)	$1,543
	(LX w/Custom Equipment Group)	$1,505
	(GT)	$1,608
	(GT w/Special Value Group)	$1,401
	(GT w/Custom Equipment Group)	$1,341
Wheel covers, wire	(LX)	$98–$193
Wheels, styled road	(LX)	178–193

Replacement Costs for Common Parts

Oil pressure sending unit		$20
Front fender	repro	$85
Front fender	original	$280
Starter		$60
Front seat belt buckle		$47
Outside door handle kit		$27
Electric window motor		$70
Window crank handle		$10
Inside door handle bezel		$23
Door lock actuator kit		$90
Lock cylinder and key		$25
Hatchback quarter window molding	pair	$100
Hatch weather stripping		$27
Trunk weather stripping		$23
Sunroof weather stripping kit		$150
Door weather stripping kit		$40
Vacuum canister		$25
Antenna kit	black	$37
Antenna kit	stainless	$23
Antenna rod		$14
Rubber fender-to-hood bumpers		$2
Hood latch assembly		$25
Wiper arm and blade kit		$40
Wiper arm		$15
Windshield washer nozzle		$9
Trunk lid	convertible and coupe	$170
Floor pan		$115
Smog pump		$60
Crankshaft pulley		$70
Water pump pulley	GT/LX	$45
Distributor cover		$10
Smog canister		$65
Heater core	A/C	$30
	exc. A/C	$35
Radiator bracket	left	$30
	right	$60
Radiator		$110
Rear-brake drum		$35
Power steering pump		$100
Front lower control arms	pair	$200
Pushrods	set of 16	$40
Harmonic balancer		$80
Radiator cap	16-pound	$6
	13-pound	$9

Thermostat	180-degree	$16
	195-degree	$7
Fuel cap		$20
Carpet		$99
Rear-wheel cylinder		$40
Temperature sending unit		$8
Four-piece T-top weather stripping kit		$230
Clutch fork		$25
Tilt wheel lever		$6
Radiator core support		$180
Convertible top boot		$80
Convertible glass rear window		$125
Convertible top		$150
Convertible top headliner		$135
Convertible sun visor	pair	$50
Convertible top motor		$200
Front inner splash shield		$90
Air check valve		$50
Motor mount	convertible	$47
Coolant temperature sensor		$30
Ignition coil		$55
Rearview mirror		$38
LX decklid emblem		$11
Fuel tank		$140
Belt tensioner		$73
Fuel tank shield		$130
Power rack and pinion steering	15:1 ratio	$200
Hydraulic roller lifters	set of 16	$130
Airbox-to-throttle body inlet tube		$35
5.0 upper intake plaque		$60
PCV adapter tube		$20
PCV hose		$9
Heater tube assembly		$70
EFI distributor		$210
Battery tray		$44
Alternator		$150
Mass air meter boot		$63
H-pipe smog tube		$100
Vacuum tree		$30
Fan shroud	repro	$90
Fan shroud	original	$110
PCV valve grommet		$4
Instrument clear lens		$40
Console arm rest pad		$80
Rear-console ashtray		$23
Emergency brake cable		$19
A/C control trim bezel		$22
Radio delete plate		$16
Console top panel		$65

Outside mirror switch		$33
Turn signal lever assembly		$70
Door speaker grille		$23
Hatch area speaker grille		$30
Convertible top switch		$50
Trunk latch		$50
Front-bumper cover	LX repro	$150
Front-bumper cover	GT repro	$140
Front-bumper cover	LX original	$250
Front-bumper cover	GT original	$400
Rear-bumper cover	LX repro	$115
Rear-bumper cover	GT repro	$140
Rear-bumper cover	LX original	$210
Rear-bumper cover	GT original	$250
Fog lamp bracket (all 3 required)	GT center	$70
	GT right	$70
	GT left	$70
Front fender apron		$120
Hood	repro	$170
Hood	original	$500
Third brake light		$45
Underhood insulator		$75
Door skin		$390
Quarter panel	hatchback right original	$680
	hatchback left original	$500
	convertible right original	$500
	convertible left original	$400
Headlight assembly	repro	$60
Headlight assembly	original	$73
Parking lamp	repro	$20
Side marker lamp	repro	$18
Fog lamp assembly	repro	$30
Fog lamp assembly	original	$35
Fog lamp lens		$18
Taillamp lens		$58
Taillamp assembly	LX	$170
Fuel tank filler neck		$40
Fuel tank sending unit		$83
Windshield washer reservoir		$40
Horn		$43
Front-brake rotor		$55
Master cylinder reservoir and cap		$33
Master cylinder	remanufactured	$65
Motor mount	coupe and hatchback	$65
Airbox-to-throttle body inlet tube		$43

What They Said in 1987–1989

Ford made a sizable effort for 1987 to improve the sound deadening in the Mustang platform. Corrugated firewall panels and sound-deadening adhesives give the 1987 Mustang a rock-solid feel. It is, in fact, one of the first things you notice when you close the door. Road noise and engine vibration are cut nearly in half, and yet you still get the benefit of the race-bred Ford small-block, as the Mustang's exhaust note puts that certain little magic in the air. . . . The Mustang's major weakness, more in terms of Showroom Stock competition than any street use, is its brakes. Ford designers chose to enlarge the front vented discs, but continued to use leftover Pinto drums on the rear. This proves all the more annoying since Ford installed the rear disc brake package on the turbocharged SVO four-cylinder Mustang that is now defunct. *—Motor Trend, October 1986*

Getting on to the Interstate was no problem. I pulled along the onramp in second gear, waiting for my spot in traffic. When I saw I had the right lane my foot went down on the gas, the stereo pipes gave a hearty "Hi-o Silver," and the car jumped into its intended place. . . . Cruising in fifth gear at 65 miles per hour takes less than 2,000 rpm and, as traffic cleared I soon found myself enjoying the end of the 85 miles per hour speedometer. This Mustang is so long-legged (2.73:1 Traction-Lok rear end is standard, 3.08 is optional) and powerful that it seems to be loping along at 85. . . . Because of its long-legged nature, I would strongly recommend the optional speed control and a good radar detector. *—Mustang Times, April 1987*

I Bought a 1987–1989 Mustang

My parents bought me a used 1987 white-on-titanium GT in 1988 during my senior year in high school. It was a five-speed with the really tall 2.73:1 rear axle gears, which meant it got pretty decent gas mileage for a V-8 but didn't have quite the acceleration I thought it should. I would definitely have opted for the 3.08:1 gears if I had known what that meant back then. The interior was a bright red that today seems sort of garish, especially against the white exterior. I had the windows tinted and installed a K&N filter to free up some horsepower. Other than those two things, I left it alone. I got married in college and sold the Mustang, but not before my brother put a new set of tires on it and took it through a high-performance driving school at a racetrack in Memphis.—*Geoff Forbus*

I couldn't resist buying my 1989 GT when I found it a couple of years ago. A coal mine engineer in Ohio had purchased the white hatchback but was too obsessed with the car's cleanliness and originality to drive it. He had the oil changed every year and ran the engine to keep gaskets and internal parts from rotting and rusting. The GT was kept on wooden blocks year round. I think it was ordered during warm weather and delivered in the winter; the owner never wanted to take it out of storage. It's clean as a whistle inside and out, and has only 275 miles on the odometer. —*Daniel Carpenter*

I was really impressed with the cars Steve Saleen was building in the mid-1980s, so I bought a black 1988 hatchback, number 0140. It ran and looked great, but I got the idea to build it into something that would be unmatched in performance by any production car. I had Ak Miller build an engine from the oil pan up with Aries 9.5:1 pistons, a Roush racing cam, special ported and polished heads, larger valves, a set of bench-flowed racing injectors, and a ported Car Tech throttle body. Feeding it all was an oil- and water-cooled Garret T-4 ceramic turbocharger that was spun by the air forced through the cast iron exhaust manifolds. Ak told me the engine produced between 550 and 575 horsepower, and I believe it! I had to run a special blend of 112-octane racing fuel that, in 1988, cost $3 a gallon. —*Mark Kemesky*

1987–1989 Mustang Ratings

Base Four-Cylinder

Model Comfort/Amenities	**
Reliability	***
Collectibility	*
Parts/Service Availability	***
Est. Annual Repair Costs	***

5.0-Liter V-8

Model Comfort/Amenities	***
Reliability	****
Collectibility	***
Parts/Service Availability	****
Est. Annual Repair Costs	***

Saleen 5.0-Liter V-8

Model Comfort/Amenities	***
Reliability	****
Collectibility	****
Parts/Service Availability	****
Est. Annual Repair Costs	***

Saleen SSC 5.0-Liter V-8

Model Comfort/Amenities	****
Reliability	****
Collectibility	*****
Parts/Service Availability	****
Est. Annual Repair Costs	***

Because the 1987 Mustang was produced nearly unchanged for the next seven years, picking a collectible out of the bunch is nearly impossible, because any of the V-8 cars is as good as another. Convertibles, GTs, and Saleens in great, low-mileage original condition will hold their value the most. Otherwise, these cars were made to be driven, and it's hard to go wrong when you buy a 1987–1989 Mustang for that purpose. The 1989 ½ Saleen SSC is the most powerful and rarest of the 1987–1989 Mustangs and currently is of great interest to collectors.

In 1987 only, V-8s equipped with automatic transmissions received slightly more restrictive mufflers than the 5-speed models, resulting in a 5-horsepower drop. The change was made in the interest of meeting certain noise-level standards, and the difference in power was not mentioned in Ford's sales literature.

Ignition switch trouble led to a recall by Ford of six years' worth of passenger car and light-duty trucks, including Mustangs. A short circuit in the switch could create fire and/or smoke.

The GT's rear bumper fascia was not properly supported from underneath, resulting in a sag just below the license plate indention. Although there was never a recall to address this issue, the aftermarket has a kit available to fix the problem.

Several interior trim pieces on GT and LX models were flimsy and self-destructed in no time. Examples include the console-mounted ashtray lid and armrest-container lock.

The Mustang LX, with 5.0-liter power, was considered by enthusiast magazines to be the best "bang for the buck" on the road in the late 1980s. It only took one look at the spec sheet to see that a comparably equipped LX V-8 would outperform the slightly heavier, more expensive GT in almost every speed test. Several published comparisons bore out this assumption.

Although it only amounted to a three-horsepower deficit, the 5.0 received a camshaft modification in mid-1988. It had little overall effect on the car's performance.

The aerodynamic Mustang headlight lenses on the 1987 through 1993 Mustangs are notorious for fogging and changing color after a few years. Ford claims there was not enough ultraviolet protection built into the clear plastic piece, and heat from the halogen bulb causes a reaction. Replacement lenses can be purchased through the aftermarket or Ford.

For the first time in Mustang history, the GT package truly looked different from the less-expensive Mustangs. Ford did a thorough job creating two different body treatments from the same chassis. These "cheese grater" taillamps were a throwback to the early hot rod practice of punching louvers into hoods for enhanced cooling.

The new-for-1987 GT "turbine" alloy wheels are not only hard to keep clean (especially the fronts, where brake dust is a problem), but the porous surface can be permanently stained if not well maintained. Don't assume wheels found at a swap meet just need a good wash to look like new.

89

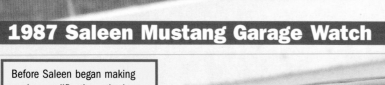

Before Saleen began making engine modifications, the best way to improve the acceleration of its Mustang was to order the optional 3.55:1 unit.

Saleens built in 1987 and 1988 could not be ordered with cruise control, as it could not be mounted to the Momo steering wheel. In 1989, the problem was rectified by the creation of a special bracket.

To emphasize the high-performance aspect of its cars, Saleen equipped every Mustang it modified in 1986 with an Escort radar detector as standard equipment. Sometime during the 1987 production year, the detector became an option.

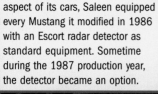

All Saleen Mustangs from the 1987 model year through today have been equipped with four-wheel disc brakes. This safety and performance feature brought with it a five-lug hub for additional strength under high-speed conditions. This basket-weave wheel design ran from its introduction in 1984 through the middle of 1989.

The Saleen Mustang gets its lowered stance and sharper handling from shorter specific-rate springs, Koni (later Monroe) shock absorbers, urethane swaybar bushings and P225/50VR16 General XP-2000Vs—all part of the standard Racecraft suspension enhancements.

The 1989½ SSC was Saleen's first Mustang with 50-state certified engine enhancements. The 5.0-liter produced 292 horsepower from an array of modifications, which included a 65-mm throttle body (the stock Mustang had a 60-mm unit), revised intake plenum, enlarged cylinder head ports, wider rocker arm ratios, stainless steel tubular headers, heavy-duty cooling system, and Walker Dynomax mufflers.

Although not officially offered by the Saleen factory in 1987, one Mustang notchback was built by request for a customer that year. Response to the coupe's appearance convinced the company to give all three body styles the Saleen treatment as of 1988 (shown).

Early 1987 Saleens had aerodynamic body pieces constructed of a plastic with very little flexibility. During the year, the change to urethane was made, which proved more resilient to occasional curb contact.

1990 to 1993 Mustangs received minor improvements from year to year, but were otherwise unchanged. Ford knew it had a complete redesign on the way for '94, so very little money was being spent on the Mustang during this period. Still, the 5.0-liter V-8 models remained the best performance bargains on the market.

Chapter 9

1990–1993 Mustang, Cobra, and Saleen

Of all the Fox-body Mustangs, the 1990 through 1993 models are the most drivable, comfortable, and reliable. All of the technology and design advances learned since 1979 were applied as the years went by, culminating in these nearly identical model years.

Ford's beloved 5.0-liter ("M" code in the VIN for 1990; "E" for 1991 through 1993) entered 1990 largely unchanged from the previous year, its standard T-5 five-speed and optional automatic overdrive four-speed still backing it up. In 1993, although no real modifications were made to the powerplant, Ford downrated it from 225 horsepower to 205, claiming the company was only changing the way it *measured* the engine's output. The 1987 V-8 was tested not only minus certain power-robbing accessories, like the air conditioner compressor (as is common practice with many car companies) but also with ignoring the restrictive airbox baffle hidden away in the passenger-side inner fender. Consideration of the baffle, taking into account a camshaft change in 1988 and Ford's tinkering with the EEC-IV engine management system, killed off 20 horsepower on paper for 1993.

On the other hand, a new head design in 1991 for the once-anemic 2.3-liter four-cylinder ("A" code in 1990; "8" for 1991 through 1993) boosted power to a more respectable 105 at 4,600 rpm. The extra steam came from a twin-spark plug head that had first been used on the Ford Ranger pickup. Outfitted with the standard five-speed, a base 2,751-pound Mustang coupe could now be considered peppy.

All 1990 Mustangs received a driver-side airbag (or "supplemental restraint system"), which put an end to tilt steering on the Fox-body line for the rest of its run. Ford improved the Mustang's handling and tire wear characteristics in 1990 with a revision to the front suspension geometry, whereby the tops of the struts were moved slightly in the direction of the car's windshield to increase caster.

The convertible underwent a linkage redesign in 1991 that reduced the stack height of a folded top by 4 inches. The V-8 Mustang also got its first 16-inch wheels that year, with a clean-looking five-spoke star design that replaced the earlier 15-inch GT turbine wheels. Four-cylinder LX models could be ordered with the older 15-inch, 10-hole alloy wheel as an option. Automatic transmission–equipped cars featured built-in shifter interlock devices that prevented a shift from park without applying the brakes. Ford also saw fit to remove the ill-designed ignition-key release mechanism from the underside of the steering column.

As the carryover models continued for 1992, Ford injected some enthusiasm into the line with a midyear Limited Edition model (LE or Summer Special). All 2,019 LEs were vibrant red convertibles with white tops, color-keyed molding, a model-specific rear spoiler (the first wing to be applied to a convertible at the factory), white interior, and white five-spoke 16-inch wheels. Otherwise, there were minimal changes to the Mustang for 1992.

Although 1993 was the final year of a long-in-the-tooth design, there were some surprises in store for the marque. Another midyear Limited Edition package, available in either canary yellow or oxford white, was produced in convertible form only, but the real excitement came from the introduction of the Special Vehicles Team's (SVT) Cobra and Cobra R models.

The Cobra, which stickered for about $2,300 more than a standard GT, had a 235-horsepower version of the 5.0-liter V-8, with its improvements due to a set of GT-40 heads, special lower intake manifold design, larger valves, freer-flowing mass airflow sensor, smaller-diameter pulleys, a recalibrated engine control computer, and less-restrictive exhaust. Suspension improvements included *softer* spring rates than the GT that, amazingly, generated better handling under most test conditions as well as a smoother ride. SVT referred to its suspension philosophy as "controlled compliance."

Exterior differences between the Cobra and GT/LX included a smoother front fascia, different rear-bumper treatment, and unique four-pedestal wing. The effect was a car sportier than the LX but less bulky than the GT. Aware of the Cobra's future collectibility, each one went to its new owner with a certificate of authenticity indicating the car's SVT-specific serial number.

The R model was lighter than the base Cobra due to absence of certain non-essential equipment, but it was also stronger by virtue of enhanced chassis components, such as convertible-style bracing. Although Ford intended for all 107 R cars to be used in competition, quite a few wound up in the garages of collectors without ever seeing the track.

The four years leading up to the end of Fox production were rough economic ones for all car companies but especially for limited-production manufacturer Saleen. Sales dropped to a low of 17 cars in 1992, but 1993 saw a climb to 102 units to close out the Fox years.

The Mustang's Special Service Vehicles (SSV) program came to an end in 1993 with the final year of the Fox body. The SN-95 design was not conceived around a patrol-friendly platform, and many law enforcement agencies switched to Ford's roomy and powerful Crown Victoria sedan. This 1990 coupe is one of an estimated 15,000 SSV Mustangs built from 1982 to 1993.

Only nine examples of the 1993 Saleen SA-10 (tenth anniversary model) were built—a car that marked the peak of that company's Fox-body Mustang development. Overall Saleen production was down during the 1990 to 1993 period, with sales of 243 cars (1990), 92 cars (1991), 17 cars (1992), and 102 cars (1993) closing out the Fox years.

Although it wore front and rear valances styled after the standard GT, there were many subtle differences. The Cobra body pieces contained no scoops built into the lower cladding, and its rear valance allowed exhaust pipes to exit horizontally (as on the LX model).

1990–1993 Mustang Specifications

Base price ('90–'93)	66B coupe LX	$9,638–$10,719
	61B hatchback LX	$10,144–$11,224
	66B convertible LX	$14,495–$17,548
	61B hatchback GT	$13,929–$15,747
	66B convertible GT	$18,303–$20,848
	61B Cobra (1993)	$18,505
	61B Cobra R (1993)	$25,692
Production ('90/'91/'92/'93)		
	66B coupe	78,728/57,777/40,093/62,077
	66B convertible	26,958/21,513/23,470/27,300
	61B hatchback	22,503/19,447/15,717/24,851
	61B Cobra (1993)	4,993
	61B Cobra R (1993)	107
Displacement (cubic inches/liters)	I-4	140/2.3
	V-8	302/5.0
Bore x stroke (inches)	I-4	3.78x3.13
	V-8	4.00x3.00
VIN code/Compression ratio	I-4 ('90)	A 9.5:1
	I-4 ('91–'93)	S 9.5:1
	V-8 ('90)	M 9.0:1
	V-8 ('91–'93)	E 9.0:1
	V-8 Cobra ('93)	D 9.0:1
Induction	I-4	SEFI
	V-8	SEFI
Valvetrain	I-4	SOHC
	V-8	OHV
Horsepower	I-4	90@3,800
	V-8 ('90–'92)	225@4,200
	V-8 ('93)	205@4,200
	V-8 Cobra ('93)	235@4,600
Transmission (std./opt.)	I-4	5-speed manual/4-speed AOD
	V-8	T-5 5-speed manual/4-speed AOD
	V-8 Cobra	T-5 5-speed manual
Rear-axle ratio	I-4, 5-speed	2.73:1
	I-4, 4-speed AOD	3.08:1
	V-8, 5-speed	2.73:1
	V-8, 4-speed AOD	2.73:1
	V-8 Cobra	3.08:1
Wheelbase (inches)		100.5
Overall width (inches)		69.1
Overall height (inches)		52.1
Overall length (inches)		179.3

Track (inches)		(front) 56.6
		(rear) 57.0
Fuel capacity (gallons)		15.4
Weight (pounds)	66B coupe LX	2,634-2,751
	61B hatchback LX	2,634-2,812
	66B convertible LX	2,871-2,973
	61B hatchback GT	3,065-3,144
	66B convertible GT	3,213-3,365
	61B Cobra (1993)	3,255
	61B Cobra R (1993)	3,195
Tires	base	P195/75R14
	V-8, GT and LX (1990)	P225/60VR15
	V-8, GT and LX (1991-'93)	P225/55ZR16
	Cobra	P245/45ZR17
Front suspension		modified MacPherson struts, coil springs
Rear suspension		live axle, four-link suspension system, Quadra-Shock
Steering	(base)	18.70:1 to 16.20:1 variable ratio rack and pinion
	(V-8)	15:1 constant ratio rack and pinion
Brakes	I-4	(front) 9.31-inch disc
	V-8	(front) 10.84-inch vented disc
	all models (exc. Cobra)	(rear) 9.0-inch drum
	Cobra	(rear) 10.07-inch vented disc
Gas mileage (EPA city/hwy., '90/'91/'92/'93)	I-4 5-speed manual	23/29, 22/30, 22/30, 22/30
	I-4 4-speed AOD	21/27, 21/28, 21/28, 22/29
	V-8 5-speed manual	17/25, 18/25, 18/25, 17/24
	V-8 4-speed AOD	16/24, 17/24, 17/24, 17/24
	V-8 Cobra 5-speed ('93)	17/24
0 to 60 (secs)	('90 GT 302/5-speed, 2.73:1 axle)*	6.4
	('93 Cobra, 302/5-speed, 3.08:1 axle)**	5.6
Standing ¼-mile (mph/secs)	('90 GT 302/5-speed, 2.73:1 axle)	94.04@14.72
	('93 Cobra, 302/5-speed, 3.08:1 axle)	98@14.3
Top speed (mph)	('90 GT 302/5-speed, 2.73:1 axle)	141
	('93 Cobra, 302/5-speed, 3.08:1 axle)	137

* *Hot Rod*, July 1990
** SVT factory info

1990–1993 Mustang

Major Options

Transmission, 4-speed AOD		$539–595
LX V-8 Sport GT Group	(1990 LX coupe, hatchback)	1,003
Power Equipment Group—inc. dual electric mirrors, power side windows, Power Lock Group, cargo tie-down net, front floor mats, speed control, AM/FM radio with cassette player and clock, styled road wheels		
	('91–'93 LX coupe, hatchback)	
		222–276
	(LX convertible)	207–306
Air conditioning		807–817
Rear defogger		150–170
Engine block heater		20
Emissions, California		100
Lighted visor mirrors		100
Radio, AM/FM w/cassette	('90–'92)	137–155
Premium Sound System		168–339
Radio, delete	credit	245–584
Speed control		191–224
Sunroof, flip-up		355
Paint, clearcoat		91
Titanium lower accent	(GT)	159
Wheel covers, wire	(standard LX)	no charge
Wheels, styled road	(LX)	178–193
Tires, WSW P195/75R14	(1990 LX four-cylinder)	82

Replacement Costs for Common Parts

Front fender	repro	$85
Front fender	original	$280
Starter		$60
Front seat belt buckle		$47
Outside door handle kit		$27
Electric window motor		$70
Window crank handle		$10
Inside door handle bezel		$23
Door lock actuator kit		$90
Lock cylinder and key		$25
Hatchback quarter window molding pair		$100
Hatch weather stripping		$27
Trunk weather stripping		$23
Sunroof weather stripping kit		$150
Door weather stripping kit		$40
Vacuum canister		$25
Antenna kit	black	$37
Antenna kit	stainless	$23
Antenna rod		$14
Rubber fender-to-hood bumpers		$2
Hood latch assembly		$25
Wiper arm and blade kit		$40
Wiper arm		$15
Windshield washer nozzle		$9
Trunk lid	convertible and coupe	$170
Floor pan		$115
Smog pump		$60
Crankshaft pulley		$70
Water pump pulley	GT/LX	$45
Distributor cover		$10
Smog canister		$65
Heater core	A/C	$30
	exc. A/C	$35
Radiator bracket	left	$30
	right	$60
Radiator		$110
Rear-brake drum		$35
Power steering pump		$100
Front lower control arms	pair	$200
Pushrods	set of 16	$40
Harmonic balancer		$80
Radiator cap	16-pound	$6
	13-pound	$9
Thermostat	180-degree	$16
	195-degree	$7

Fuel cap		$20
Carpet		$99
Rear-wheel cylinder		$40
Temperature sending unit		$8
Clutch fork		$25
Convertible top boot		$80
Convertible glass rear window		$125
Convertible top		$150
Convertible top headliner		$135
Convertible sun visor	pair	$50
Convertible top motor		$200
Front inner splash shield		$90
Air check valve		$50
Motor mount	convertible	$47
Coolant temperature sensor		$30
Ignition coil		$55
Rearview mirror		$38
LX decklid emblem		$11
Fuel tank		$140
Belt tensioner		$73
Fuel tank shield		$130
Power rack and pinion steering		
	15:1 ratio	$200
Hydraulic roller lifters	set of 16	$130
5.0 upper intake plaque		$60
PCV adapter tube		$20
PCV hose		$9
Heater tube assembly		$70
EFI distributor		$210
Battery tray		$44
Alternator		$150
Mass air meter boot		$63
H-pipe smog tube		$100
Vacuum tree		$30
Fan shroud	repro	$90
Fan shroud	original	$110
PCV valve grommet		$4
Console arm rest pad		$80
Rear-console ashtray		$23
Emergency brake cable		$19
A/C control trim bezel		$22
Radio delete plate		$16
Console top panel		$65
Outside mirror switch		$33
Turn signal lever assembly		$70
Door speaker grille		$23
Hatch area speaker grille		$30
Convertible top switch		$50
Trunk latch		$50
Front-bumper cover	LX repro	$150
Front-bumper cover	GT repro	$140
Front-bumper cover	LX original	$250
Front-bumper cover	GT original	$400
Rear-bumper cover	LX repro	$115
Rear-bumper cover	GT repro	$140
Rear-bumper cover	LX original	$210
Rear-bumper cover	GT original	$250
Fog lamp bracket (all 3 required)		
	GT center	$70
	GT right	$70
	GT left	$70
Front-fender apron		$120
Hood	repro	$170
Hood	original	$500
Third brake light		$45
Underhood insulator		$75
Door skin		$390
Quarter panel	hatchback right original	$680
	hatchback left original	$500
	convertible right original	$500
	convertible left original	$400
Headlight assembly	repro	$60
Headlight assembly	original	$73
Parking lamp	repro	$20
Side marker lamp	repro	$18
Fog lamp assembly	repro	$30
Fog lamp assembly	original	$35
Fog lamp lens		$18
Taillamp lens		$58
Taillamp assembly	LX	$170
Fuel tank filler neck		$40
Fuel tank sending unit		$83
Windshield washer reservoir		$40
Horn		$43
Front-brake rotor		$55
Master cylinder reservoir and cap		$33
Master cylinder	remanufactured, exc. Cobra	$65
	Cobra	$100
Motor mount	coupe and hatchback	$65
Airbox-to-throttle body inlet tube		$43
Instrument clear lens		$40
Speed control switches		$65
Hatch cargo cover		$130
Radiator core support		$200
Oil pressure sending unit		$27
Steering wheel	$100 core charge	$270
Front fender	repro	$90
Front fender	original	$300
16x7-inch 5-spoke wheel		$140
Rearview mirror		$19
Starter		$155

What They Said in 1990–1993

The Ford Mustang is another car that polarized our drivers. Some of our people couldn't forgive the Mustang for its protracted braking distances, stiff shifter, and non-supportive driver's seat. The rest of us loved the car for its limitless supply of rich, creamy torque at any rpm and all the wonderful things that made it possible. The boosted steering feels a little dead, but who cares? Once you're in a turn with the Mustang, you steer with the throttle anyway. It's a marvelous slider, right up to the point of no return. We passed that point numerous times, so we ought to know. —*Motor Trend,* **November 1989**

Over the past six years, we've driven one of everything Saleen Autosport has produced. That includes one of each body style of Saleen Mustang, the short-lived Ranger-based Sportruck, a few one-off prototypes, and last year's supercar, the 290-horsepower SSC. Because the SSC was Saleen's first product with a horsepower increase (approved by the EPA and everything), it got an enormous amount of attention and was enthusiastically received by Mustangers. Steve Saleen said from the start the SSC would be a one-year-only model, never to be repeated to ensure rarity and collector status. True to his word, Saleen has completely redesigned his supercar package this year to include more horsepower, seating for four, a stiffer chassis, more color choices, and a new name—the SC. —*Mustang Illustrated,* **October 1990**

Much of the Cobra variant is, first, carryover, including most of the chassis and metal body panels. Cosmetic changes are, for once, genuine upgrades in most eyes. They tone down the raucous "boy racerhood" that still hounds the rear-drive musclecar, even though the high school kids commonly held to be the Mustang's chief clientele presumably were frozen out of the market long ago by rising prices. A Mustang GT can go out the door in the high teens to about $20,000, and the Cobra package is expected to add a rather small $2,500 bump. For that you get a freshened powerplant, new grille, tastefully refined trim, decorous rear-deck spoiler, and a few minor but effective suspension changes that soften the ride yet improve the handling. —*Motor Trend,* **October 1992**

I Bought a 1990 Mustang

I bought one of the first Saleen SCs built in 1990, number 0012. My SC was red and, in stock form, had much of the performance equipment from the previous year's all-white SSC model. It had the 304-horsepower 5.0-liter that Saleen had gotten certified in 1989, a heavy-duty Borg-Warner T-5 transmission, Auburn-built Traction-Lok rear axle, and 3.55:1 gears. The chassis upgrades from the factory included Z-rated XP2000 General tires (P225/50R16 front, P245/50R16 rear) on five-spoke alloy wheels, extra stiffening in the form of a triangular shock tower brace and subframe connectors, and Racecraft suspension components. The interior had FloFit seats and a 200 miles per hour speedometer, but the stock Ford steering wheel, because it was the first year for an airbag and no one in the aftermarket had much experience working around them yet. At the time it came out, the SC was the fastest late-model Mustang produced. I installed a full rollcage, onboard fire extinguisher system, shaved tires, and fiberglass racing seats for some weekend track visits. —*Kerry Peterson*

I come from an all-Ford family, so there was really no discussion about what kind of car I would drive when I got my license at 16. My father had been building, modifying, and racing Mustangs since before I was born. He and I shopped Ford dealers for two weeks in 1993 looking for a well-maintained, slightly used V-8 Mustang. We were really exhausted one day sitting on a dealer lot, when this older gentleman drove by us in a 1993 green coupe. He was in the process of trading it for a new truck and was turning it in. It was a five-speed 5.0 LX with 10,000 miles on the odometer. I didn't have much experience driving something so powerful, so I did a 360-degree spin in the rain pulling out of the lot for the first time. Since that day 10 years ago, I have grown to love my green Mustang, which now has 160,000 miles on it. I work on it myself, making sure the fluids, plugs, and belts are inspected or changed on a strict schedule. The only thing I've ever had to replace is the alternator. I intend to keep driving it until smoke comes out of the tailpipe, at which point my father will probably rebuild the V-8 for another round of driving. The only thing that could tempt me to sell it is the 2005 Mustang I've seen photos of in magazines. —*Shannon Wright*

1990–1993 Mustang Ratings

Base Four-Cylinder

Model Comfort/Amenities	***
Reliability	****
Collectibility	*
Parts/Service Availability	***
Est. Annual Repair Costs	***

5.0-Liter V-8

Model Comfort/Amenities	****
Reliability	****
Collectibility	***
Parts/Service Availability	****
Est. Annual Repair Costs	***

Cobra 5.0-Liter V-8

Model Comfort/Amenities	****
Reliability	****
Collectibility	****
Parts/Service Availability	****
Est. Annual Repair Costs	***

Saleen 5.0-Liter V-8

Model Comfort/Amenities	****
Reliability	****
Collectibility	****
Parts/Service Availability	***
Est. Annual Repair Costs	***

Saleen SC 5.0-Liter V-8

Model Comfort/Amenities	****
Reliability	****
Collectibility	*****
Parts/Service Availability	***
Est. Annual Repair Costs	***

These cars are the best of the Fox years in terms of daily driving and owning. V-8 models are extremely popular used cars. Younger drivers have modified many for performance, but finding adult-driven, well-maintained examples is not too difficult—yet. The four-cylinder's power increase in 1991 makes it an enjoyable alternative, but not exactly what collectors are seeking. The true collectibles will likely be V-8 convertibles with low miles, especially the single-year packages such as the Canary Yellow or Oxford White 1993 ½ Limited Edition convertibles. The debut SVT Cobra and Cobra R models, along with Saleen's 1990–1993 SC and 1993-only 15th Anniversary supercharged car, are the rarest and most desirable of this bunch.

Several 5.0-liter V-8 Mustangs built in April and May 1993 had inadequately formed fuel rails feeding the injectors. Because of their potential to fracture and leak, Ford issued a recall for these cars.

The year 1990 was the first for Mustang production to see a driver-side supplemental restraint system (SRS) in the form of an airbag. Such cars feature a "C" in the fourth spot of the VIN. There is no way for the average driver to tell if the airbag has been properly replaced after a previous accident; it is necessary to consult a Ford dealer or specialized body shop.

Automatic transmission–equipped Mustangs built in October 1990 may have been fitted with a park cam that is too soft to keep the car from rolling when left on an incline. Ford issued a recall to replace the entire parking rod assembly.

Another performance component first came to the Mustang line in 1991 when 5.0-liter cars gained 16-inch wheels and tires as standard equipment. A five-spoke "star" wheel came shod with P225/55ZR16 Goodyear GT all-season radials (LX) or Gatorbacks (GT). The turbine wheel was dropped from the line, and the 10-hole alloy rim introduced on the 1985 GT was offered to four-cylinder buyers.

Slow to make the Mustang list of optional equipment was a compact disc player, which had been offered with other Ford, Lincoln, and Mercury division cars for several years. When ordered, the $629 option took the place of a cassette player.

The last Limited Edition to be built in the Fox body style was a run of 1993½ Canary Yellow or Oxford White convertibles. The yellow option, which was $1,488 (under the name Preferred Equipment Package Order Code 415), included monochromatic paint, chromed 16-inch wheels, color-keyed interior, and a black or white top. The white option was $976, with painted wheels instead of chrome.

Another safety feature introduced in 1990 was the three-point restraint for rear passengers. The new belts and airbag added weight that Ford had to reduce in other areas, so for much of 1990, the armrest disappeared from the rear of the console.

Goodyear's Gatorback tires gave the 5.0-liter Mustangs some great traction on dry pavement, but they made the car a handful when it rained. Starting in late 1989, Ford started putting P225/60VR15 Eagle GT+4 all-season high-performance tires on LX V-8 cars as standard and on GTs as an option.

1990–1993 Cobra Garage Watch

The SVT Cobra's front was a distinctive combination of LX, SVO, and GT styling. The lower valance resembles that of the GT, including the identical fog lamps, but it has been cleaned up to remove the busy scoops. The LX- and SVO-like elements work together above the bumper to create an efficient face featuring a "mail slot" grille intake.

The Cobra brought with it some improvements for the regular 5.0-liter Mustang line, specifically in the gearbox. The T-5 five-speed received a phosphate-coated cluster gear and tapered roller bearings, which greatly improved the transmission's durability and reliability.

The Cobra was the first production V-8 Mustang to combine four-wheel disc brakes, a five-lug bolt pattern, and 17-inch wheels. Under test conditions, the Cobra was found to stop from 60 miles per hour in 15 feet less than a comparably equipped GT.

Because they were produced in limited numbers on a mass-production system, first-year Cobras were turned out in batches based on color. Black cars were made first (1,854 in all), followed by red Cobras (1,891, including the 107 R models), and the eye-catching teal finished the run at 1,355 units.

Probably the stoutest of the Fox chassis was the Cobra R, which benefited from several braces and assembly line modifications normally reserved for V-8 convertibles.

Because some sanctioning bodies had rules against deleting equipment from production cars intended for competition, the components missing from the Cobra R were simply never installed. On the Ford assembly line, the R cars were not equipped with backseats, fog lamps, air conditioning, and sound-deadening material.

With 30 more horsepower than the LX/GT models, the Cobra's 5.0-liter took the Fox-body Mustang to a new level of performance. Zero to 60 times were close to a second faster than a stock GT, and quarter-mile runs could be accomplished a half second quicker.

The empty fog lamp openings became sources of extra cooling for the engine and brakes on the Cobra R. The driver-side opening allows air to flow through a power steering fluid cooler.

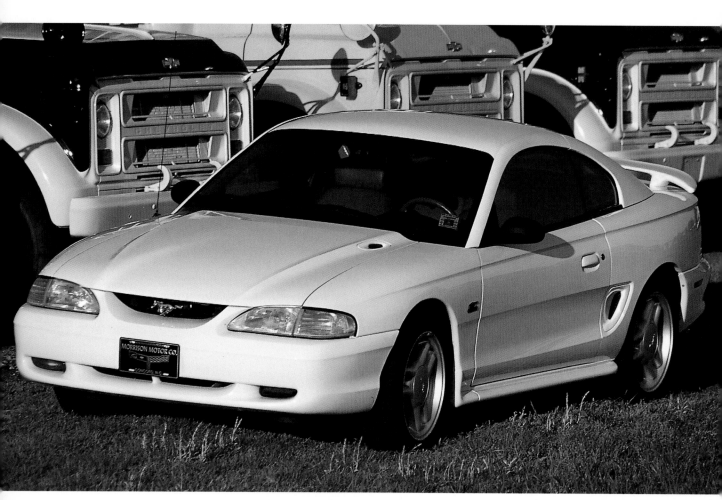

Stiffer than ever, the new 1994 body was a huge improvement over the Fox cars that preceded it. Noise, vibration and harshness (NVH) levels were much lower than before, even in the convertible.

Chapter 10

1994–1995 Mustang, Cobra, and Saleen

On Oct. 15, 1993, the Mustang entered its fourth generation and thirtieth anniversary with a slick new redesign that Ford engineers and marketers referred to as the Fox-4 or SN-95, ending a seven-year run of identical models.

What looked like an all-new model was really a high-tech body and suspension draped over an evolved version of the Fox chassis. Mustang engineers did not have the luxury of starting with a clean slate. In order to meet production and sticker-cost goals, the Fox floor pan, K-member, and other "hidden" components were carried over from the 1993 model, along with a mildly revised version of the 5.0-liter engine. Everything else—or at least 1,330 out of 1,850 parts, according to a source at Ford—was created specifically for the new-generation Mustang.

Because the early Fox cars suffered from flexible bodies, structural integrity was the Mustang team's primary focus. To reach its objective, Ford dropped the hatchback from its lineup, having realized that such a body style could never be satisfactorily stiff without an unacceptable amount of weight for reinforcement. Heavy-gauge metal and thicker sections were incorporated into the new coupe and convertible, as were some components borrowed from the thriving Mustang aftermarket, such as strut-tower braces and X braces.

The results spoke for themselves, with the coupe gaining 44 percent in torsion and 56 percent in bending, with the convertible improving an impressive 150 percent and 76 percent, respectively.

At 181.5 inches, the SN-95 was 2.4 inches longer than the 1993 model, although the more aerodynamic body looked smaller. Its 101.3-inch wheelbase had grown by 0.9 inches, and its girth gained 2.8 inches over the original Fox car to measure 71.9 inches. Modifications allowed for 1.5 to 4.0 degrees of adjustable suspension settings, which appealed to weekend racers who would be fitting wider tires and dialing in their own handling specifications.

Under the GT's sloping new hood sat a 5.0-liter V-8 ("E" code in the VIN) rated at 215 horsepower, a 10-horsepower gain over 1993. The increase was due to a low-profile, low-restriction intake manifold borrowed from the Thunderbird. A T-5 five-speed manual transmission was standard equipment, and the tried-and-true AOD automatic was optional with the V-8.

An old engine returned to Mustang duty with the dropping of the four-cylinder for 1994. The 3.8-liter V-6 ("4" code), which had not been available in the Mustang line since 1986, was the base engine. With 145 horsepower on tap, the new V-6 became the most powerful base Mustang model ever, clocking 0 to 60 times in the nine-second range. The powerplant benefited from development in the Thunderbird and Probe during its absence[em]that and some well-chosen aluminum parts here and there. Transmission choices were the same for the V-6 as the V-8.

SVT followed the GT's introduction with its one-step-better Cobra. Also powered by the carryover 5.0-liter ("O" code), the Cobra's V-8 produced 240 horsepower and was available only with a slightly modified T-5 five-speed manual transmission. It boasted bigger brakes than the GT (13-inch fronts versus the GT's 10.8 inchers) and wider tires (P255/45ZR17s vs. P245/45ZR17), but softer springs and a smaller front swaybar.

Saleen built a modern musclecar on the SN-95 platform by installing normally aspirated and supercharged 351-cid V-8s into coupes and convertibles. The S-351 took the new Mustang to new levels of performance—5.9-second 0 to 60, 14.3-second quarter mile, and 0.97g on the skidpad—and price—$34,990 as a coupe; $40,990 as a convertible).

In 1995, SVT repeated its Cobra R-model formula (first seen in 1993), only this time with a 300-horsepower 351-cid V-8 ("C" code). Just 250 were built, all in white and stripped of unnecessary equipment such as air conditioning, rear seat, soundproofing materials, fog lamps, and radio. The 1995 R was largely built from the corporate parts bin, which proved to be a blessing when SVT convinced the EPA that the 351 was nothing more than an already certified 302 with a longer stroke, thereby saving much time and money for the project.

Ford knew its 5.0-liter, which was enjoying its final year as a Mustang engine, had a strong following among the marque's longtime fans. Its roots went all the way back to the 260-cid V-8 that powered the 1965 Mustang, and the 302 itself was introduced in 1968. The Windsor engine had only been out of Mustang production for three of those 30 years—in 1974, 1980, and 1981—and was replaced for 1996 by a high-tech modular 4.6-liter.

As a nod to its enthusiasts, the company produced the GTS, a 1995-only model that was essentially a GT without the sports seats, rear spoiler, and fog lamps. It rode on the GT's stock 16-inch alloy wheels and was available in coupe only for $16,910, or nearly $1,000 less than the GT.

The 1995-only Cobra R featured Ford's only modern use of a 351-cid V-8 in one of its Mustangs. Because it was built for competition, it could only be ordered by someone with an active race license. At $37,599, all 250 were sold within a 10-hour period.

Ford's Mach 460 stereo was one bit of evidence that the company was serious about the new Mustang's creature comforts. Speakers were placed according to the specifications of acoustic engineers.

Saleen produced a limited run of V-6 Sport Mustangs in 1994 that were not part of the company's serialized line. The 29 coupes benefited from Racecraft suspension pieces, 17x8-inch wheels, and a short-throw Hurst shifter. The coupe pictured was fitted with Saleen's supercharger and dual-exhaust system.

1994–1995 Mustang Specifications

Base price ('94–95)	40 coupe V-6	$13,355–$14,330
	44 convertible V-6	$20,150–$20,795
	42 coupe GT	$17,270–$17,905
	45 convertible GT	$21,960–$22,595
	42 coupe Cobra	$20,765–$21,300
	45 convertible Cobra	$26,845–$25,605
	42 coupe Cobra R (1995)	$35,499
Production ('94–'95)	40 coupe	73,475–137,722
	44 convertible	43,714–48,264
	42 coupe Cobra	5,009–4,005
	45 convertible Cobra	1,000–1,003
	42 coupe Cobra R (1995)	250
Displacement (cubic inches/liters) V-6		232/3.8
	V-8	302/5.0
	V-8 Cobra R (1995)	351/5.8
Bore x stroke (inches)	V-6	3.80x3.40
	V-8	4.00x3.00
	V-8 Cobra R	4.00x3.50
VIN code/Compression ratio V-6		4 9.0:1
	V-8	E 9.0:1
	V-8 Cobra	0 9.0:1
	V-8 Cobra R	C 9.0:1
Induction	V-6	TPI
	V-8	SEFI
Valvetrain	V-6	OHV
	V-8	OHV
Horsepower	V-6	145@4,000
	V-8	215@4,200
	V-8 Cobra	240@4,800
	V-8 Cobra R	300@4,800
Transmission (std./opt.)	V-6	5-speed manual/4-speed AOD
	V-8	5-speed manual/4-speed AOD
	V-8 Cobra	T-5 5-speed manual
	V-8 Cobra R	TR-3550 5-speed manual
Rear-axle ratio	V-6	2.73:1
	V-8, 5-speed	2.73:1
	V-8, 4-speed AOD	3.27:1
	V-8 Cobra	3.08:1
Wheelbase (inches)		101.3
Overall width (inches)		71.8
Overall height (inches)		53.1
Overall length (inches)		181.5
Track (inches)		(front) 60.1
		(rear) 58.7
Fuel capacity (gallons)		15.4
Weight (pounds)	40 coupe V-6	3,055–3,077
	44 convertible V-6	3,193–3,257
	42 coupe GT	3,258–3,280
	45 convertible GT	3,414–3,451
	42 coupe Cobra	3,365–3,365
	45 convertible Cobra	3,567–3,567
	42 coupe Cobra R ('95)	3,280
Tires	base	P205/6515
	GT standard	P225/55ZR16
	GT optional	P245/45ZR17
	Cobra	P255/45ZR17
Front suspension		modified MacPherson struts, lower A-arms, coil springs, tube shocks, anti-roll bar
Rear suspension		live axle, angled upper and lower trailing arms, coil springs, tube shocks, anti-roll bar
Steering		14.7:1 constant ratio rack and pinion
Brakes	all models (exc. Cobra)	(front) 10.8-inch vented disc
	all models (exc. Cobra)	(rear) 10.5-inch disc
	Cobra	(front) 13-inch vented disc
	Cobra	(rear) 11.65-inch vented disc
Gas mileage (EPA city/hwy.) V-6 5-speed manual		20/30, 20/30
	V-6 4-speed AOD	19/29, 19/29
	V-8 5-speed manual	17/25, 17/25
	V-8 4-speed AOD	17/25, 17/24
	V-8 Cobra 5-speed	17/25, 17/25
	V-8 Cobra R 5-speed ('95)	14/22
0 to 60 (secs)	(V-6/auto, 2.73:1 axle)*	9.9
	(GT 302/5-speed, 3.08:1 axle)**	6.7
	(Cobra, 302/5-speed, 3.08:1 axle)***	6.9
	(Saleen S-351)****	4.9
Standing ¼-mile (mph/secs)	(V-6/auto, 2.73:1 axle)	81.3@17.3
	(GT 302/5-speed, 3.08:1 axle)	92.5@15.2
	(Cobra, 302/5-speed, 3.08:1 axle)	93@15.3
	(Saleen S-351)	111.9@13.2
Top speed (mph)	(GT 302/5-speed, 3.08:1 axle)	140
	(Cobra, 302/5-speed, 3.08:1 axle)	140
	(Saleen S-351)	177.1

* *Motor Trend*, May 1995
** *Road & Track*, Jan. 1994
*** *Road & Track*, June 1994
**** *Road & Track*, June 1995

1994–1995 Mustang

Major Options

Transmission, 4-speed AOD		$790–$815
Optional axle ratio	(GT only)	$45
Mustang 241A	(includes A/C, AM/FM stereo cassette)	$565
Mustang 243A	(includes A/C; power side windows, door locks,	
	decklid release; speed control, dual lighted visor mirrors, 15-inch aluminum wheels, AM/FM stereo radio w/cassette and Premium Sound, remote keyless entry and cargo net)	
	(coupe)	$1,825–$2,030
	(convertible)	$1,415–$1,625
Cobra coupe 250A	(includes A/C, rear-window defroster, front floor	
	mats, speed control)	$1,260
Cobra convertible 250C	('95, includes A/C, rear-window defroster, front floor mats, speed control, remote keyless entry,Mach 460 stereo w/cassette and CD, leather seats)	
		$2,755
		$1,185–$1,260
Emissions, California		$95
Wheels, 15-inch aluminum	(V-6 only)	$265
Wheels, 17-inch aluminum	(GT only)	$380
Seats, leather sport bucket	(GT)	$500
	(convertible)	$500
	(Cobra coupe)	$500
Air conditioning		$780–$855
Brakes, anti-lock	(std. Cobra)	$565
Anti-theft system		$235-$145
Convertible hardtop	(available '95 only)	$1,825
Rear-window defroster		$160
Front floor mats		$30
Engine block heater	(N/A Cobra)	$20
Bodyside moldings	(V-6 and GT only)	$50
CD player	(N/A coupe)	$475-$375
Mach 460 AM/FM stereo		$375
AM/FM stereo w/cassette	(std. Cobra, N/A coupe)	$165

Replacement Costs for Common Parts

Pushrods	set of 16	$40
Harmonic balancer		$80
Radiator cap	16-pound	$6
	13-pound	$9
Thermostat	180-degree	$16
	195-degree	$7
Fuel cap		$20
Carpet		$99
Temperature sending unit		$8
Clutch fork		$25
Coolant temperature sensor		$30
Ignition coil		$55
Hydraulic roller lifters	set of 16	$130
Roller rockers	Cobra, set of 16	$250
Starter		$155
Hydraulic roller lifters	set of 16	$130
Temperature sending unit		$8
Pushrods	set of 16	$40
Harmonic balancer		$80
Radiator cap	16-pound	$6
	13-pound	$9
Thermostat	180-degree	$16
Indy Pace Car decklid emblem		$37
Convertible glass rear window		$165
Underhood insulator		$63
GT fender emblem		$10
EGR-to-header tube		$50
Idler pulley		$18
Oil pressure sending unit		$13
Distributor cover		$13
Airbox-to-throttle body inlet tube		$70
Radiator		$160
Power rack and pinion steering	14:1 ratio	$245
Motor mount	left	$53
	right	$84
Radiator core support		$200
Radiator-to-grille cover		$65
Fuel tank sending unit		$77
Fuse box cover		$13
Battery tray		$13
Radio and A/C bezel		$120
Rearview mirror		$20
Convertible top motor		$240
Front-bumper cover	Cobra repro	$230

Part	Spec	Price	Part	Spec	Price
Front-bumper cover	GT/V-6 repro	$180	Convertible top		$190
Front inner splash shield		$40	Turn signal lever assembly		$40
Front fender	repro	$90	Trunk weather stripping		$35
Front fender	original	$210	Convertible top headliner		$150
Hood	GT/V-6 repro	$200	Factory headlight knob		$12
Hood	GT/V-6 original	$500	Mach 460 speaker grille		$20
Third brake light		$80	Convertible top boot		$300
Rubber fender-to-hood bumpers		$2	Convertible top switch		$20
Headlight assembly	GT/V-6	$70	Electric window motor		$110
Headlight assembly	Cobra	$100	Antenna rod		$12
Side marker lamp		$23	Wiper arm		$35
Fog lamp kit		$240	Space-saver wheel and tire		$40
Pony grille emblem		$22	Front-brake rotor	GT	$40
Heater core		$49	Front-brake rotor	Cobra	$160
Clutch fork		$27	Outside mirror switch		$45
Instrument clear lens		$70	Tilt wheel lever		$6
Console arm rest pad		$70	SVT emblem	Cobra	$12
Utility compartment		$18	Convertible glass rear window		$165
Fog lamp switch		$19			

What They Said in 1994–1995

Performance-car history settles on the Mustang like morning dew. Was it really almost 30 years ago[em]April 17, 1964, in fact, at the New York World's Fair[em]that the original Ford Mustang was introduced? It spawned the entire pony-car craze. . . . The 1994 Mustang is a full and legitimate descendant of the car and the excitement spawned in 1964. Performance will get a healthy augmentation next spring with the introduction of a 245-horsepower Cobra "pony express" variant, but for now, the new Mustang is about as much fun as you can have without breaking the law. *—Motor Trend,* **November 1993**

It may require a double-take before you're sure, but trust your instincts that the 1994 Mustang Cobra is a threat to be taken seriously. The powertrain engineers swear there's only been some recalibration work performed on the GT40-fortified 5.0-liter since last year, but it feels significantly stronger in the lower rpm ranges. Ford's spec chart states that the 1994 Cobra motor produces five horsepower more than in 1993, but the same amount of peak torque. . . . More horsepower at a lower rpm is a good thing, but we can feel that the torque curve was widened a bit as well. . . . Gradual highway grades no longer require a downshift just to maintain momentum, and same-gear passing on a two-lane can be accomplished without a last will and testament. *—Motor Trend,* **April 1994**

I Bought a 1995 Mustang

In 1997, I drove my 1994 Impala SS from North Carolina to Denver and back on a two-week vacation. On every scenic drive I took, I saw new Mustang convertibles and realized that putting the windows down on my big Impala was nowhere near the experience their owners were enjoying. The day after I returned, I drove to CARMAX and saw a teal 1995 GT convertible with only 25,000 miles and a brand new set of Nitto tires on the stock 17-inch wheels. The only defects in the car were a broken thigh support on the driver's seat (fixed under warranty), a glitch in the cruise control that occasionally caused it to accelerate without driver input (never fixed) and a Mach 460 radio face that stopped working due to too much exposure to the sun. My only modifications included a K&N replacement filter, removal of the fender air baffle, installation of a Pro 5.0 short-throw shifter, and a set of FlowMaster mufflers. **—Brad Bowling**

My wife, Karen, and I were trading in our black 1992 5.0 LX Mustang in 1996 because we entered it in a lot of car shows and were really tired of trying to keep that black paint clean. We had dropped by CARMAX in Charlotte, North Carolina, and were stopped in our tracks when we entered the showroom to find a beautiful black 1995 Cobra on display with the super-rare removable hardtop. The Cobra had 6,300 miles on the odometer and was flawless. In spite of the color, Karen and I told the salesperson we wanted to take it for a test drive. He was a little suspicious of joy riders, since it was difficult to remove from its indoor display rack (he said someone had driven it that morning and decided not to buy). We took it for a spin and the sales guy asked if he needed to put it back in the lobby. We told him to take it straight to prep[em]it was going home with us! The first owner, in Indiana, ordered it with a light bar, and he installed an Alpine equalizer and subwoofer as well. Our other Mustangs include a 1970 Grabber Green Mach 1, a 1988 LX four-cylinder track car (also my daily driver), and a 2003 Mach 1. **—Norm Demers**

1994–1995 Mustang Ratings

Base V-6

Model Comfort/Amenities	****
Reliability	****
Collectibility	**
Parts/Service Availability	***
Est. Annual Repair Costs	**

5.0-Liter GT

Model Comfort/Amenities	*****
Reliability	****
Collectibility	***
Parts/Service Availability	****
Est. Annual Repair Costs	**

5.0-Liter Cobra

Model Comfort/Amenities	*****
Reliability	****
Collectibility	*****
Parts/Service Availability	****
Est. Annual Repair Costs	**

Saleen S-351

Model Comfort/Amenities	****
Reliability	**
Collectibility	****
Parts/Service Availability	***
Est. Annual Repair Costs	***

The new-for-1994 Mustang breathed life into what had become a very stagnant marque. Today, both V-6 and V-8 cars still make great daily drivers, but when compared to later, more powerful models built on the same platform, their value among collectors is not so strong. Ford concentrated on building a good basic Mustang in these two years, so there are very few standouts for collectibility. GT convertibles and SVT Cobras, especially the Indy pace car convertibles, are the top of the Mustang hierarchy for these years. Considering they are the very last 5.0-liter Mustangs built, collectors will always have a soft spot for the 1994 and 1995 models. The 170 S-351s built by Saleen during these two years retain their value well despite quality problems with their limited-production 351-cid V-8s.

Structural stiffness increased tremendously in the SN-95 body versus the earlier Fox platform. One of the many chassis reinforcements that made the 1994 and 1995 Mustangs such good handlers was a cowl support brace that tied the tops of the shock towers to the firewall.

Some Mustangs built between July 1994 and January 1995 for the North American market were fitted with odometers that indicated distance in kilometers instead of miles—even though the speedometers read miles per hour.

The year 1994 was the first for any mass-produced Mustang to be sold with standard four-wheel disc brakes and five-lug rotors. Antilock braking (ABS) was available, but only as an extra-cost option.

Incorrect taper ball studs on the outer tie rod ends were discovered on Mustangs built in February 1995. This improper part could fracture around the 50,000-mile mark, resulting in loss of vehicle control.

Although they were extremely comfortable, the articulated GT seats had a couple of problems. The adjustable side bolster brace was weak and tended to break easily, and the power lumbar feature, on cars built from May 1993 to June 1994, had potential to catch fire because of its proximity to the cushion supports.

The biggest wheels ever put on a production Mustang as of 1994 were these 17-inch six-spokes that measured 8 inches wide and were optional equipment for the GT. The 245/45Z-R17 tires looked unbelievably low in profile for the time; now such sidewall measurements are commonplace.

The Mach 460 stereo option was the best factory Mustang sound system to date. For just an additional $375, most buyers stepped up to 460 watts of eight-speaker (six-speaker in convertibles) concert sound.

Gone was the square layout of the Fox Mustang's interior. In its place was a cabin of soft curves and gentle arches reminiscent of the first Mustang's dual-cowl design.

Ford recalled a number of 1994 and 1995 Mustangs for inspection because the inner and outer hood panels were separating after minor accidents and not being repaired correctly. The condition could lead to complete separation at speed.

The new-for-1994 passenger-side airbag experienced a recall in 1995. It was discovered that the igniter cap on Mustangs built in January and February of that year could become separated in the event of an accident, leading to a failed inflation and/or ignition of nearby materials.

1994–1995 Cobra Garage Watch

The 1994 Cobra began a tradition of using white-face gauges with black numbers and markings that continues to the present. Appropriately, the Cobra speedometer reads to 160 miles per hour, 10 higher than the speedo on the production GT.

SVT installed a unique engine oil cooler to all Cobras. It used the engine's liquid cooling system to cool the oil instead of flowing the lubricant through its own radiator.

Under the hood, the 1994 and 1995 Cobras were missing the strut tower bracing that was standard on the GT. SVT's application of the taller 1993 intake manifold prevented its use. For 1996, that brace returned to the Cobra equipment list.

To provide maximum power to its 13-inch front discs and 11.65-inch rears, the Cobra had its own specific brake booster.

One of the many details upgraded by the SVT crew was in the area of seating. All Cobra front seats received magnesium seat cushion frames, while the GT components were made of heavier steel.

Original serpentine belts for the Cobra featured the name stamped in white ink to prevent confusion on the Ford assembly line. Replacement belts are missing this stamping, which makes the originals very valuable to collectors.

SVT built 1,003 convertible Cobras in 1994, all of which were Rio Red Indy Pace Car replicas with saddle tan interiors. As with many past replicas of this sort, the race-specific decals were shipped to the dealership in the trunk, allowing the buyer to decide if they should be installed.

The removable hardtop Ford advertised as available for 1994 Mustangs and Cobras did not actually reach production cars until 1995, when it became a Cobra-only option. Weighing 90 pounds, the factory piece is not interchangeable with regular convertibles.

While production Cobras got by with the Mustang's stock 15.4-gallon gas tank, the 1995 R-model received a 20-gallon competition Kevlar fuel bladder housed in black aluminum. Considering its 14 miles per gallon EPA city rating, the R's range with the larger tank was probably not increased over the standard Cobra.

The Saleen SR was available only in coupe form. It added a dual-plane rear wing, carbon-fiber hood, and scooped body-side enhancements to the supercharged S-351 model. The interior received a four-point chassis stiffener, four-point safety belts, a rear seat delete tray, and racing Recaro seats.

In 1994, which was a short production year for the company, Saleen sold 30 S-351 coupes, 14 S-351 convertibles, and 2 SR coupes. For 1995, those numbers more than doubled, with 84 S-351 coupes, 42 S-351 convertibles, and seven SR models finding new homes.

All Saleens built from 1994 through the end of the 1995 production run, regardless of exterior color, were fitted with blacked-out taillight surrounds. The purpose of the effect is to visually widen the rear of the car.

As is often the case when a limited-production manufacturer tools up for a model year, a few early 1994 S-351s were built with fiberglass body kits. Once the supply line was brought up to speed, stronger, more pliable Centrex pieces were fitted.

This two-point interior chassis stiffener would have been called a rollbar in the old days. It was one of several components Saleen installed to make the S-351 chassis stiffer for stronger handling.

S-351s wore 18x8.5-inch five-spoke Saleen wheels with BFGoodrich Comp T/A radials (P235/40R18 front, P245/40R18 rear), but the optional wheel package brought with it magnesium rims and Dunlops measuring P255/40R18 in the front and 285/40R18 in the rear.

Only mild cosmetic changes were in store for the 1996 Mustang (the most prominent being a new taillamp design), but that model opened the door for overhead cam performance with the introduction of Ford's 4.6-liter V-8.

Chapter 11

1996–1998 Mustang, Cobra, and Saleen

Ford's 4.6-liter V-8 ("W" code in the VIN), introduced in the 1996 Mustang GT, was the marque's first entirely new powerplant since 1965. Although it replaced the beloved 5.0-liter and suffered from initial skepticism among traditional buyers, the 4.6 was the platform that would drive the Mustang into the twenty-first century at high speed.

The 4.6 was a member of Ford's innovative "modular" family of engines, designed with the idea that future four-, six-, eight-, and 10-cylinder formats could share components and cut the cost of developing new cars. The first version of the 4.6 saw duty in the 1991 Lincoln Town Car. As fitted in the Mustang, it featured single overhead camshafts actuating two valves per cylinder, which greatly reduced the reciprocal weight of moving parts and allowed a broader powerband with a higher redline.

Every aspect of the 4.6 was carefully engineered for efficiency, strength, cost, and emissions. No carryover parts here, as the iron block was designed for maximum rigidity with a unique system of head-to-block bolt placement, which prevented block distortion under high-performance use, and four-bolt main bearing caps. Lightweight pistons and connecting rods were developed for the modular motors, as was a special plastic intake manifold that flowed more air but took up less room than the old 5.0 unit. The alternator, air conditioning compressor, and power steering pump were all directly mounted to the block, greatly reducing the amount of brackets and wiring. The serpentine belt and platinum-tipped spark plugs were designed to go 100,000 miles before replacement. Ford's second-generation onboard diagnostic program (OBD II) and a redesigned distributorless ignition took the engine's computer management to a new level of sophistication.

Even though it displaced 31 fewer cubic inches, the 4.6-liter debuted in the GT breathing through a 65-mm throttle body and 80-mm mass airflow sensor with a rating of 215 horsepower at 4,400 rpm—the same as the previous year's 5.0 but at a higher engine speed. With a nearly square bore and stroke of 3.55x3.54 inches, the SOHC engine maintained the 1993's torque output of 285 lbs-ft.

Because its taller and wider heads took up more room in the engine compartment, all V-8 Mustangs for 1996 came equipped with a new hydraulic brake boost system that worked through the power steering pump and was much more compact than the previous vacuum-activated units. Other V-8 equipment for 1996 included a strut tower triangulated brace, Ford's key-encoded passive anti-theft system (PATS, became standard on all Mustangs in 1997), a new five-spoke 17-inch wheel design, and "GT 4.6L" fender badges.

The base 3.8-liter V-6 ("4" code) also received some mechanical attention, acquiring a stiffer block from the Thunderbird Super Coupe and a rating increase to 150 horsepower.

The sturdy, long-serving T-5 five-speed was retired in 1996 in favor of Borg-Warner's T-45, with its thicker gears, integral bell housing, and a host of other improvements. The automatic overdrive four-speed was replaced with a 4R70W unit managed by more computer programming than any previous Ford transmission. Not only was it the first performance-oriented automatic from Ford in many years, engines equipped with the 4R70W would later qualify for low-emission vehicle (LEV) status. Rear-axle ratios for both transmissions were 2.73:1 and 3.27:1.

External changes to the SN-95 body were few, the most noticeable being three-element taillights in a vertical format and a screen in the grille to hide the radiator. For 1997, the grille was revised to flow more air to a higher-capacity radiator.

Of course, SVT leapfrogged corporate Ford's efforts with an aluminum-block, double overhead cam 4.6-liter ("V" code) that generated a remarkable 305 horsepower at 5,800 rpm. The alloy block, poured by Teksid in Italy, was so light that when fully dressed with heads and accessories, the Cobra's DOHC 4.6 weighed no more than the GT's SOHC 4.6. Assembled by hand in the Romeo, Michigan, plant, each engine received six-bolt nodular iron main bearing caps, twin 57-mm throttle bodies, 80-mm mass airflow sensors, and a signed plaque on the passenger-side valve cover stating the names of the two-man crew that built it.

The new-for-1996 T-45 five-speed was the only transmission available on the Cobra.

Saleen's product line increased by one model in 1996 with the debut of the S-281—GT- or Cobra-based coupes and convertibles with stock engines but highly tuned suspensions (including 18-inch wheels) and bodywork. The S-281 was created in response to Saleen enthusiasts who wanted a less-expensive option built around the company's original 1984 formula. The model was such a hit that Budget Rent A Car ordered S-281 convertibles for its customers.

The largely hand built S-351 continued with some changes, most significant being the move to Trick Flow heads.

By 1996 (1998 model shown), Ford had finally caught on that the Mustang was viewed by its buyers as a performance car, even when equipped with a base engine. Gone were the whitewall tires and faux wire wheel hubcaps. In their place were polished aluminum alloy wheels and 205/65R15 blackwalls.

The 150-horsepower 3.8-liter V-6 even had a high-performance look as it sat under the Mustang hood. Its tuned intake runners looked like a scaled-down version of the old 5.0-liter V-8's manifold. All that's missing to make this engine compartment look like it houses a mini-V-8 is a set of polished valve covers.

Wheels for the 1996 and 1997 Cobra were the five-spoke design with the openings between the spokes painted a dark gray metallic, as seen on the 1994 Indy pace cars. In 1998, SVT introduced a replica of its 1995 Cobra R alloy rim as standard equipment. Both designs measured 17x8 inches.

1996–1998 Mustang Specifications

Base price ('96–'98)	40 coupe V-6	$15,180–$15,970
	44 convertible V-6	$21,060–$20,470
	42 coupe GT	$17,610–$19,970
	45 convertible GT	$23,495–$23,970
	42 coupe Cobra	$24,810–$25,335
	45 convertible Cobra	$27,580–$28,135
Production ('96/'97/'98)	40 coupe V-6	61,187/56,812/99,801
	44 convertible V-6	15,246/11,606/21,254
	42 coupe GT	31,624/18,464/28,789
	45 convertible GT	17,917/11,413/17,024
	42 coupe Cobra	7,496/6,961/5,174
	45 convertible Cobra	2,510/3,088/3,480
Displacement	V-6	232/3.8
(cubic inches/liters)	V-8	281/4.6
Bore x stroke (inches)	V-6	3.80x3.40
	V-8	3.55x3.54
VIN code/Compression ratio	V-6	4 9.0:1
	V-8	W 9.0:1
	V-8 Cobra	V 9.85:1
Induction	V-6	TPI
	V-8	SEFI
Valvetrain	V-6	OHV
	V-8	SOHC
	V-8 Cobra	DOHC
Horsepower	V-6	150@4,000
	V-8	215@4,400
	V-8 Cobra	305@5,800
Transmission (std./opt.)	V-6	T-45 5-speed manual/4-speed AOD
	V-8	T-45 5-speed manual/4-speed AOD
	V-8 Cobra	T-45 5-speed manual
Rear-axle ratio	V-6	2.73:1
	V-8, 5-speed	2.73:1
	V-8, 4-speed AOD	3.27:1
	V-8 Cobra	3.27:1
Wheelbase (inches)		101.3
Overall width (inches)		71.8
Overall height (inches)		53.1
Overall length (inches)		181.5
Track (inches)		(front) 60.1
		(rear) 58.7
Fuel capacity (gallons)		15.4
Weight (pounds)	40 coupe V-6	3,057–3,065
	44 convertible V-6	3,269–3,210
	42 coupe GT	3,279–3,227
	45 convertible GT	3,468–3,400
	42 coupe Cobra	3,445–3,446
	45 convertible Cobra	3,620–3,620
Tires	base	P205/6515
	GT standard	P225/55ZR16
	GT optional	P245/45ZR17
	Cobra	P245/45ZR17
Front suspension		modified MacPherson struts, lower A-arms, coil springs, tube shocks, anti-roll bar
Rear suspension		live axle, angled upper and lower trailing arms, coil springs, tube shocks, anti-roll bar
Steering		14.7:1 constant ratio rack and pinion
Brakes		all models (exc. Cobra) (front) 10.8-inch vented disc
		all models (exc. Cobra)(rear) 10.5-inch disc
	Cobra	(front) 13-inch vented disc
	Cobra	(rear) 11.65-inch vented disc
Gas mileage (EPA city/hwy.)	V-6 5-speed manual	20/30, 20/30, 20/20
	V-6 4-speed AOD	20/30, 20/30, 19/28
	V-8 5-speed manual	18/27, 17/26, 17/25
	V-8 4-speed AOD	17/24, 17/24, 17/24
	V-8 Cobra 5-speed	18/26, 18/26, 17/26
0 to 60 (secs)	(GT 4.6/5-speed, 2.73:1 axle)*	6.8
	(Cobra cvt., 4.6/5-speed, 3.27:1 axle)**	5.8
Standing 1/4-mile (mph/secs)	(GT 4.6/5-speed, 2.73:1 axle)	89@15.3
	(Cobra cvt., 4.6/5-speed, 3.27:1 axle)	100.3@14.3
Top speed (mph)	(GT 4.6/5-speed, 2.73:1 axle)	140
	(Cobra cvt., 4.6/5-speed, 3.27:1 axle)	150

* *Road & Track*, April 1996
** *Road & Track*, June 1996

1996–1998 Mustang

Major Options

Transmission, 4-speed AOD	(exc. Cobra)	$815
Optional axle ratio	(GT only)	$200
Mustang 241A ('96–'97)	(includes A/C, AM/FM stereo cassette)	$670-615
Mustang 243A ('96–'97)	(includes A/C; power side windows, door locks, decklid release; speed control, dual lighted visor mirrors, 15-inch aluminum wheels, AM/FM stereoradio w/cassette and Premium Sound, remote keyless entry and cargo net)	
	(coupe)	$2,020-$2,115
	(convertible)	$1,590-$1,615
Cobra 250A ('96–'97)	(includes A/C, rear-window defroster, front floor mats, speed control)	$1,335
Emissions, California		$100-$170
Wheels, 15-inch aluminum	(V-6 only)	$265
Wheels, 17-inch aluminum	(GT only)	$400-$500
Seats, leather sport bucket	(GT)	$500
	(convertible)	$500
	(Cobra coupe)	$500
Spoiler		$195
Air conditioning		$895
Brakes, anti-lock	(std. Cobra)	$500-$570
Anti-theft system	(opt. 1996, standard '97–'98)	$145
Rear-window defroster	(standard Cobra)	$170-$190
Front floor mats	(standard Cobra)	$30
Engine block heater	(N/A Cobra)	$20
Speed control	(standard Cobra)	$215
CD player		$295
Mach 460 AM/FM stereo		$395-$690
AM/FM stereo w/cassette		

Replacement Costs for Common Parts

Fuel cap		$20
Carpet		$99
Radiator core support		$200
Radiator-to-grille cover		$65
Fuel tank sending unit		$77
Fuse box cover		$13
Battery tray		$13
Radio and A/C bezel		$120
Rearview mirror		$20
Convertible top motor		$240
Front-bumper cover	Cobra repro	$230
Front-bumper cover	GT/V-6 repro	$180
Front inner splash shield		$40
Front fender	repro	$90
Front fender	original	$210
Hood	GT/V-6 repro	$200
Hood	GT/V-6 original	$500
Third brake light		$80
Rubber fender-to-hood bumpers		$2
Headlight assembly	GT/V-6	$70
Headlight assembly	Cobra	$100
Side marker lamp		$23
Fog lamp kit		$240
Pony grille emblem		$22
Heater core		$49
Clutch fork		$27
Instrument clear lens		$70
Console arm rest pad		$70
Utility compartment		$18
Fog lamp switch		$19
Convertible top		$190
Turn signal lever assembly		$40
Trunk weather stripping		$35
Convertible top headliner		$150
Factory headlight knob		$12
Mach 460 speaker grille		$20
Convertible top boot		$300
Convertible top switch		$20
Electric window motor		$110
Antenna rod		$12
Wiper arm		$35
Space-saver wheel and tire		$40
Front-brake rotor	GT	$40

Front-brake rotor	Cobra	$160	Underhood insulator	GT/V-6		$60
Outside mirror switch		$45	Underhood insulator	Cobra		$63
Tilt wheel lever		$6	Taillamp assembly			$80
SVT emblem	Cobra	$12	GT 4.6 fender emblem			$10
Convertible glass rear window		$165	Engine oil cooler	Cobra		$200
Grille		$70	Radiator core support			$200
Hood	Cobra repro	$280	Radiator-to-grille cover			$25
Hood	Cobra original	$500	Fuse box cover			$10

What They Said in 1996–1998

Ford's better idea is camshafts. The vacancy left by the demise of the Mustang's thumping 5.0-liter pushrod engine will be filled by the New Wave: a pair of overhead-cam 4.6-liter V-8s. Mustang GT models will now be powered by a 215-horsepower SOHC two-valve-per-cylinder V-8, and the Cobra's hiss will come from a 305-horsepower DOHC four-valve drivetrain. . . . The NVH improvements of the 4.6-liter cammer over the 5.0-liter pushrod V-8 were to a large extent free because of the care and feeding bestowed on the modular engine before it was approved for Lincoln duty. The heart of the matter is a cast-iron deep-skirt block with cross-bolted main bearings. Long cylinder head bolts screw into the block's foundation instead of into its deck surface, to avoid cylinder-bore distortion. . . . The tougher task was making the 4.6-liter engine perform like a hard-charging 5.0-liter V-8. —*Motor Trend,* **September 1995**

I Bought a 1997 SVT Cobra

I'm the second owner of my yellow 1997 SVT Cobra coupe. The first owner was a local doctor who was a fanatic about keeping it immaculate. He used to put magnetic vinyl bumpers on his doors if he ever parked it anywhere that other cars might hit it. One day, he stopped by Wal-Mart on his way home from work, and, even though he wasn't near any other cars—he was about a half-mile from the store itself—he put those door bumpers on. When he came out, a shopping cart had rolled from the high part of the parking lot into his Cobra. Apparently, it was going quite fast, because it knocked the heck out of the passenger-size quarter panel. He got it repaired, but couldn't stand knowing it had been damaged and traded it for a 1999 Cobra convertible. I feel like I got a real bargain, because the body shop did a great job on the repair and matched the paint beautifully. —**Jack Roker**

1996–1998 Mustang Ratings

Base V-6

Model Comfort/Amenities	****
Reliability	****
Collectibility	**
Parts/Service Availability	****
Est. Annual Repair Costs	**

4.6-Liter GT

Model Comfort/Amenities	*****
Reliability	****
Collectibility	***
Parts/Service Availability	****
Est. Annual Repair Costs	**

4.6-Liter Cobra

Model Comfort/Amenities	*****
Reliability	****
Collectibility	*****
Parts/Service Availability	****
Est. Annual Repair Costs	**

Saleen S-281

Model Comfort/Amenities	****
Reliability	****
Collectibility	****
Parts/Service Availability	***
Est. Annual Repair Costs	***

Saleen S-351

Model Comfort/Amenities	****
Reliability	****
Collectibility	****
Parts/Service Availability	***
Est. Annual Repair Costs	***

For everyday driving, there are no bad choices here. With continued refinement to the platform and powertrains, everything from an automatic-equipped V-6 to a fire-breathing S-351 will provide a fun, reliable drive to work. Once again, though, the rarest and most desirable of this bunch from a long-term collector standpoint is the Saleen S-281s and S-351s. Buying a used Cobra from this period is a great way to get behind the wheel of an incredibly powerful musclecar for a relatively small amount of money.

1996–1998 Mustang Garage Watch

The 1996 through 1998 Mustang coupes benefited from rear-seat cushions that could be folded forward or locked into place, depending on the owner's need at the time. When down, the seats created a surface that merged with the trunk for a seamless, carpeted floor.

Overall, reviewers heaped praise on the 1996 through 1998 Mustangs' interior creature comforts and quality of components. Complaints focused on the driver's seat, which could not travel far enough to comfortably accommodate people over 6 feet tall; inadequate storage space (glove box, console compartment, cup holders); and stereo controls that required an unreasonable amount of dexterity and attention to manipulate.

Mustangs built from August through November 1997 may have had inadequate or missing braze joints between the fuel rail body and the mounting brackets. Ford recalled and fixed these cars as the condition could result in an engine fire.

Ford's modular 4.6-liter V-8 was not a welcome sight to traditional Mustang buyers at first, as they questioned its potential for increased power output. Once the aftermarket began developing speed parts for the single overhead camshaft engine, it became as popular as the 5.0-liter it replaced.

The 1997 and 1998 grille opening was designed for more airflow to a new radiator in all Mustangs. The background screen that appeared on the 1996 was absent on these models. This change greatly improved the cooling characteristics of the engine.

A small number of Mustangs with September 1997 build dates may have been fitted with damaged rack and pinion input shaft bearings. If not corrected, owners may notice a stronger than normal steering effort is required to turn the wheel, but severe cases could lead to a loss of control.

More than any other car, the late-model Mustang—with its various scoops and indentions—is difficult to wash, as there are many areas for water to hide and pool. Because of high plastic content and better rustproofing, this is more a matter of appearance than concern for corrosion.

1996–1998 Cobra Garage Watch

For reasons known only to Ford Motor Company, 1996 was the only year SVT replaced the grille-mounted running pony emblem with one depicting a coiled snake on its Cobra. The grille emblems are very easy to remove, so many owners have installed their own snake (or other) identification.

Mystic was a 1996-on paint option for Cobras. $815, a buyer could ha GAF-developed color scheme that alternate between green, purple, blue, and black, depen on the viewer's angle o site. This was a popula option with the "look a me" crowd, and 1,999 were ordered with it.

The taller and wider double overhead camshaft 4.6-liter that powered the Cobra required a special hood built for additional clearance. Although the bulge is necessary, the twin scoops are non-functional. This hood is a popular modification for GT and V-6 Mustang owners.

The triangulated shock tower brace returned for 1996 and 1997, but it was absent from the 1998 Cobra.

Despite the T-45 five-speed's increased torque capacity, it was often no match for a hard-driving Cobra. Owners complained of prematurely worn synchronizers and bent shift forks. Installing an aftermarket shifter with positive shift stops reduced occurrences of fork damage, but SVT's fix came in 1999 with a beefier version of the T-45 built by Tremec.

The rear spoiler—for 1996 through 1998 a stock GT piece—was standard equipment on 1996 Cobras but was optional on 1997 and 1998 models. Many buyers left off the $198 wing in order to make their cars stand out from the Mustang crowd.

Cobra models between 1996 and 1998 suffered from serpentine belts that squealed, ticked, or, in some instances, came off the pulleys. SVT suggested dealers replace the pulleys or belt tensioner, but the real fix seemed to come with a new tensioner design for 1999.

Starting in 1996, the Cobra received exhaust tips that were 3 inches in diameter, up from the previous year's 2.75 and more in keeping with the car's improved horsepower and torque ratings.

Uncharacteristically, tires for the 1996 through 1998 Cobras were actually narrower than the 1995 model. SVT found it saved a pound per tire of unsprung weight by returning to the 245/45ZR17, the same rolling stock as the GT.

131

Most Saleen S-351s began life as V-6 Ford Mustangs. The Saleen facility stripped the cars nearly to their shells before installing all model-specific engine, suspension, and body components. That's why this manufacturer decal on S-351 97-0001 shows a "4" (VIN code for V-6) in its eighth spot.

Racecraft is Saleen's own brand of suspension components applied to its high-performance Mustangs. Although the specific pieces have changed over the years, the system generally contains springs to lower the chassis, stiffer bushings, and premium struts and shock absorbers.

Saleen officially blended the SR model (offered for 1994 and 1995) into the supercharged S-351 line in 1996. This shot under the lightweight composite hood of the first 1997 S-351 built illustrates just how different Saleen's hand-built S-351 was from a standard Mustang GT.

In 1997, the S-351 took on a six-speed manual transmission as standard equipment. Also starting that year, all S-351s came equipped with Vortech superchargers and the magnesium 18-inch wheels.

This S-351 convertible is equipped with the Speedster package, a Saleen option that included the two-point "light bar" and one-piece fiberglass rear-seat cover. The hard tonneau effectively turns the convertible into a two-seater and is held in place by the seat belt receivers. Unfortunately, the cover is nearly impossible to transport inside the car in the case of rain.

An extremely rare option on S-351s is the Widebody package, which makes the car resemble more of a race car than street car. Such models include a different front fascia, fenders, rear quarter panels, rear valance, carbon-fiber lightweight hood, and dual-plane rear wing.

In its introductory year of 1996, Saleen's S-281 proved to be enormously popular, with 436 sales (including 30 for Budget) as compared to the more expensive S-351, of which 20 were built. In 1997 Saleen sold 327 S-281s (including 88 convertibles sold to Budget) and 40 S-351s. The final year of this body style, 1998, saw 186 S-281s (including 10 for Budget) and 22 S-351s go to customers.

An upgrade in the S-351 program for 1997 improved the powerplant's reliability. It included forged pistons, a Saleen/Cosworth engine management computer, and high-flow 36 pounds/hour fuel injectors.

Although there are many S-281 Mustangs with Vortech superchargers on the road, Saleen did not have certification to install them at the factory. Until 1999, it was up to Saleen's dealer network or aftermarket shops to supercharge customers' cars.

Despite a nearly $10,000 premium over the "standard" S-281, Saleen found several buyers for its Cobra-based products. In 1996, 11 Saleen-Cobras were sold; 18 were built in 1997; and the California company manufactured 35 such models for 1998.

SALEEN

The Mustang's first redesign since its 1994 overhaul came in 1999 with a style Ford referred to as its "New Look." Instead of looking like a smooth bar of soap, the Mustang gained sharp, creased lines that suggested muscular performance.

Chapter 12 1999–2000 Mustang, Cobra, and Saleen

Following the changeless years of 1987 through 1993, the Mustang's two- to three-year evolutionary jumps through the late 1990s brought renewed enthusiasm and some great models to the marque's followers.

For 1999—not coincidentally the thirty-fifth anniversary of the Mustang—Ford endowed its pony car with a raft of performance improvements.

The 3.8-liter V-6 ("4" code in the VIN) gained 40 horsepower and 10 lbs-ft of torque through the use of a new intake manifold, cylinder head flow improvements, and new, high-tech piston coatings that reduced operating friction. Smoother running was achieved at all engine speeds through Ford's development work on a balance shaft. The V-6 could be mated to the T-45 five-speed manual or four-speed automatic overdrive transmission. Each ultimately connected to a 3.27:1 rear-axle gear.

Ford found 35 more horsepower and 10 more lbs-ft of torque in its 4.6-liter V-8 ("X" code). The increase was due to new higher-lift camshafts with longer duration, bigger valves, and revised intake manifold runners that increased intake airflow above 2,000 rpm. More-complete burning of the air/fuel mixture was accomplished through better flow and an improved combustion-chamber shape. A coil-on-plug ignition system helped the GT meet power and emissions goals by providing a higher-energy spark. GTs came standard with the T-45 five-speed manual transmission, and the four-speed automatic overdrive was an option. The 1999 model year marked the first that both V-6 and V-8 engines received the same rear-axle ratio (3.27:1) regardless of transmission choice.

Not to be outshined, SVT boosted the Cobra's 4.6-liter aluminum-block V-8 ("V" code) to 320 horsepower by way of new intake ports and combustion chambers that increased the tumbling effect of the air/fuel mixture. The Cobra also received the coil-on-plug ignition system Ford installed on the lesser GT, as well as an improved knock sensor. Stronger bearings prepared the bottom end for a life of hard launches and high revs.

Probably the most significant development for any late-model Mustang was SVT's application of independent rear suspension (IRS) to the 1999 Cobra. The system took the place of the standard Mustang's ancient live axle, but, amazingly, bolted to the same mounting points. Although IRS added 80 pounds to the Cobra platform, it reduced the all-important unsprung weight by 125 pounds for vastly improved handling over irregular surfaces. SVT shaved 95 pounds from the chassis' front end to bring the overall weight back in line and managed to create a desirable 55/45 distribution in the process.

Unfortunately, owners and car magazines immediately noticed the new Cobras, which boasted 15 more horsepower than the 1998 models, were no faster and were registering lower-than-expected dynamometer readings. The culprits turned out to be an intake manifold that was cast to lower standards than SVT's test motors and mufflers that were more restrictive than original specs called for. In order to please its customers and maintain its reputation for quality products, SVT stopped production of the Cobra until cars on the line could be built with the proper equipment. SVT spent all of 2000 fixing customer cars and did not produce "base" Cobras that year.

Instead, SVT's 2000 production was limited to 300 very special Cobras that were more deserving than ever of the R designation. The centerpiece of the R was the 5.4-liter DOHC V-8 ("H" code), which produced 385 horsepower without turbochargers or superchargers. One of the most noticeable visual features of the 2000 R was the side-exit exhaust system, which was chosen in order to clear room under the rear of the car for a 20-gallon fuel cell. The first six-speed manual transmission in a production Mustang belonged to the 2000 R, for which there was no automatic transmission option. Surprisingly, the stock 11-inch Cobra clutch proved stout enough to handle the R's amazing horsepower, and rear-axle gears were raised numerically to 3.55:1 for better acceleration through all six gears. The R received the base Cobra's four-wheel discs but with four-piston calipers on the front.

The Saleen camp continued to improve its Mustang-based products. Certification was obtained in 1999 for Saleen to install its own superchargers, which had formerly been the domain of aftermarket shops and Ford service departments. The S-351, still built from stripped-down V-6 coupe and convertible chassis, was enjoying its last year of production, as federal emissions certification ran out with the end of the 1999 model run. Because there were no Cobras being built in 2000 and the S-351 was no longer in production, Saleen offered only the S-281. Available in coupe and convertible body styles (with or without supercharger), the 2000 model experienced record sales, with 974 models finding new homes.

The 1999 V-6 Mustang is a good example of how far engine technology has evolved since the 1970s. With 190 horsepower on tap, it was more powerful than the small-block V-8s offered in Mustangs from 1972 through 1984.

After a rash of highly publicized kidnappings and carjackings in which owners were forced into trunk compartments of their cars, manufacturers began installing an "escape" handle in many models. All Mustangs received their interior trunk releases starting in 1999.

Not one to miss an anniversary, Steve Saleen produced 10 special yellow SA-15 convertibles in 1999. For the year, the company sold 373 S-281s and 45 S-351s. In 2000, 974 S-281s were built.

1999–2000 Mustang Specifications

Base price ('99–'00)	40 coupe V-6	$16,470–$16,520
	44 convertible V-6	$21,070–$21,370
	42 coupe GT	$20,870–$21,015
	45 convertible GT	$24,870–$25,270
	42 coupe Cobra (1999)	$27,470
	45 convertible Cobra (1999)	$31,470
	42 coupe Cobra R (2000)	$54,995
Production	40 coupe V-6	73,180–121,026
	44 convertible V-6	19,299–41,368
	42 coupe GT	19,634–32,328
	45 convertible GT	13,699–20,224
	42 coupe Cobra (1999)	4,040
	45 convertible Cobra (1999)	4,055
	42 coupe Cobra R (2000)	300
Displacement (cubic inches/liters)		
	V-6	232/3.8
	V-8	281/4.6
	V-8 Cobra R	330/5.4
Bore x stroke (inches)	V-6	3.80x3.40
	V-8	3.55x3.54
	V-8 Cobra R	3.55x4.17
VIN code/Compression ratio	V-6	4 9.36:1
	V-8	X 9.0:1
	V-8 Cobra	V 9.85:1
	V-8 Cobra R	H 9.6:1
Induction	V-6	SEFI
	V-8	SEFI
Valvetrain	V-6	OHV
	V-8	SOHC
	V-8 Cobra and R	DOHC
Horsepower	V-6	190@5,250
	V-8	260@5,250
	V-8 Cobra	320@6,000
	V-8 Cobra R	385@6,250
Transmission (std./opt.)	V-6 T-45 5-speed manual/4-speed AOD	
	V-8 T-45 5-speed manual/4-speed AOD	
	V-8 Cobra	T-45 5-speed manual
	V-8 Cobra R	T-56 6-speed manual
Rear-axle ratio	V-6	3.27:1
	V-8	3.27:1
	V-8 Cobra	3.27:1
	V-8 Cobra R	3.55:1
Wheelbase (inches)		101.3
Overall width (inches)		71.8
Overall height (inches)		53.4
Overall length (inches)		181.5
Track (inches)		(front) 60.1
		(rear) 58.7
Fuel capacity (gallons)		15.4
	Cobra R (fuel cell)	21
Weight (pounds)	40 coupe V-6	3,069–3,064
	44 convertible V-6	3,211–3,203
	42 coupe GT	3,273–3,227
	45 convertible GT	3,429–3,375
	42 coupe Cobra ('99)	3,340
	45 convertible Cobra ('99)	3,560
	42 coupe Cobra R (s'00)	3,590
Tires	base	P205/6515
	GT (standard)	P225/55HR16
	GT (optional)	P245/45ZR17
	Cobra	P245/45ZR17
	Cobra R	P265/40ZR18
Front suspension		modified MacPherson struts, lower A-arms, coil springs, tube shocks, anti-roll bar
Rear suspension (base, GT)		live axle, angled upper and lower trailing arms, coil springs, tube shocks, anti-roll bar
Rear suspension (Cobra and R)		independent rear suspension, upper and lower control arms, coil springs, tube shocks, anti-roll bar
Steering		15:1 constant ratio rack and pinion
Brakes	all models (exc. Cobra) (front)	10.8-inch vented disc
	all models (exc. Cobra)(rear)	10.5-inch disc
	Cobra and R (front)	13-inch vented disc
	Cobra and R (rear)	11.65-inch vented disc
Gas mileage (EPA city/hwy.)	V-6 5-speed manual	20/29, 20/29
	V-6 4-speed AOD	20/27, 20/27
	V-8 5-speed manual	17/24, 17/25
	V-8 4-speed AOD	17/23, 17/24
	V-8 Cobra 5-speed	18/26
	V-8 Cobra R 6-speed	13/18
0 to 60 (secs)	(GT 4.6/5-speed, 3.27:1 axle)*	5.4
	(Cobra, 4.6/5-speed, 3.27:1 axle)**	5.4
	(Cobra R)***	4.8
	(Saleen S-281 coupe)****	5.2
	(Saleen S-351 coupe) *****	4.7
Standing ¼-mile (mph/secs)	(GT 4.6/5-speed, 3.27:1 axle)	100@14
	(Cobra, 4.6/5-speed, 3.27:1 axle)	102@13.8
	(Cobra R)	109.1@13.2
	(Saleen S-281 coupe)	98@14.1
	(Saleen S-351 coupe)	111.7@13.0
Top speed (mph)	(GT 4.6/5-speed, 3.27:1 axle)	140
	(Cobra, 4.6/5-speed, 3.27:1 axle)	150
	(Cobra R)	170

* *Road & Track*, April 1999
** SVT factory info
*** *Road & Track*, April 2000
**** Saleen factory info
***** *Motor Trend*, May 1999

1999–2000 Mustang

Major Options

Transmission, 4-speed AOD	(exc. Cobra)	$815
Convenience Group	(including front floor mats, rear-window defroster, speed control, power driver's seat)	$550
GT Sport Group	(including 17-inch 5-spoke aluminum wheels, hood stripe, wraparound fender stripes, leather-wrapped shift knob, engine oil cooler)	$595
V-6 Sport Appearance Group	(including 15-inch cast aluminum wheels, rear spoiler, leather-wrapped steering wheel, lower bodyside accent stripe)	$310
35th Anniv. Package ('99)	(including 17-inch 5-spoke aluminum wheels, black appliqué, black and silver leather seats, silver door trim inserts, silver/black floor mats, shift knob)	$2,695
Brakes, anti-lock	(std. Cobra)	$500
Rear spoiler	(std. GT)	$195
Rear-window defroster	(standard Cobra)	$190
Emissions, California		no charge
Seats, leather sport bucket		$500
Air conditioning		$895
Front floor mats	(standard Cobra)	$30
Mach 460 AM/FM stereo		$395
AM/FM stereo w/cassette		$165
Wheels, 17-inch aluminum	(GT only)	$500

Replacement Costs for Common Parts

Console arm rest pad		$70
Utility compartment		$18
Fog lamp switch		$19
Convertible top		$190
Turn signal lever assembly		$40
Trunk weather stripping		$35
Convertible top headliner		$150
Factory headlight knob		$12
Mach 460 speaker grille		$20
Convertible top boot		$300
Convertible top switch		$20
Electric window motor		$110
Antenna rod		$12
Wiper arm		$35
Space-saver wheel and tire		$40
Front-brake rotor	GT	$40
Front-brake rotor	Cobra	$160
Outside mirror switch		$45
Tilt wheel lever		$6
Convertible glass rear window		$165
Engine oil cooler	Cobra	$200
Radiator-to-grille cover		$25
Fuse box cover		$10
Hood scoop	35th Anniversary Edition	$130
"35th Anniversary" fender emblem		$13
Headlight assembly		$130
Hood	Cobra repro	$350
Underhood insulator	Cobra	$63
Fog lamp bezel	Cobra	$17
Taillamp assembly	Cobra	$150
SVT Cobra emblem	Cobra	$11
Instrument clear lens		$30
Leather steering wheel		$160
Convertible top motor		$185
Front-bumper cover	GT/V-6 repro	$200
Front-bumper cover	Cobra original	$300
Front-bumper cover	V-6 original	$400
Front-bumper cover	GT original	$470
Grille		$90
Front fender	original	$210
Hood	GT/V-6 original	$500
Hood	Cobra original	$500
Third brake light		$75
Underhood insulator	GT/V-6	$57
Rubber fender-to-hood bumpers		$5

Replacement Costs for Common Parts

Radiator core support		$290
Fog lamp kit		$205
Taillamp assembly	GT/V-6	$70
Front splitter	Cobra R original	$500
Hood	Cobra R repro	$320
Hood	Cobra R original	$500

What They Said in 1999–2000

All Mustangs now sport four-wheel discs with aluminum twin-piston calipers in front. This year, revisions to the master cylinder and the pedal ratio provide more precise modulation, important in the wet and on the track. And for 1999, an all-speed traction-control system will be offered that manages fuel, ignition retard, cylinder cut-out, and rear caliper actuation for slippery conditions and takeoffs. . . . Other minor, but much appreciated chassis improvements include more noise-attenuating mastics under the floor, expandable foam in the rockers, improved on-center steering feel, a three-foot-shorter turning circle, and underbody rail extenders for reducing the convertible's shake. —*Motor Trend,* **October 1998**

When you lean on the gas in the 1999 Saleen S-351, you'd better be securely buckled in, because you're about to go on a very quick ride. Senior Road Test Editor Mac DeMere put it this way: "Driving either of the new Saleen Mustangs is mostly an exercise in tire-spin control." With up to 495 supercharged horsepower on tap, that's an understatement, Mac! While the supercharged S-281 has more power than required to dust most like-priced competition, driving the S-351 is a real hoot. Around town, it's easy to get the S-351 sideways, spinning the tires, without even going past quarter throttle. —*Motor Trend,* **May 1999**

I Bought a 2000 Mustang

I owned a really nice 1995 Mustang GT several years ago, but carpool duty called, so I traded it for a more suitable car. My plan was to turn in the carpool vehicle at the end of its lease in order to buy a V-6 Mustang, which I would drive for a few years and give to my son when he got his driver's license at 16. When I saw the V-6's horsepower jump in 1999, I was happy to know that it was enough to make the car peppy, but not so much that it would be dangerous for a novice driver such as my son. I bought a 2000 V-6 with a five-speed transmission off the dealer's lot and have used it every day as my transportation. My son now has his learner's permit, so he has been getting acquainted with the Performance Red coupe in anticipation of it becoming his. I've put 42,000 trouble-free miles on the Mustang, and I have to say the V-6 performance is not bad at all with the manual transmission. The gas mileage in town could be better, but I guess that's the price you pay for more power. Unlike a lot of people in my local Mustang club, I've never really gotten into the practice of competing at shows; I just bought it for driving. When the 2000 is no longer mine, I will consider one of the redesigned 2005 Mustangs—a V-8 this time! —**Dr. Larry Vandeventer**

1999–2000 Mustang Ratings

Base V-6

Model Comfort/Amenities	****
Reliability	*****
Collectibility	**
Parts/Service Availability	****
Est. Annual Repair Costs	**

4.6-Liter GT

Model Comfort/Amenities	*****
Reliability	*****
Collectibility	***
Parts/Service Availability	****
Est. Annual Repair Costs	**

4.6-Liter Cobra

Model Comfort/Amenities	*****
Reliability	****
Collectibility	*****
Parts/Service Availability	****
Est. Annual Repair Costs	**

Saleen S-281

Model Comfort/Amenities	****
Reliability	****
Collectibility	****
Parts/Service Availability	***
Est. Annual Repair Costs	***

Saleen S-351 (1999)

Model Comfort/Amenities	****
Reliability	****
Collectibility	****
Parts/Service Availability	***
Est. Annual Repair Costs	***

5.4-Liter Cobra R (2000)

Model Comfort/Amenities	**
Reliability	***
Collectibility	*****
Parts/Service Availability	***
Est. Annual Repair Costs	***

The Mustang just kept getting better in the late 1990s, with Ford treating the 1999 and subsequent Mustangs to chassis tweaks, minor facelifts, and power boosts. The 3.8-liter V-6 became a very sporty choice for enthusiasts on a budget when its horsepower rating jumped to 190 that year, especially when equipped with the standard five-speed manual. Cobras from this period make excellent used musclecars, but be certain SVT's warranty work has been performed to ensure the 4.6-liter V-8 is putting out its claimed 320 horsepower. The 2000-only 5.4-liter Cobra R probably occupies top spot on any late-model Mustang collector's must-have list. The 1999 model marked the final year for Saleen's S-351 and included such boy racer fantasy equipment as a 22-gallon fuel cell, standard Vortech supercharger, six-speed manual transmission, and 495 horsepower.

1999–2000 Mustang Garage Watch

For 1999, the California version of the 3.8-liter V-6 qualified as a Low Emission Vehicle (LEV), and the California 4.6-liter V-8 was considered a Transitional Low Emission Vehicle (TLEV). In a year when both engines received power increases, these environmentally friendly labels proved that greenhouse gases and performance automobiles were not mutually exclusive.

Changes to the suspension geometry improved low-speed agility and turning. V-6 models decreased their turning circles from just over 40 feet to 37 feet. The GT radius went from 40 feet, 8 inches to 37 feet, 11 inches.

The redesigned headlamp/turn signal assembly was not just an exercise in cosmetic updating. The reflector-type arrangement and clear plastic lens provided a brighter white light than previous models.

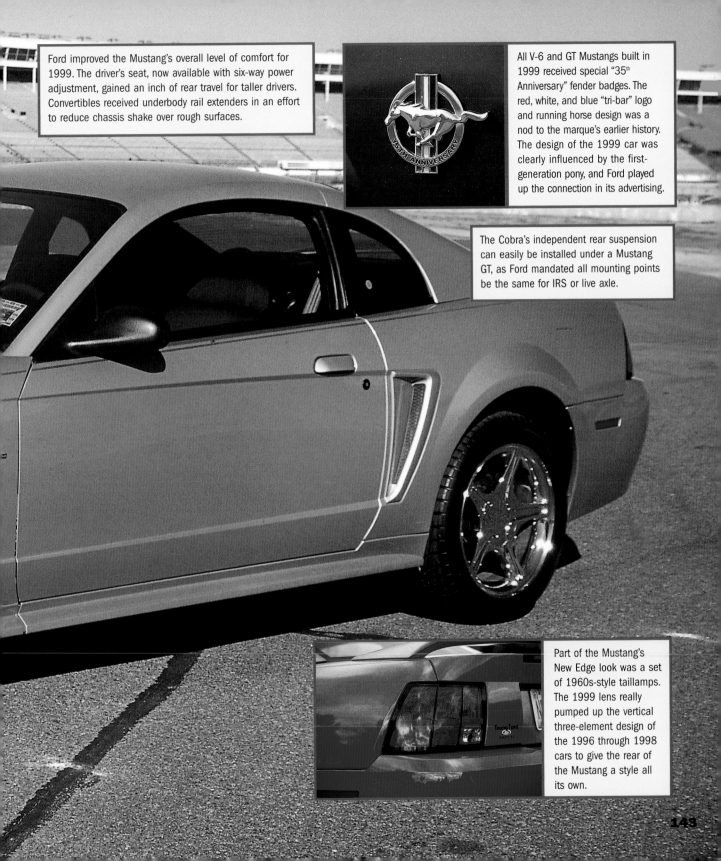

Ford improved the Mustang's overall level of comfort for 1999. The driver's seat, now available with six-way power adjustment, gained an inch of rear travel for taller drivers. Convertibles received underbody rail extenders in an effort to reduce chassis shake over rough surfaces.

All V-6 and GT Mustangs built in 1999 received special "35th Anniversary" fender badges. The red, white, and blue "tri-bar" logo and running horse design was a nod to the marque's earlier history. The design of the 1999 car was clearly influenced by the first-generation pony, and Ford played up the connection in its advertising.

The Cobra's independent rear suspension can easily be installed under a Mustang GT, as Ford mandated all mounting points be the same for IRS or live axle.

Part of the Mustang's New Edge look was a set of 1960s-style taillamps. The 1999 lens really pumped up the vertical three-element design of the 1996 through 1998 cars to give the rear of the Mustang a style all its own.

143

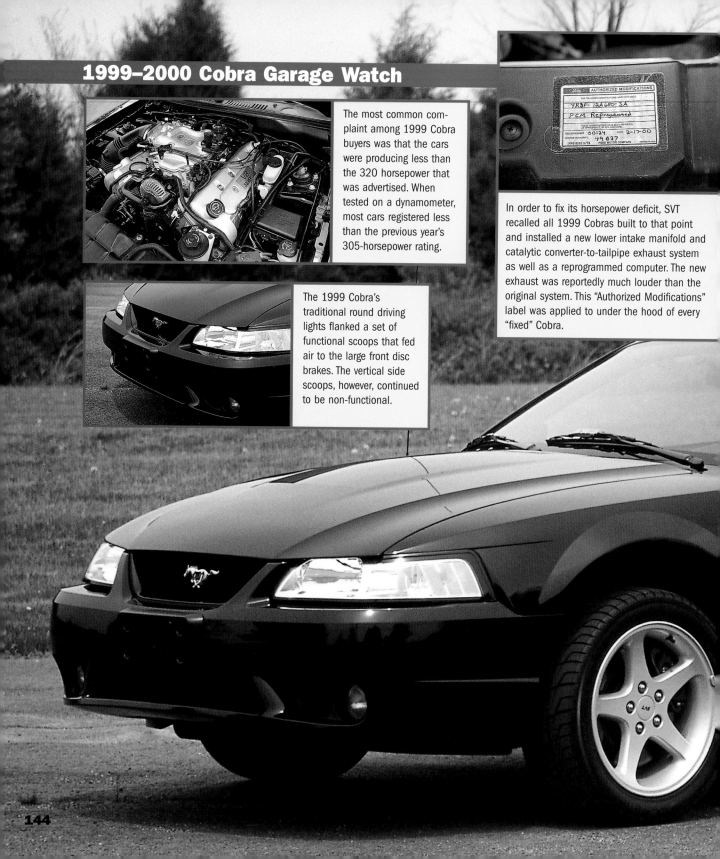

1999–2000 Cobra Garage Watch

The most common complaint among 1999 Cobra buyers was that the cars were producing less than the 320 horsepower that was advertised. When tested on a dynamometer, most cars registered less than the previous year's 305-horsepower rating.

The 1999 Cobra's traditional round driving lights flanked a set of functional scoops that fed air to the large front disc brakes. The vertical side scoops, however, continued to be non-functional.

In order to fix its horsepower deficit, SVT recalled all 1999 Cobras built to that point and installed a new lower intake manifold and catalytic converter-to-tailpipe exhaust system as well as a reprogrammed computer. The new exhaust was reportedly much louder than the original system. This "Authorized Modifications" label was applied to under the hood of every "fixed" Cobra.

The Cobra's T-45 five-speed manual transmission was revised for 1999 to fix customer complaints of broken gears and synchronizers. The heavier-duty tranny can be identified from the outside by the name "Tremec" stamped into the housing.

A driveline vibration was observed by many 1999 Cobra owners when driving between 55 and 70 miles per hour in any gear. SVT offered a set of matched driveline components to fix the problem.

Most car companies can't claim what SVT accomplished in 1999—a near balance between sales of coupes and convertibles. Of the 8,095 Cobras sold, 4,040 were coupes and 4,055 were convertibles. The only Cobras sold in 2000 were the 300 R models.

In its first year (1999), the Cobra's independent rear suspension (IRS) went a long way toward fixing the Mustang's chronic tail-happy handling. It also was the source of some owner complaints because of a tendency to allow wheel hop during hard launches.

The S-281's Racecraft suspension made a tremendous difference to the car's handling ability. A stock GT measured .83g on a test skid pad, and the S-281 posted a .93g result.

The Saleen Speedster package—available only on convertibles—provided a great place to store small items out of the sun with the top down. Unfortunately, the one-piece cover could not easily be transported if not in use.

Massive Pirelli P7000 tires (P255/35ZR18 front, P265/35ZR18 rear) were standard equipment on the S-281 and S-351. An upgrade substituted PZeros measuring P265/35ZR18 on the front and P295/35ZR18 on the rear.

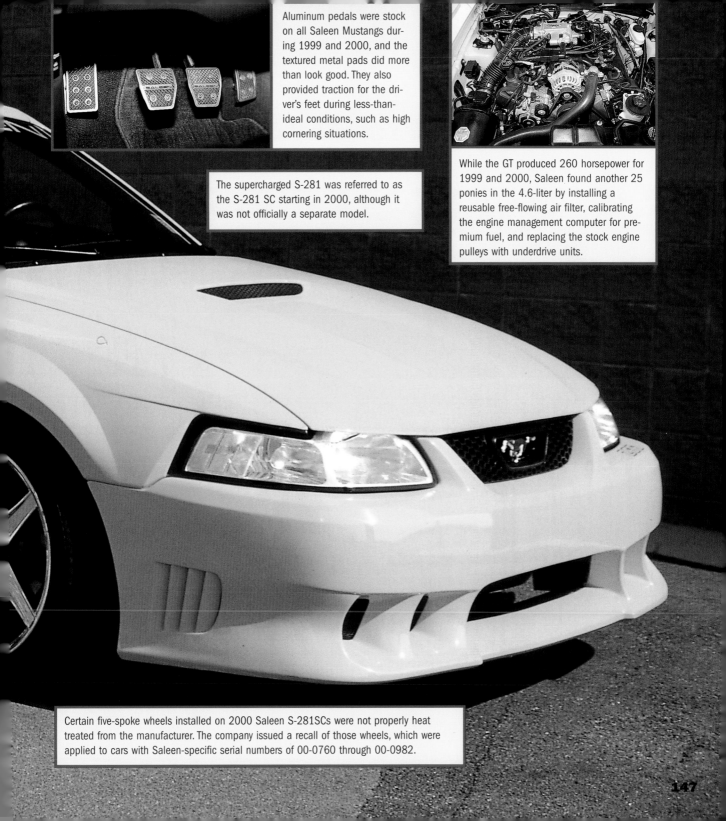

Aluminum pedals were stock on all Saleen Mustangs during 1999 and 2000, and the textured metal pads did more than look good. They also provided traction for the driver's feet during less-than-ideal conditions, such as high cornering situations.

While the GT produced 260 horsepower for 1999 and 2000, Saleen found another 25 ponies in the 4.6-liter by installing a reusable free-flowing air filter, calibrating the engine management computer for premium fuel, and replacing the stock engine pulleys with underdrive units.

The supercharged S-281 was referred to as the S-281 SC starting in 2000, although it was not officially a separate model.

Certain five-spoke wheels installed on 2000 Saleen S-281SCs were not properly heat treated from the manufacturer. The company issued a recall of those wheels, which were applied to cars with Saleen-specific serial numbers of 00-0760 through 00-0982.

Ford continued to add content to its Mustang in 2001, a practice that made even the base V-6 a desirable sporty car. The GT gained some scoops to separate it visually from the V-6 version.

Chapter 13

2001–2002 Mustang, Cobra, and Saleen

In 2001, Ford made few changes to its Mustang from a performance standpoint, but the GT received new body add-ons similar to those first seen on the limited-edition 1999 35th Anniversary Mustang. The cosmetic upgrades, which included a non-functional forward-facing hood scoop, fake side vents, and a stand-alone rear wing, helped distinguish the more expensive GT from the V-6 models and mimicked the Bosses and Mach 1s of the past.

The company also whittled the number of separate Mustang order combinations from the previous year's 2,600 to roughly 50 for 2001. In simple terms, a Mustang buyer could decide on paint color (10 choices), body style (coupe or convertible), engine (V-6 or V-8), transmission (five-speed manual or four-speed automatic), and equipment level (base, deluxe, or premium). Otherwise, there was a very short list of individual options, all of which were available bundled in the deluxe or premium packages.

The Traction Control System introduced as an option in 1999 was standard GT equipment in 2001, but it was only available at extra cost for the V-6 model. All models came standard with a rear-window defroster, but the smoker's package and block heater were dealer-installed accessories. New for 2001 was an in-dash six-disc CD changer, an option that required the Mach 460 sound system.

Arguably, the most enthusiast attention was given in 2001 to a limited-edition run of GT coupes ordered with the Bullitt package. Available only in dark highland green, true blue, or black, the cars were designed to recall Steve McQueen's silver-screen chase in 1968 down the streets of San Francisco in a Mustang GT as fictional police detective Frank Bullitt. Although the Bullitt engine upgrades of twin 57-mm throttle bodies, cast aluminum intake manifold, and high-flow mufflers only produced an increase of 5 horsepower, the exhaust sound and lowered suspension combined to make the car feel as though it fit squarely between Ford's GT and SVT's Cobra, in terms of performance. Thirteen-inch Brembo brake rotors and red performance calipers were installed, along with several unique suspension components. The Bullitt package also included 17-inch aluminum American Racing wheels—modern interpretations of the Torq-Thrust rims McQueen's fastback wore in the movie—which were standard equipment on the GT when ordered with the premium trim level.

All 5,582 Bullitt cars were fitted with a model-specific front fascia, blacked-out grille, quarter-panel molding, side scoop, and brushed aluminum filler cap, but they could not be ordered with a rear wing. Interiors were fitted with vintage-style gauges, a retro vinyl pattern in the seats, and an aluminum shift knob.

In GT form, the 4.6-liter SOHC V-8 ("X" code in VIN) again put out 260 horsepower. The V-8 came standard with a five-speed manual or optional four-speed automatic transmission.

The 3.8-liter V-6 ("4" code) was a carryover powerplant with the same transmission choices of the V-8. No matter the engine or transmission, 3.27:1 gears were installed in the rear axle.

SVT's Cobra changed very little from the 1999 model. Its 4.6-liter DOHC V-8 ("V" code) turned out a solid 320 horsepower, as all "fixes" from 1999 were incorporated into 2001 production. SVT offered eight exterior color choices for the Cobra this year, the most it had ever made available in the model's history. The only options on the high-dollar Cobra were a rear spoiler, floor mats, and polished wheels.

No Cobra model was offered for the 2002 production year. Instead, the next generation of supercharged coupes and convertibles would be introduced as early 2003 models.

Saleen had another banner year in 2001, with sales of its largely unchanged S-281 reaching 910 units. In 2002, the company introduced its S-281E model, which included the standard Saleen performance upgrades as well as a screw-type intercooled supercharger sitting atop a Saleen-built, 50-states-certified 4.6-liter V-8 that was rated at 425 horsepower. A quick-ratio six-speed manual transmission and a Maxgrip 8.8-inch differential that housed 3.27:1 gears backed up the E's engine. Pirelli PZero tires (P265/35ZR18 front, P295/35ZR18 rear) were mounted on 18-inch, five-spoke alloy wheels.

The E's performance was available at a premium, though, with coupes stickering at $60,190 and convertibles starting at $64,089. Popular options included the $2,979 Speedster package (for convertibles only), $1,119 chrome alloy wheels, $6,000 custom paint ($11,500 for the Extreme Rainbow treatment), and $1,375 for enclosed transport to the dealer.

When compared to the price tag on the E, the regular S-281 coupe ($34,194) and convertible ($38,194) seem like bargains. For 2002, Saleen sold 781 S-281s and 54 of its premium S-281Es.

With the addition of extra scoops and vents on the GT, the sporty V-6 model (seen here) took on a style of its own. Some have argued that the simple, uncluttered lines of the base model have more appeal than the GT's attention-grabbing exterior. Sixteen-inch wheels became standard on the V-6 convertible in 2001.

Where Ford puts one fake scoop, Saleen puts three. This non-functional side vent is one of the subtle details that makes the Saleen Mustangs stand out from the garden-variety GTs. When combined, the upgrades to front fascia, bumper cover, rocker moldings, hood scoop, wing, and rear quarter windows give the Saleens a totally different appearance.

Air conditioning became standard equipment across the board in 2000. By 2001, the list of one-time options that jumped to the standard list included single-disc CD stereo, power door locks, power windows, and rear window defroster.

2001–2002 Mustang Specifications

Base price	P40/100A standard V-6 coupe	$16,995–$17,475
	P40/110A deluxe V-6 coupe	$17,560–$18,080
	P44/150A deluxe V-6 convertible	$22,410–$23,000
	P40/120A premium V-6 coupe	$18,790–$19,195
	P44/160A premium V-6 convertible	$24,975–$25,585
	P42/130A deluxe GT coupe	$22,630–$23,220
	P45/170A deluxe GT convertible	$26,885–$27,475
	P42/140A premium GT coupe	$23,780–$24,390
	P45/180A premium GT convertible	$28,035–$28,645
	P42/135A Bullitt coupe (2001)	$26,320
	P48/300A Cobra coupe (2001)	$28,605
	P49/350A Cobra convertible (2001)	$32,605
Production	P40 V-6 coupe	75,321
	P44 V-6 convertible	30,399
	P42 GT coupe	32,511
	P45 GT convertible	18,336
	P48 Cobra coupe	3,867
	P49 Cobra convertible	3,384
Displacement (cubic inches/liters)		
	V-6	232/3.8
	V-8	281/4.6
Bore x stroke (inches)		
	V-6	3.80x3.40
	V-8	3.60x3.60
VIN code/Compression ratio		
	V-6	4 9.36:1
	V-8	X 9.40:1
	V-8 Cobra	V 9.85:1
Valvetrain	V-6	OHV
	V-8	SOHC
	V-8 Cobra	DOHC
Horsepower	V-6	193@5,550
	V-8	260@5,250
	V-8 ('01 Bullitt)	265@5,000
	V-8 Cobra	320@6,000
Transmission	V-6 standard	5-speed manual
	V-6/V-8 optional	4-speed automatic
	V-8 standard	5-speed
	V-8 Cobra	5-speed
Wheelbase (inches)		101.3
Overall width (inches)		73.1
Overall height (inches)		(coupe) 53.1
		(convertible) 53.2
Overall length (inches)		
	V-6/V-8	183.2
	V-8 Cobra	183.5
Track (inches) V-6/V-8		(front) 60.2
		(rear) 60.6
	V-8 Cobra	59.9

Weight (pounds)		
	P40/100A standard V-6 coupe	3,064
	P40/110A deluxe V-6 coupe	3,066
	P44/150A deluxe V-6 convertible	3,208
	P40/120A premium V-6 coupe	3,066
	P44/160A premium V-6 convertible	3,208
	P42/130A deluxe GT coupe	3,241
	P45/170A deluxe GT convertible	3,379
	P42/140A premium GT coupe	3,241
	P45/180A premium GT convertible	3,379
	P42/135A Bullitt coupe (2001)	3,241
	P48/300A Cobra coupe (2001)	3,430
	P49/350A Cobra convertible (2001)	3,560
Tires	V-6	P205/65R15
	V-8	P245/45ZR17
	V-8 Cobra	P245/45ZR17
Front suspension	modified MacPherson struts, lower A-arms, coil springs, tube shocks, anti-roll bar	
Rear suspension (base, GT)	live axle, angled upper and lower trailing arms, coil springs, tube shocks, anti-roll bar	
Rear suspension (Cobra)	independent rear suspension, upper and lower control arms, coil springs, tube shocks, anti-roll bar	
Steering	15.0:1 power rack-and-pinion	
Brakes	V-6	(front) 10.5-inch disc (rear) 8.0-inch drum
	V-8	(front) 10.8-inch disc (rear) 10.0-inch disc
	V-8 Cobra	(front) 13.0-inch disc (rear) 11.65-inch disc
Gas mileage (EPA city/hwy.)		
	V-6 5-speed manual	19/29, 20/29
	V-6 4-speed AOD	19/27, 19/27
	V-8 5-speed manual	18/25, 18/26
	V-8 4-speed AOD	18/25, 17/24
	V-8 Cobra 5-speed	17/25
0 to 60 (secs) (Cobra coupe)*		5.4
	(2001 Bullitt)**	5.9
	(GT coupe)***	6.0
Standing ¼-mile (mph/secs)		
	(Cobra coupe)	102@13.8
	(2001 Bullitt)	99.5@14.4
	(GT coupe)	96.4@14.7
Top speed (mph)(Cobra coupe)		150

* SVT factory info
** www.edmunds.com 2001
*** *Road & Track*, Dec. 2001

2001–2002 Mustang

Major Options

Automatic transmission	(N/A Cobra)	$815
V-6 Sport Appearance Group	(15-inch wheels, side stripes, leather-wrapped steering wheel, rear spoiler)	$250
Convenience Group	(front floor mats, speed control, power driver's seat)	$550
Bullitt Package ('01)	(265-hp V-8; unique stabilizer bars, performance calipers, side scoops, rocker panel moldings, C-pillar and glass, brushed aluminum fuel door, badging, leather-surfaced seat trim, Heritage instrument cluster, brushed aluminum accents, underhood clearcoat paint, charcoal interior and serialized identification)	$3,695
Emissions, California		no charge
Anti-lock brakes	includes Traction Control	$730
Mirrors, dual visor		$95
Traction control		$230
Rear spoiler	(std. deluxe, GT)	$195
Mach 460 radio system changer–460 watts	AM/FM stereo, 6-disc CD	$550
Wheels, 17-inch aluminum	(GT only)	$500
Seats, leather bucket		$500

Replacement Costs for Common Parts

Carpet		$99
Turn-signal lever assembly		$40
Trunk weather stripping		$35
Convertible top headliner		$150
Factory headlight knob		$12
Mach 460 speaker grille		$20
Convertible top boot		$300
Convertible top switch		$20
Electric window motor		$110
Antenna rod		$12
Wiper arm		$35
Space-saver wheel and tire		$40
Front-brake rotor	GT	$40
Front-brake rotor	Cobra	$160
Outside mirror switch		$45
Tilt wheel lever		$6
Convertible glass rear window		$165
Engine oil cooler	Cobra	$200
Radiator-to-grille cover		$25
Fuse box cover		$10
Hood	Cobra repro	$350
Underhood insulator	Cobra	$63
Fog lamp bezel	Cobra	$17
Taillamp assembly	Cobra	$150
SVT Cobra emblem	Cobra	$11
Instrument clear lens		$30
Leather steering wheel		$160
Convertible top motor		$185
Front-bumper cover	GT/V-6 repro	$200
Front-bumper cover	Cobra original	$300
Front-bumper cover	V-6 original	$400
Front-bumper cover	GT original	$470
Grille		$90
Front fender	original	$210
Hood	GT/V-6 original	$500
Hood	Cobra original	$500
Third brake light		$75
Underhood insulator	GT/V-6	$57
Rubber fender-to-hood bumpers		$5
Radiator core support		$290
Fog lamp kit		$205
Taillamp assembly	GT/V-6	$70
SVT emblem	Cobra R	$8

Replacement Costs for Common Parts		
Bullitt decklid emblem		$20
Bullitt pedals	automatic and manual trans	$90
Bullitt fuel door		$80
Bullitt 17x8-inch wheel		$160
Bullitt door scuff plate		$70
Bullitt shift knob		$35
Bullitt shifter trim bezel		$70
Fog lamp switch		$20
Convertible top		$200
Headlight assembly		$130
Hood scoop	GT	$130
Saleen S281 emblems	pair	$60
Saleen door stripe kit		$140
Saleen S281 hood decals		$5

What They Said in 2001–2002

On the performance front, the Bullitt is snappier off the line and sharper in the corners than the GT, but gives away significant horse-power and handling advantages to the SVT entry. What it has that the Cobra lacks is mojo. The Bullitt GT makes you feel like an ado-lescent in a darkened theater watching Steve McQueen fling a Mustang around the streets of San Francisco with abandon and élan. The magic of movies in a Mustang—who would have thought it possible? —*Road & Track,* **August 2001**

Let's get something straight right now: The Mustang GT is not a sports car. It's not even a grand touring car, despite the GT initials that adorn it. It's a musclecar, with the forte of straight-line speed, achieved by big horsepower and even bigger torque; the kind of V-8 power that makes leaving a pair of long black stripes from a stoplight as easy as falling in love. . . . Mustangs have always been about performance, and this one carries on the tradition. . . . Unfortunately, Ford has not addressed many of the problems enthusiasts have with this car, including a lack of independent rear suspension and a strange seating position that's too high. . . . Despite being a mus-clecar, the GT handles the twisty stuff just fine. The Quadra Shock rear setup keeps the rear planted, and you really have to work to make the tail slide out.—*Road & Track,* **December 2001**

I Bought a 2001 Mustang

Two factors convinced me to become a Mustang owner for the third time in 2001: The introduction of the color Zinc Yellow, and Ford's decision to install the retro-style 17-inch American Racing Torq-Thrust wheels on the Premium GT. Considering my wife and I share green as a favorite color, and I am a huge fan of the movie *Bullitt,* it might seem odd we didn't spring for the commemorative edition, but the package—attractive though it is—only delivered five more horsepower for the additional $3,700. I bought a yellow GT coupe instead, figuring someday I'll spend the money I saved on some engine, suspension, and axle upgrades. So far, all I've done to the car is tint the windows, install a K&N filter, and replace the rubbery black shift knob for a yellow ball. One other modification I made that Ford should consider as an option is the removal of the nearly useless back seat. I installed a Cobra R-style delete kit, which consists of two aluminum panels covered in matching carpet. Now my luggage and other cargo can ride flat when I travel, and I don't have to worry about scratching the leather. **—Brad Bowling**

I've never actually seen the movie *Bullitt,* but I was still in college in 2001 when Ford produced its version of Steve McQueen's car, and I had saved enough money to put a down payment on a new Mustang. My friend's 1999 GT had plenty of power and handled well, so I had been thinking about a 2001 coupe when I saw a Bullitt car on my dealer's lot. The Bullitt was supposed to be a hot item, so I was surprised when the salesman told me it had been sitting there for more than a month. It was not the popular green color, but blue, which I think may have turned off some buyers. Despite the lack of other immediate offers, the dealership was sticking to a figure just above MSRP. I took it for a test drive and really started to like the unique sound it made and its crisp handling. After two days of bargaining, I drove the car home for just under sticker. **—Steven Short**

2001–2002 Mustang Ratings

V-6

Model Comfort/Amenities	***
Reliability	****
Collectibility	**
Parts/Service Availability	*****
Est. Annual Repair Costs	*

GT

Model Comfort/Amenities	***
Reliability	*****
Collectibility	***
Parts/Service Availability	*****
Est. Annual Repair Costs	**

Saleen S-281

Model Comfort/Amenities	***
Reliability	****
Collectibility	*****
Parts/Service Availability	*****
Est. Annual Repair Costs	***

SVT Cobra (2001)

Model Comfort/Amenities	***
Reliability	****
Collectibility	****
Parts/Service Availability	*****
Est. Annual Repair Costs	**

Some add-on, non-functional body pieces (hood and side scoops) helped visually distinguish the 2001 GT from its less-powerful V-6 stablemate—a fact that traditionally affects collector value in later years. While the performance of the 2001 Bullitt cars was not greatly upgraded beyond that offered by the GT, its nod to the most famous Mustang movie in history has made it popular with collectors. With its refined independent rear suspension and a true 320 horsepower, the 2001 Cobra is an excellent bet for a future collectible, but it also is a perfectly civilized daily driver as well. Another record-setting sales year for Saleen's S-281 in 2001 means the coupes and convertibles are not as rare as other model years but are just as desirable from the collector's standpoint.

2001–2002 Mustang Garage Watch

With the 2001 model, the amount of plastic on the Mustang's exterior surfaces reached a new high. Starting in 1999, Ford began making the decklid, hood, and door skins from plastic. In 2001, the GT received more in the form of its various scoops and vents.

The new-for-2001 six-disc in-dash CD changer was a welcome option for Mustangers who had tired of the earlier, less-convenient trunk-mounted unit. Shortly after its introduction, Ford began warning owners not to play homemade CDs with self-adhesive labels, as the heat inside the unit was peeling them off and causing damage.

Called by many "the Bullitt wheels" because of their association with the 2001 package of that name, the origin of these American Racing Torq-Thrust wheels can be traced to the mid-1960s aftermarket when Chevy, Ford, Mopar, and AMC musclecars wore them to reduce unsprung weight and increase brake cooling.

The Mustang gained some practical interior storage space in 2001 with the redesign of the center console. It contained two cup holders (the rear-most one larger), a power plug for accessories such as cell phones, a tissue holder, and relocated parking brake boot.

It's not pretty, but the dirt-simple, old-fashioned V-6 benefits from those tuned intake runners. Improved airflow was the major key to massaging 193 horsepower and 225 lbs-ft of torque from the pushrod V-6. When equipped with the standard five-speed manual transmission, the 3.8-liter can achieve 29 miles per gallon on the highway.

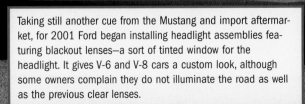

Taking still another cue from the Mustang and import aftermarket, for 2001 Ford began installing headlight assemblies featuring blackout lenses—a sort of tinted window for the headlight. It gives V-6 and V-8 cars a custom look, although some owners complain they do not illuminate the road as well as the previous clear lenses.

Ford's Traction Control System works with the antilock brakes and the engine management computer to decrease rear wheel spin in slippery conditions. Since some aspects of high-performance driving or racing (such as burnouts) can induce traction control at unwanted times, Ford installed an on/off switch for the system at the base of the console.

2001–2002 Saleen Garage Watch

One of the places Saleen "found" extra horsepower for its S-281 was through the use of underdrive pulleys, an idea that was developed and made popular in the 5.0-liter Mustang aftermarket. The idea of freeing power by installing smaller pulleys has been used on a limited basis by some manufacturers.

Since its inception in 1984, Saleen has aligned the front of its high-performance Mustangs with unique specs. The top of this strut tower is one point that is adjusted to get Saleen-specific caster and camber angles. Such alignment mods can greatly reduce the tendency of the front-heavy Mustang to understeer.

Although the S-351 was retired in 1999, Saleen found a new use for the 351-cid V-8 it had developed for that model. The company offered to build a 505-horsepower coupe, the SR, which featured an independent rear suspension, complete roll cage, and Saleen-unique composite body panels. For only $158,000, you could have a car capable of four-second 0 to 60 times that pulled 1.09g on the skid pad.

The 2002 S-281E's 425-horsepower engine was not simply a modification of an existing 4.6-liter SOHC powerplant. Like the S-351 before it, the E motor was new from the block up. It included a Saleen-specified forged steel crankshaft, rods, aluminum pistons, aluminum heads, and camshafts; a 90-mm mass air sensor; water-to-air intercooler and heat exchanger; and a cold air induction system.

Adding the optional Roots-type supercharger to an S-281 added nearly $5,000 to the price but cut almost a half a second from the car's 0 to 60 time. Normally aspirated S-281s could make the trip in 5.2 seconds; the blown version did it in 4.8 seconds.

A ventilated hood made of composite materials was optional for the S-281. It was lighter than the stock plastic GT unit and offered slightly more clearance.

With the return of the Cobra for 2001, Saleen once again offered its customers an S-281 built on the SVT platform. Although the figures for that combination have yet to be broken out of the production numbers, it is reported that quite a few of the $41,600 Saleen Cobra coupes and $45,500 convertibles were built.

Knowing its customers have a soft spot for nostalgia, in 2003 Ford mined its old parts bins and revived the Mach 1 nameplate. With its unique Shaker hood scoop and model-specific 305-horsepower DOHC powerplant, the Mach 1 quickly regained the respect it deserved.

Chapter 14

2003–2004 Mustang and Saleen

ord entered the last two years of its SN-95 platform with the mindset, "If it ain't broke, don't fix it."

The least-expensive Mustang offered for 2003 was the V-6 coupe with a sticker price of $17,695, which might sound like a lot of money for a base model if it weren't for the extensive list of standard equipment and safety features.

Even the lowly price leader came equipped with air conditioning, power windows and door locks, 80-watt single-disc CD stereo, power steering, power four-wheel disc brakes, tilt-steering column, console, remote keyless entry system, rear-window defroster, dual front airbags, fold-down rear seat (coupe only), dual vanity mirrors, and a lit trunk compartment.

Upgrading to the Premium package ($1,845) and adding equipment from the Pony group ($595) turned the bottom-rung pony from an airport rental car into a GT look-alike, with a leather steering wheel, six-disc CD Mach 460 stereo system, ABS/traction control, a racing stripe, GT hood and scoop, and 16-inch polished wheels.

After the demise of Chevrolet's Camaro and Pontiac's Firebird, Ford was obviously enjoying having the ponycar segment to itself again—in addition to nearly 18 percent of the convertible market—so changes to the middle- and bottom-rung Mustangs were minimal. The GT and V-6 models each benefited from stiffer accessory drive brackets and improved bearings underhood, refined weather stripping, and a retuned suspension with new shock absorbers. Other than these improvements, the 3.8-liter V-6 engine ("4" code on VIN) continued without change for 2003 and 2004, as did the very popular 4.6-liter SOHC V-8 ("X" code) that came standard in the GT.

Several safety improvements were put into place for 2003. Head-impact crash studies resulted in a new design for the A-pillar, headliner, and sun visors. Air bags and safety belts were recalibrated and/or upgraded. For the first time, anchors were installed in the backseat area so drivers could implement the LATCH child safety-seat system.

Overshadowing the GT in 2003 was the limited-edition Mach 1, a styling throwback to the 1969 and 1970 high-performance package created by the same in-house enthusiasts responsible for the 2001 Bullitt. From the outside, the average 10-year-old could spot the new Mach 1 by its modernized Shaker air-intake scoop, which stood a couple of inches above the surface of the hood. That scoop fed air to a 305-horsepower DOHC 4.6-liter V-8 ("R" code), which, like the Cobra, requires premium gasoline. The new scoop's shaking was the result of some clever spring and vacuum hose work—not an engine torquing against its mounts.

Unlike the Bullitt and Cobra, the Mach 1 could be outfitted with a four-speed automatic transmission (in place of the standard five-speed), which was coupled to a 3.55:1 rear axle. Special springs lowered the car a ½ inch all around and bigger brakes—13-inch Brembos in front, 11.7-inch Brembos in the rear—kept the extra horsepower in check. Subframe connectors, a mainstay of the Mustang aftermarket, came standard on the torquey Mach 1.

Further Mach 1-specific equipment included a chin spoiler, a tape stripe running from the leading edge of the hood to the cowl vent, and a free-standing rear wing—all in black, regardless of the exterior color—as well as a set of 17-inch five-spoke alloy wheels that mimicked the Magnum 500. From the driver seat, which is nicely trimmed in a vintage-looking vinyl, the Bullitt-like gauge cluster, stainless steel pedal covers, and aluminum shifter ball give a lucky owner a real sense of "new-stalgia." Only 6,500 of these retro-Stangs were planned, with final production numbers unknown at the time of this writing.

Anticipating Ford's all-new 2005 Mustang, Saleen entered its twentieth year of continuous production offering its three different 4.6-liter packages almost without change, other than increased power, for 2003 and 2004.

The base Saleen remained the S-281, which could be ordered on either the GT or Cobra platform. In GT trim, Saleen underdrive pulleys, low-restriction exhaust, and a recalibrated computer boosted S-281 horsepower to 290 (from 260 stock) and required the use of premium unleaded fuel. S-281s built from Cobras retained SVT's 390-horsepower rating.

The S-281SC was a GT-based 4.6-liter with a Saleen Series IV twin-screw supercharger, special intake manifold, intercooler, and tweaked engine management computer. Also running on premium, the SC registered 375 horsepower.

At the top of the Saleen hierarchy sat the S-281E, with its hand-built, supercharged 4.6-liter producing 445 horsepower, which it managed through a six-speed transmission.

All S-281s wore 18-inch five-spoke wheels with Pirelli P7000 or PZero Rosso high-performance tires. They also received all of the company's usual upgrades to suspension, interior, and cosmetics.

Gauges in the 2003 Mach 1 were similar to those found in the 2001 Bullitt GT. The style was chosen because it mimics the look and functionality of the high-performance Mustangs of the late 1960s and early 1970s.

Just about all high-performance versions of the 2003 and 2004 V-8 Mustang include some kind of pedals with metallic surfaces for better grip during spirited driving. Shown here are the Mach 1's pedals, which were first seen on the Bullitt Mustang.

Conventional thinking maintains the 295/35ZR18 high-performance radial tire (such as the Pirelli PZeros on this Saleen S-281) is the widest rubber that will fit in the wheelwell of the 1994 through 2004 Mustang for street applications.

2003–2004 Mustang Specifications

Base price	P40/100A standard V-6 coupe	$17,695
	P40/110A deluxe V-6 coupe	$18,425
	P44/150A deluxe V-6 convertible	$23,395
	P40/120A premium V-6 coupe	$19,540
	P44/160A premium V-6 convertible	$25,980
	P42/130A deluxe GT coupe	$23,680
	P45/170A deluxe GT convertible	$27,985
	P42/140A premium GT coupe	$24,850
	P45/180A premium GT convertible	$29,155
	P42/145A premium Mach 1 coupe	$28,680
Production	P40/100A standard V-6 coupe	not available
	P40/110A deluxe V-6 coupe	not available
	P44/150A deluxe V-6 convertible	not available
	P40/120A premium V-6 coupe	not available
	P44/160A premium V-6 convertible	not available
	P42/130A deluxe GT coupe	not available
	P45/170A deluxe GT convertible	not available
	P42/140A premium GT coupe	not available
	P45/180A premium GT convertible	not available
	P42/145A Mach 1 coupe	not available
Displacement (cubic inches/liters)		
	V-6	232/3.8
	V-8	281/4.6
Bore x stroke (inches)		
	V-6	3.80x3.40
	V-8	3.60x3.60
VIN code/	V-6	4 9.36:1
Compression ratio	V-8	X 9.40:1
	V-8 Mach 1	R 10.1:1
Valvetrain	V-6	OHV
	V-8	SOHC
	V-8 Mach 1	DOHC
Horsepower	V-6	190@5,250
	V-8	260@5,250
	V-8 Mach 1	305@5,800
Transmission	V-6 standard	5-speed manual
	V-6/V-8 optional	4-speed automatic
	V-8 standard	Tremec TR3650 5-speed
Wheelbase (inches)	101.3	
Overall width (inches)	73.1	
Overall height (inches)		(coupe) 53.1
		(convertible) 53.2
Overall length (inches)		V-6/V-8
		183.2
Track (inches)	V-6/V-8	(front) 60.2
		(rear) 56.0
Weight (pounds)	V-6	(coupe) 3,066

		(convertible) 3,208
Tires	V-6	P225/55R16
	V-8	P245/45ZR17
	V-8 Mach 1	P245/45ZR17
Front suspension	independent, modified MacPherson strut with separate spring on lower arm and stabilizer bar	
Rear suspension	non-independent four-bar link with coil springs on lower arm and stabilizer (GT only)	
Steering	15.0:1 power rack-and-pinion	
Brakes	V-6	(front) 10.5-inch disc
		(rear) 8.0-inch drum
	V-8	(front) 10.8-inch disc
		(rear) 10.0-inch disc
	V-8 Mach 1	(front) 13.0-inch disc
		(rear) 11.65-inch disc
Gas mileage (city/highway)		V-6 coupe manual
		20/29
	V-6 coupe automatic	19/27
	V-8 coupe manual	18/26
	V-8 coupe automatic	18/24
	V-8 coupe Mach 1 manual	17/25
	V-8 coupe Mach 1 automatic	17/23
	V-8 Cobra coupe manual	16/22
0 to 60 (secs)	(S-281)*	5.1
	(S-281E)*	4.5
	(Mach 1)**	5.2
Standing ¼-mile (mph/secs)		(S-281)
		99@14.0
	(S-281E)	113@12.5
	(Mach 1)	105@12.97
Top speed (mph)	(Mach 1)	151

* Saleen factory info
* *Car and Driver*, Dec. 2002

2003–2004 Mustang

Major Options

Automatic transmission	(N/A Cobra)	$815
Interior Upgrade Package	(N/A base standard)	$345
	aluminum finish door lock posts, shift boot trim ring, stainless steel pedals, leather-wrapped shift knob,	
4-way head restraint		
Pony Package	(base deluxe and premium)	$645
	polished aluminum wheels, unique side stripes, unique rear fascia, leather-wrapped steering wheel	
Sport Appearance Group	(base deluxe coupe)	$175
	side stripes, leather-wrapped steering wheel, bright alloy wheels	
Anti-lock brakes	includes Traction Control	$730
Mach 460 radio system 460 watts	AM/FM stereo, 6-disc CD changer,	$550
Mach 1000 radio system 1,000 watts	AM/FM stereo, 6-disc CD changer,	$1,295
Convertible boot	(std. Cobra convertible)	$95
Leather-surfaced seats		$595

Replacement Costs for Common Parts

Trunk weather stripping		$35
Convertible top headliner		$150
Factory headlight knob		$12
Mach 460 speaker grille		$20
Convertible top boot		$300
Convertible top switch		$20
Electric window motor		$110
Antenna rod		$12
Wiper arm		$35
Space-saver wheel and tire		$40
Front-brake rotor	GT	$40
Front-brake rotor	Cobra	$160

Outside mirror switch		$45
Tilt wheel lever		$6
Convertible glass rear window		$165
Radiator-to-grille cover		$25
Fuse box cover		$10
Instrument clear lens		$30
Leather steering wheel		$160
Convertible top motor		$185
Front-bumper cover	GT/V-6 repro	$200
Front-bumper cover	Cobra original	$300
Front-bumper cover	V-6 original	$400
Front-bumper cover	GT original	$470
Grille		$90
Front fender	original	$210
Hood	GT/V-6 original	$500
Hood	Cobra original	$500
Third brake light		$75
Underhood insulator	GT/V-6	$57
Rubber fender-to-hood bumpers		$5
Radiator core support		$290
Fog lamp kit		$205
Taillamp assembly	GT/V-6	$70
Fog lamp switch		$20
Convertible top		$200
Headlight assembly		$130
Hood scoop	GT	$130
Mach 1 decklid emblem		$23
Mach 1 chin spoiler		$70
Mach 1 grille		$50
Mach 1 rocker stripes	pair	$60
Mach 1 hood stripe		$60
Mach 1 wheel		$150
Hood	Cobra repro	$320
Hood	Cobra original	$500
Outer door mirror	Cobra	$160
Steering wheel	Cobra	$170
Shifter knob	Cobra	$65
Wheel center cap	Cobra	$15
Saleen S281 emblems	pair	$60
Saleen door stripe kit		$140
Saleen S281 hood decals		$5

What They Said in 2003–2004

A 300-mile drive in a GT convertible was a reminder that the Mustang is a throwback to another era, but still a very enjoyable car. It was gorgeously sunny during the day, brilliantly starry after midnight. We dropped the top and kept it there the whole time. We had our new Bonnie Raitt CD along and discovered the MACH speed-sensitive sound system is fantastic with the top down. But a Beach Boys tape might have been more in tune with the wonderful rumble of the engine. Throwback time. **—www.newcartestdrive.com, 2003**

Among the various Mustangs produced during the muscle car era of the late 1960s and early 1970s, the Mach 1 stood out from the rest—and still does to this day. . . . Anyone who's acclimated to the standard 4.6 in the GT will notice the Mach 1's extra juice immediately. Unlike the revisions in the Bullitt Mustang that resulted in barely discernable differences in power, the Mach's substantial improvements return results you can feel. The Mach 1 is also aided by a shorter 3.55:1 final drive ratio, so sub-14 second quarter-mile times shouldn't be much of a problem. **—www.edmunds.com, December 2003**

I Bought a 2003–2004 Mustang

When I saw pictures of the Mach 1 prototype on stangnet.com last year, I decided I had to get one if it ever saw production. My wife and I even wrote Ford to tell them how much we wanted to own a new Mach 1 to go with our Grabber Green 1970. When the company announced it would go into production, we went to Tindol Ford in Charlotte, North Carolina, to let them know we wanted to place our order as soon as possible. In May 2002, we got the call and put down a deposit for a Grabber Blue model with the only available option—he interior dress-up package. We were given a projected delivery date of January 2003, which became February, which rolled into March. We saw plenty of them on the road, even blue ones like ours was supposed to be. At one point, the dealer called to see if we would take a black one that was in stock, but we were adamant about getting the car we had ordered. Finally, on April 17, of all dates, we picked up our new Mach. **—Norm Demers**

I've been crazy about high-performance cars all of my life; I remember drawing a Formula 1 racer at Monaco when I was four years old. My wife and friends call me a car "nit," because I am probably the pickiest person alive about my cars in terms of neatness and preventing them from being damaged. My first Mustang was a 1967 GT-500, which I kept for three years and sold for double what I paid for it, but I sure wish I had kept it! I also had a new 1984 Mustang GT five-speed coupe. Since I was the sales manager for Hendrick Porsche, I've owned about 15 of those, including a 1996 twin-turbo model that put out 630 horsepower to all four wheels. I got the itch to buy another Mustang and looked at the Roush cars but, despite the great performance, didn't care too much for the overall package, especially the body kit. I briefly considered one of the Roush Classic models because it addressed some of the issues I disliked, but then I saw an S-281 and knew the Saleen's visual impact was exactly what I was looking for. I bought a supercharged 2003 S-281 coupe in Shadow Gray Metallic, and I must say, I am enjoying it more than my last 911. I may make some performance modifications in the future, but for now it is a real thrill to drive every day. **—Darrell Smith**

2003–2004 Mustang Ratings

V-6

Model Comfort/Amenities	***
Reliability	****
Collectibility	*
Parts/Service Availability	*****
Est. Annual Repair Costs	*

GT

Model Comfort/Amenities	****
Reliability	*****
Collectibility	***
Parts/Service Availability	*****
Est. Annual Repair Costs	**

Saleen S-281

Model Comfort/Amenities	****
Reliability	****
Collectibility	*****
Parts/Service Availability	*****
Est. Annual Repair Costs	***

Mach 1 (2003)

Model Comfort/Amenities	****
Reliability	*****
Collectibility	***
Parts/Service Availability	*****
Est. Annual Repair Costs	**

The Mach 1 is no doubt the future collectible among the production Mustangs. Saleen's S-281 continues to enjoy the lowest production numbers of any Mustang line, and collectors will single out the E model as an historical car from that 20-year-old company.

2003–2004 Mustang Garage Watch

The Mach 1's Comfortweave seat pattern recalls the look of the 1969 through 1973 Mustangs. Today's version, however, offers considerably more lumbar and lateral support and six-way adjustable power.

Wind noise was attacked by Ford engineers for 2003 by the use of expandable foam seals around the body. Particular attention was paid to the outside door handles and belt molding on the doors.

While the GT's four brake rotors are carryovers in service for several years, the Mach 1 received 13-inch Brembo discs in the front and 11.6-inchers in the rear. Contrasting the Bullitt's bright red calipers, the Mach 1 stoppers were painted black.

The federal government gave the 2003 and 2004 Mustang a five-star rating—its highest—for front passenger safety. Improvements such as recalibrated airbags, redesigned A-pillars and safety belts with pretensioners, and energy-management retractors reduce the chances of injury in a collision.

Unlike in the old days, the Mach 1's protruding hood scoop does not shake in direct relation to the engine beneath it. Because the 4.6-liter DOHC's noise/vibration/harshness is kept to a minimum by special engine mounts, the V-8 does not torque like the 1968 through 1970 big blocks. Instead, a special vacuum-and-spring mechanism provides the show when revs go up.

All V-6 and V-8 Mustangs received some suspension tuning from Ford for 2003. New shocks and urethane jounce bumpers gave the chassis a more progressive engagement over bumps, and rear axle travel was reduced by the addition of a pinion snubber.

Ford was criticized for producing its 2001 Bullitt Mustang with no real power increase from the 4.6-liter V-8. The 2003 Mach 1 package was centered around a 305-horsepower double overhead cam V-8 with 10.1:1 compression and 3.55:1 rear axle gears for stump-pulling acceleration.

2003–2004 Saleen Garage Watch

Saleen celebrated its twentieth anniversary in the Mustang-modifying business in 2003. A limited-production, special-edition car has been planned, the details currently under wraps.

A boost and intercooler temperature gauge come with the supercharger in the Saleen S-281. They sit in the middle of the dash above the stereo and climate controls.

For 2003 and 2004, Saleen offered a base S-281, supercharged S-281, supercharged S-281E, and an S-281 built from the 390-horsepower supercharged SVT Cobra. All were available in coupe or convertible form.

Saleens benefited from the improvements made in 2003 to the production Mustang in the interest of passenger safety. Improvements such as recalibrated airbags, redesigned A-pillars, and safety belts with pretensioners and energy-management retractors reduce the chances of injury in a collision.

Saleen's custom-spec supercharger adds more than 100 horsepower to the Mustang's 4.6-liter V-8. This engine is the base supercharged V-8. The E package adds many internal modifications to produce 445 horsepower from the 4.6.

In order to provide clearance for the tall Roots-type supercharger, this S-281 is equipped with the slightly roomier, ventilated hood.

171

With no competition in the showroom, the 2003 SVT Cobra was a real standout in terms of performance and presentation.

Chapter 15

2003–2004 Cobra

Fans of the marque are loath to admit it, but the Mustang had trailed slightly behind the Camaro and Firebird in terms of sheer horsepower output and cubic inches of displacement since Ford rejoined the musclecar competition in 1982. For every single horsepower the Mustang gained, GM seemed to find 1.5 horsepower. When the Camaro/Firebird twins got corporate permission to use a Corvette-based 350-cid powerplant, Ford resisted market pressure to respond with a modern version of its 351, instead choosing to sit tight on its 302- and, later, 281-cid engines.

While it underperformed against the competition in head-to-head acceleration comparisons, magazines generally gave the Mustang the nod for its greater real-world attributes, such as long-term comfort, greater drivability, and friendlier ergonomics. Despite better quarter-mile times, enthusiasts were not surprised when GM discontinued its slow-selling F-bodies at the end of 2002, eliminating the last of the pony car pretenders. What was surprising, however, was that SVT chose the next year to introduce the most powerful production Mustang ever, a car that would have soundly defeated the Camaro in every category!

The 2003 Cobra platform and equipment were very similar to the 1999 through 2001 models, including the independent rear suspension, 13-inch Brembo disc brakes with twin-piston calipers in the front, 11.65-inch discs in the rear, and 3.55:1 rear-axle gears. The engine layout was the same—dual overhead camshafts tickling four valves per cylinder—but it was the addition of a Roots-type supercharger that produced an astounding 390 horsepower at 6,000 rpm and 390 lbs-ft of torque at 3,500 rpm.

The Cobra's 4.6-liter V-8 (VIN code "Y") was backed up by a stout TTC T-56 six-speed manual transmission (fifth and sixth gears are overdrives), an aluminum driveshaft with hardened yoke and special U-joints, and increased-capacity 31-spline halfshafts. Because SVT cast this version of the 4.6 in iron (as opposed to 1996 through 2001, when aluminum was used), the greater weight in front required stiffer springs and suspension components.

For perhaps the first time since the horsepower wars of the late 1960s, there is evidence that SVT is *understating* the horsepower of its product. The company claims a net 390-horsepower rating for the supercharged 4.6 DOHC in its Cobra, which refers to the amount of power generated at the flywheel with certain accessories turned off or disconnected. Rear-wheel horsepower, on the other hand, is generally 15 to 17 percent less due to parasitic losses from friction associated with the transmission, driveshaft, and rear axle. In the case of the 2003 Cobra, some enthusiasts have reported a solid 390 to 400 horses at the rear wheels instead of the expected 325 to 335!

Other changes from the previous year include an LED third brake light, color-keyed side-mirror housings, smooth rocker panels, and side scoops designed to complement the heat-extracting openings in the hood. Cobra convertibles received an upgraded top for 2003, similar to what corporate cousin Jaguar produced for its XK-8.

The Cobra received some safety upgrades applied to all Mustangs in 2003, including a new A-pillar and improved headliner as well as better sun visors and a revised D-ring seat belt attachment, all in the name of reducing head injuries in the event of an impact. The firing logic of both driver and passenger airbags was reconfigured to take into account various body types. Pretensioners were applied to the front passenger seat belts for the purpose of tightening the lap and shoulder belts during the first thousandths of a second of a crash. Retractors manage the initial energy of the belt's use in an emergency in order to reduce the amount of pressure placed against the driver's or passenger's torso. Child seat installation was made easier and more secure in 2003 with the addition of anchors designed to work with the LATCH system.

Inside, the most obvious change is the boost gauge that monitors the pressure generated by the supercharger. The Cobra's six-speed shifter is topped with a leather-wrapped knob topped off by a brushed-aluminum insert inscribed with the transmission's pattern. Metal-trimmed pedals (including a "dead" one at the far left) give the driver more traction for his feet during tricky maneuvers on the road or track.

To celebrate its tenth year of producing high-performance Mustangs, SVT released a special anniversary edition in the summer of 2003. It was available in either coupe or convertible body style with 17x9-inch argent wheels, red-leather seating surfaces, carbon fiber-look interior trim, and special anniversary badging on the floor mats and decklid. Only 2,003 of the anniversary Cobras—available in red, black or silver—were schedule for production.

As a yardstick of how far the Cobra name has come since the dark days of the 1970s, realize that the 2003 model puts out more than three times the horsepower of the 1976 through 1978 Cobra II and King Cobra V-8s.

Even though the Cobra's aluminum block was replaced by a cast iron unit for 2003 and later, all SVT Mustang V-8s are still assembled in the Romeo, Michigan, plant's niche production line. This plaque was signed by the DOHC's two-man team of builders.

The 2003's and 2004's gigantic Goodyear Eagle F1 GS high-performance tires (P275/40ZR17 all around) are necessary in order to put the Cobra's 390 horsepower and 390 lbs-ft of torque to the ground with minimal slippage.

The Cobra's six-speed contains two overdrive gears. Fifth and sixth gear ratios are .80 and .63, respectively, which account for the supercharged car's relatively efficient 22-miles per gallon highway rating. The Cobra's rear-axle ratio is 3.55:1.

2003–2004 Cobra Specifications

Base price	P48/300A Cobra coupe	$33,440
	P49/350A Cobra convertible	$37,780
Production	P48/300A Cobra coupe	N/A
	P49/350A Cobra convertible	N/A
Displacement (cubic inches/liters)		281/4.6
Bore x stroke (inches)		3.60x3.60
VIN code/Compression ratio		Y 8.50:1
Valvetrain		DOHC
Supercharger		Eaton Roots-type, aluminum case and internal rotors
Block/heads		iron/aluminum
Horsepower		390@6,000
Transmission		TTC T-56 6-speed manual
Wheelbase (inches)	101.3	
Overall width (inches)	73.1	
Overall height (inches)	(coupe) 53.1	
	(convertible) 53.2	
Overall length (inches)		183.5
Track (inches)		60.3
Weight (pounds)		(coupe) 3,665
		(convertible) 3,780
Tires		P275/40ZR17
Front suspension		independent, modified MacPherson strut with separate spring on lower arm and stabilizer bar
Rear suspension		multi-link independent system, cast-iron upper control arms, aluminum lower control arms, fixed toe-controltie rods, aluminum spindles, gas-charged shocks and stabilizer bar
Steering	15.0:1 power rack-and-pinion	
Brakes		(front) 13.0-inch disc
		(rear) 11.65-inch disc
Gas mileage (city/highway)		16/22
0 to 60 (secs)	*	4.6
Standing ¼-mile (mph/secs)		112@12.9
Top speed (mph)		155

* *Car and Driver*, April 2003

2003–2004 Cobra

Major Options

10th Anniversary Package	
('03 Cobra only, summer delivery)	$1,495
unique badging, unique leather seat trim,	
7-spoke cast aluminum wheels	
Mach 1000 radio system AM/FM stereo, 6-disc CD changer,	
1,000 watts	$1,295
Chrome alloy wheels (Cobra only)	$695

Replacement Costs for Common Parts

Trunk weather stripping		$35
Convertible top headliner		$150
Factory headlight knob		$12
Mach 460 speaker grille		$20
Convertible top boot		$300
Convertible top switch		$20
Electric window motor		$110
Antenna rod		$12
Wiper arm		$35
Space-saver wheel and tire	$40	
Front-brake rotor	Cobra	$160
Outside mirror switch		$45
Tilt wheel lever		$6
Convertible glass rear window		$165
Radiator-to-grille cover		$25
Fuse box cover		$10
Instrument clear lens		$30
Convertible top motor		$185
Front-bumper cover	original	$300
Grille		$90
Front fender	original	$210
Hood	original	$500
Rubber fender-to-hood bumpers		$5
Radiator core support		$290
Fog lamp switch		$20
Convertible top		$200
Headlight assembly		$130
Hood	repro	$320
Hood	original	500
Outer door mirror		160
Steering wheel		170
Shifter knob		65
Wheel center cap		15
Rear wing	repro	260
Fog lamps	each	100
Third brake light		51
Chrome SVT emblem		13

What They Said in 2003–2004

If you're a driver whose No. 1 priority is straight-line speed, look no further than the SVT Mustang Cobra. . . . Nor is the Cobra a one-trick pony. Although its platform was designed before Super Bowl XXXVII's MVP, Dexter Jackson, was born, this ultimate Mustang acquits itself well in the corners. It easily turned the quickest lap time [of three competitors] at the Streets of Willow road-racing circuit in Southern California, owing to the balanced way it was able to apply its superb power. —*Car and Driver*, **April 2003**

We can't say enough about the Cobra's supercharged power. Just ease into the throttle, and the Cobra surges forward in a luscious rush of torque. Need to pass a slow-moving tractor trailer? Don't even worry about downshifting. Heck, you'll only need part throttle. At full throttle, the sensation and sound of shifting through the six gears can be compared to an Indy car; the shifts come fast and furious, while the Eaton supercharger emits a mechanical whine that mixes with the toned-down exhaust.—*Mustang Monthly,* **June 2003**

I Bought a 2003–2004 Cobra

I knew I was going to have to trade my red 1997 Cobra for a 2003 when I read that SVT was putting a supercharger on it and that it would put out 390 horsepower. I ordered my coupe in Sonic Blue Clearcoat Metallic, which makes the car seem very subdued. It's been extremely reliable, despite my frequent burnouts and hard launches, although Ford had to replace the rear end under warranty in its first year. —**Bob Cox**

2003–2004 SVT Cobra Ratings

Model Comfort/Amenities	*****
Reliability	*****
Collectibility	*****
Parts/Service Availability	*****
Est. Annual Repair Costs	**

Since 2003 is the first year for the supercharged 390-horsepower SVT Cobra, it will likely bring a premium in years to come from collectors, especially if stored and undriven. With an all-new Mustang design on the boards for 2005, SVT's supercar will only have a two-year run in its current format. The 2003 10th anniversary editions are the most likely to retain strong value.

Owners can't resist taking the powerful Cobra to the drag strip, where it regularly runs in the low 13-second range. A common performance complaint is the notchy six-speed shifter. Aftermarket shifters can improve the smoothness between gears.

If there is a weak point to the 2003 Cobra package, it is the car's independent rear suspension (IRS). Although components were beefed up after complaints from owners of 1999 and 2001 Cobras, the addition of 70 horsepower may push the upgrades to the limit, especially if drag raced.

Although they might look familiar, the four-valve heads are an entirely new design for 2003, with a higher flow rate than previous models. Valve size did not change (37-mm intake, 30-mm exhaust), but the camshaft was reprofiled to boost low-end torque.

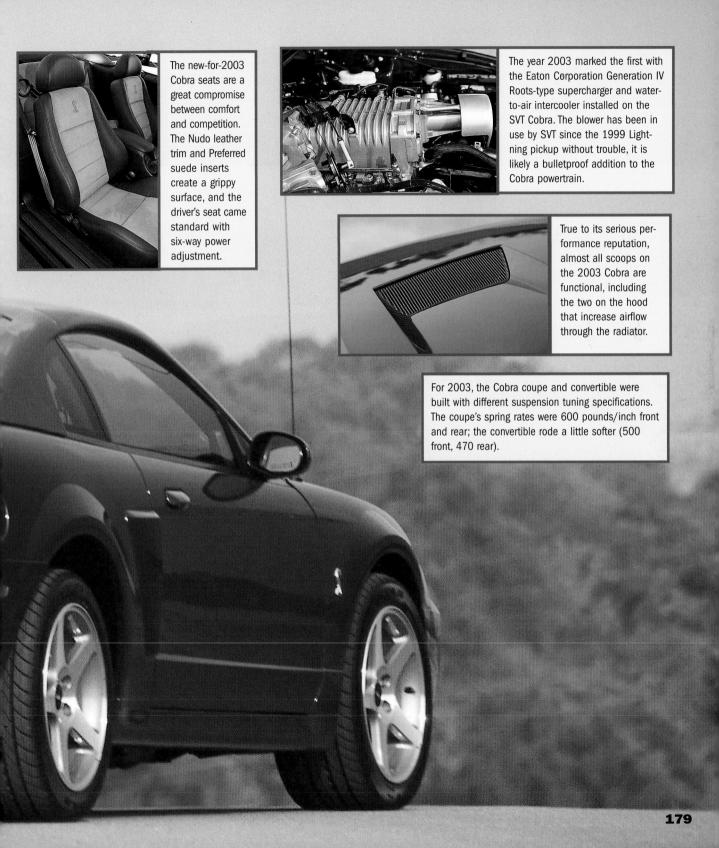

The new-for-2003 Cobra seats are a great compromise between comfort and competition. The Nudo leather trim and Preferred suede inserts create a grippy surface, and the driver's seat came standard with six-way power adjustment.

The year 2003 marked the first with the Eaton Corporation Generation IV Roots-type supercharger and water-to-air intercooler installed on the SVT Cobra. The blower has been in use by SVT since the 1999 Lightning pickup without trouble, it is likely a bulletproof addition to the Cobra powertrain.

True to its serious performance reputation, almost all scoops on the 2003 Cobra are functional, including the two on the hood that increase airflow through the radiator.

For 2003, the Cobra coupe and convertible were built with different suspension tuning specifications. The coupe's spring rates were 600 pounds/inch front and rear; the convertible rode a little softer (500 front, 470 rear).

Jack Roush's name carries with it a certain hushed awe among NASCAR fans. His development work for Ford during the last couple of decades has given him a platform on which to build some of the most powerful and well-designed Mustangs available.

Chapter 16

Roush

Many NASCAR enthusiasts already recognize Jack Roush's name from his ownership of several Winston Cup Ford teams, not the least of which have Mark Martin and Jeff Burton in the driver's seat. His company, Roush Industries, employs more than 2,000 people at 50 locations in Michigan, California, North Carolina, Mexico, and England.

For several decades, Roush has had his hands in every aspect of the performance world, including research and development for the Big Three automakers and engine building for motorsports, street, aviation, and marine applications. Roush Performance Products is the corporate arm that was created in 1995 for the development and sale of go-fast parts and crate motors for Ford products that include the F-150 pickup, Mercury Cougar, and, of course, Mustang. In 1997, Roush began producing a series of performance packages for V-6 and V-8 Mustangs that could be ordered through special Ford dealerships around the country. Packages have evolved or been replaced by newer versions, but as of this writing, the least-expensive Roush model is the Sport, which can be applied to either V-6 or V-8 Mustangs and includes no powerplant modifications. The $3,875 Sport equipment consists mostly of a complete body kit, side-exit exhaust, and the nifty trunk-mounted tool kit. A laundry list of optional components, such as the Roush rear spoiler, V-8 suspension, and brake package can take the Sport that much closer to high-performance territory.

The next step in the Roush ladder, the Stage 1, is also available for V-6 or V-8 buyers. An expansion of the Sport theme, Stage 1 makes the rear spoiler standard and includes a set of 17x8-inch argent wheels and tires. The V-6 package, which retails for $6,569, also adds a lowered suspension, but the $6,020 V-8 model maintains the GT components.

Stage 2, for GT-based conversions only, adds 18-inch argent wheels and tires plus a lowered performance suspension to the Stage 1 package for $9,860.

The first engine upgrade comes at the Stage 3 level, where the stock 4.6-liter V-8 increases output to 379 horsepower (360 when introduced in 2001) by virtue of an Eaton supercharger and computer recalibration. Stage 3 Sport delivers the more powerful engine combined with an aluminum flywheel, sub-frame connectors, 17-inch argent wheels, Cobra hood and cosmetic package, as well as Roush's brake system, all for $17,645 over the cost of a GT. For $21,612 above base, the Stage 3 Rally starts with the Sport and adds a lowered suspension system, 18-inch wheels, racing-style alloy pedals, and white-face gauges. The pinnacle of Stage 3 performance and price is the $27,550 Premium package, which takes the Sport and Rally equipment and adds the Alcon brake system and Roush-specific sport leather seating. All Stage 3 Roush Mustangs receive individual serial-numbered plaques to indicate order and year of production.

In all Roush applications, the 379-horse engine also benefits from a modified mass-airflow sensor, Bosch fuel injectors, and a BBK throttle body. The supercharger can create boost to 6 psi thanks to an Allied-Signal dual-core air-to-liquid intercooler and electric water pump. Any 379-horse Roush ordered with an automatic transmission is fitted with a mandatory fluid cooler.

For Mustang enthusiasts whose cutting-edge performance does not have to be laser sharp, the $18,525 Classic package (also advertised by the company as the Jack Roush Classic) combines the 379-horse supercharged 4.6 with Roush brakes, 17-inch chrome wheels, a Cobra hood, billet pedals, serial-numbered plaque, white gauges, and complete body kit, but leaves the stock GT suspension in place. Only 50 Classics are scheduled for production in 2003.

On the other side of the Roush coin is the $16,800 380R, which began life as the 360R. The 380R features the supercharged engine, Cobra hood, cosmetic upgrades, serial-numbered plaque, Roush brake system, and a nostalgic stripe package meant to evoke memories of Carroll Shelby's GT-350s. Roush anticipates production of 200 380Rs per year.

For 2003, Roush teamed with legendary hot rod builder and custom wheel designer Boyd Coddington to produce a run of 100 convertibles. Marketed as the Boyd Coddington California Roadster, the 25 supercharged and 75 normally-aspirated droptops feature Roush cosmetic pieces, serial-numbered plaques, sport leather seats, convertible light bars, lowered suspension, and chrome 18-inch wheels designed by Coddington. The California hot rodder's autograph appears on the white-face gauges. Each car features a two-tone paint scheme, with a black hood against a red, yellow, or silver body. The Boyd Coddington California Roadster package lists for $11,942.

Just like with Shelbys and Saleens, the Roush Mustangs feature individual serial-numbering separate from Ford's VIN. Such identification can be found next to the driver-side strut tower (seen here) and at the base of the console, as well as some hidden locations.

First glances can be deceiving. Those leather-covered seats are not stock GT inventory. They are more thickly padded than the GT or Cobra buckets, which makes for a more comfortable ride with plenty of lateral support should the road get twisty.

Roush's body kit gives the company's cars a unique look, from the squared-off front spoiler to this rear wing. The wing is styled to continue the upward sweep of the Mustang's profile.

Roush Specifications

Base price *			
	Stage 2 (coupe)		$34,520
	Stage 2 (convertible)		$38,825
	Stage 3 Sport (coupe)		$42,305
	Stage 3 Sport (convertible)		$46,610
	Stage 3 Rally (coupe)		$46,260
	Stage 3 Rally (convertible)		$50,565
	Stage 3 Premium (coupe)		$52,210
	Stage 3 Premium (convertible)		$56,515
	380R (coupe)		$41,460
	380R (convertible)		$45,765
	Boyd Coddington California Roadster		$40,907
	Classic Edition		$43,185

*2003 model prices calculated by adding Roush-package MSRP to GT MSRP

Displacement (cubic inches/liters)			V-8
			281/4.6
Bore x stroke (inches)	V-8		3.60x3.60
VIN code/Compression ratio			V-8
			X 9.40:1
Valvetrain	V-8		SOHC
Horsepower	V-8		260@5,250
	V-8 (360 supercharged)		360@5,250
	V-8 (380 supercharged)		379@5,250
Transmission	standard		Tremec TR3650 5-speed
	optional		4R70W 4-speed automatic
Wheelbase (inches)			101.3
Overall width (inches)			73.1
Overall height (inches)	380R, Classic		53.1
	Stage 2, Stage 3		51.6
Overall length (inches)			183.2
Track (inches)		(front)	60.2
		(rear)	56.0
Weight (pounds)	Stage 3, manual	(coupe)	3,468
		(convertible)	3,602
	Stage 3, auto	(coupe)	3,487
		(convertible)	3,625
Tires	Stage 2, Stage 3	(front)	P265/35ZR18
		(rear)	P295/35ZR18
	380R, Classic	(front)	P245/45ZR17
		(rear)	P245/45ZR17

Front suspension — Stage 2, Stage 3 independent Bilstein struts, Roush springs, Roush anti-roll bar 380R, Classic independent, modified MacPherson strut with separate spring on lower arm and stabilizer bar

Rear suspension — Stage 2, Stage 3 solid axle with Bilstein shocks, Roush springs, Roush lower control arms, factory Mustang sway bar 380R, Classic non-independent four-bar link with coil springs on lower arm and stabilizer (GT only)

Steering			15.0:1 power rack-and-pinion
Brakes (all ABS)	Stage 2	(front)	12-inch ventilated disc
		(rear)	10.5-inch disc
	Stage 3	(front)	14-inch slotted disc, four-piston Alcon caliper
		(rear)	13-inch slotted disc, two-piston PBR caliper

380R (front) 13-inch cross-drilled disc, two-piston PBR caliper (rear) 10.5-inch cross-drilled disc

Classic (front) 13-inch cross-drilled disc, two-piston PBR caliper (rear) 10.5-inch cross-drilled disc

Gas mileage (city/highway)	Stage 2, manual	18/26
	Stage 2, auto	18/26
	Stage 3, manual	17/25
	Stage 3, auto	18/23
	380R, manual	17/25
	380R, auto	18/23
	Classic, manual	17/25
0 to 60 (secs)	Stage 2*	5.7
	Stage 3**	5.1
Standing ¼-mile (mph/secs)	Stage 3**	107@13.6
	Classic***	111.6@12.73
Top speed (mph)	Stage 2*	146
	Stage 3*	173

* Roush factory info
** *Car and Driver*, December, 2001
*** *Muscle Mustangs & Fast Fords*, April, 2003

Roush

Major Options

Handling package	incl.18-inch arent wheels, BFGoodrich g-Force KD tires (265/35ZR18 front, 295/35ZR18 rear), Alcon brakes (14-inch front, 13-inch rear), Bilstein struts, Roush springs and anti-roll bars	$5,400
Alcon brake package		$2,700
PBR brake package		$2,275
Sub-frame connectors	Stage 2	$425
V-8 suspension kit	Stage 3 Sport	$1,875
Supercharger	Boyd Coddington edition	$7,900
Custom leather seats		$1,890
Sport leather seating	Stage 2	$1,690
White-face gauges		$340
Vintage-style shifter		$275
Short-throw shifter		$340
Magna Pac mufflers		$450
Trunk-mounted Roush tool kit		$300
Rear wing		$775
Billet aluminum pedals		$150
Convertible light bar		$910
Red-fire paint upgrade	Stage 3 Premium	$1,000
Roush windshield banner		$30
Locking lug nuts		$60
Embroidered floor mats		$130
18-inch chrome wheels/tires	Stage 3 Premium	$981
17-inch argent wheels/tires	Classic	$1,350
18-inch argent wheels/tires	Classic	$1,475
18-inch chrome wheels/tires	Classic	$2,456

Replacement Costs for Common Parts

Console arm rest pad		$70
Utility compartment		$18
Fog lamp switch		$19
Convertible top		$190
Turn signal lever assembly		$40
Trunk weather stripping		$35
Convertible top headliner		$150
Factory headlight knob		$12
Mach 460 speaker grille		$20
Convertible top boot		$300
Convertible top switch		$20
Electric window motor		$110
Antenna rod		$12
Wiper arm		$35
Space-saver wheel and tire		$40
Front-brake rotor	GT	$40
Outside mirror switch		$45
Tilt wheel lever		$6
Convertible glass rear window		$165
Hood	Cobra repro	$280
Hood	Cobra original	$500
Underhood insulator	GT/V-6	$60
Underhood insulator	Cobra	$63
Taillamp assembly		$80
Radiator core support		$200
Radiator-to-grille cover		$25
Fuse box cover		$10
Headlight assembly		$130
Instrument clear lens		30
Leather steering wheel		160
Convertible top motor		185
Front-bumper cover	GT/V-6 repro	200
Front-bumper cover	GT original	470
Grille		90
Front fender	original	210
Third brake light		75
Rubber fender-to-hood bumpers		5
Radiator core support		290
Fog lamp kit		205
Taillamp assembly	GT/V-6	70
Fog lamp switch		20
Convertible top		200
Headlight assembly		130
Hood scoop	('01-'04) GT	130
Hood	('03-'04) Cobra repro	320
Hood	('03-'04) Cobra original	500

What They Said About Roush Mustangs

Slap the Stage III Roush powertrain on a dyno, and the readouts bear no resemblance to the stock GT's. Peak horsepower swells from 215 at 4,400 rpm, to a heady new crest of 315 horses at 5,500—a gain of 100 horsepower. There's great news in the torque department, too, with an increase from 285 pound-feet at 3,500 in stock form to 345 pound-feet at 3,750 rpm in Roush trim. That's a jump of 21 percent, backed up with mesa-flat torque delivery that beats 275 pound-feet all the way from 2,000 to 5,500 rpm. This is not the sort of power Roush suggests plopping into an otherwise-stock Mustang GT. —*Motor Trend,* **July 1998**

This is a serious car, a worthy contestant to a stock C5 Corvette, if falling a bit short of Z06 performance. The price of $48,975 (for the "Premium" Stage 3 with every conceivable mechanical and cosmetic option available) is as steep as its acceleration curve. We'd certainly opt for the $9,500-cheaper base Stage 3, a car that does without some of the Premium's bodywork (side skirts, rear wing), reworked suspension, and 14.0-inch front brakes clamped by Alcon four-piston calipers (it has 13.0-inch rotors and Brembo calipers instead). —*Road & Track,* **December 2001**

When it first came out, the Roush 360R was billing itself as the most powerful car under $40,000. It was an interesting combo, giving you some of the best features of the Roush Stage 3 Mustang—including the 360-horsepower supercharged 4.6—but without some of the costlier pieces that hike up the price, like the electroluminescent gauges and sidepipes. —*Muscle Mustangs & Fast Fords,* **September 2002**

I Bought a Roush Mustang

On June 6, 2001, I took delivery of a True Blue Stage III Premium Roush Mustang with parchment top. After dating a Mustang owner for a few years and participating in the Carolinas Regional Mustang Club as secretary, co-chair of our national show, and vice president, I decided it was time to own one! No more cleaning other people's ponies—I wanted to enter mine in shows. My Roush has the 360-horsepower 4.6-liter V-8 with supercharger and intercooler. All that engine required more clearance, so it has a Cobra hood. Other performance features include 18-inch wheels (9 inches wide in front, 10 rear) and Roush disc brakes (14 inches front, 13 rear). I won trophies in all national Mustang Club of America shows last year. The Roush folks have used my car as an exhibit car at several shows. It is a daily driver I would not trade for any other car in the world. Jack Roush has signed the engine and the dash. —**Carol Barker**

Roush Mustang Ratings

360R/380R

Model Comfort/Amenities	****
Reliability	****
Collectibility	*****
Parts/Service Availability	****
Est. Annual Repair Costs	***

Stage 3

Model Comfort/Amenities	****
Reliability	****
Collectibility	*****
Parts/Service Availability	****
Est. Annual Repair Costs	***

The Roush name is one of the most respected in motorsports, especially among Ford fans. It stands to reason that the company's serial-numbered Stage 3 and 360R models will be attractive to enthusiasts in years to come, but for now, the collector value of such new series is difficult to predict.

Rousch Garage Watch

Stage 2 Roush cars receive bone-stock 4.6-liter V-8s. It's the Stage 3, Stage 3 Premium, 360/380R, and Classic Edition that get boosted by the Eaton supercharger. Stage 2 Mustangs can run on regular unleaded, but the others require premium.

Tremec's 3650 five-speed transmission, the stock GT's gearbox, has the strength to handle the Roush's 379 horsepower. The T-5 five-speed Ford installed in Mustangs for more than 15 years would not have been sufficient.

Side-exit exhaust pipes, not seen on Mustangs since the 1965 Shelby GT-350, made a comeback on Jack Roush's cars. Drivers usually feel strongly one way or the other about the half-an-engine exhaust sound that comes from splitting the pipes this way.

The supercharged engine in this 2001 Roush Stage 3 Premium convertible puts out 360 horsepower at 5,250 rpm and 375 lbs-ft at 3,000 rpm. The Eaton Roots-type blower creates a maximum 6.0 pounds of boost on premium unleaded gas. For 2003, horsepower was increased to 379.

Surprisingly, the Roush speedometer only registers to 150 miles per hour. Many manufacturers use that gauge as a marketing tool, as it's been a long time since a performance car could bury its own needle.

Super-size, cross-drilled, and ventilated Alcon brakes are part of a $5,400 handling package that includes the 18-inch wheels. The Alcons measure 14 inches in the front and 13 inches in the rear.

Part of the Stage 3's appeal is its tremendous handling ability over the stock Mustang, the result of careful suspension tuning and these giant high-performance tires. Roush stuffs the front wheel wells of his Stage 3 Mustang with 265/35ZR18 BFGoodrich radials, and the rears measure 395/35ZR18.

Appendix I

Which 1979–2004 Mustang Do I Want?

Year	Body	Automatic Transmission	Manual Transmission	Number of Cylinders	Special Models
1979	CP, HB	3-sp	4-sp	4	
	HB	3-sp	4-sp	4 Turbo	Indy Pace Car, Cobra
	CP, HB	3-sp		6	
	CP, HB	3-sp	4-sp	8	
	HB	3-sp	4-sp	8	Indy Pace Car, Cobra
1980	CP, HB	3-sp	4-sp	4	
	HB	3-sp	4-sp	4 Turbo	Cobra
	CP, HB	3-sp		6	
	CP, HB	3-sp	4-sp	8	
	HB	3-sp	4-sp	8	Cobra
1981	CP, HB	3-sp	4-sp	4	
	CP, HB	3-sp		6	
	CP, HB	3-sp	4-sp	8	
	HB	3-sp	4-sp	8	Cobra
1982	CP, HB	3-sp	4-sp	4	
	CP, HB	3-sp		6	
	CP, HB	3-sp	4-sp	8	
	HB		4-sp	8	GT
1983	CP, HB	3-sp	4-sp	4	
	HB		5-sp	4 Turbo	Turbo GT
	CP, HB, CV	3-sp		6	
	CP, HB, CV		5-sp	8	
	HB, CV		4-sp, 5-sp	8	GT

Year	Body	Automatic Transmission	Manual Transmission	Number of Cylinders	Special Models
1984	CP, HB	3-sp	4-sp	4	
	HB, CV		5-sp	4 Turbo	20th Anniv., Turbo GT
	HB		5-sp	4 Turbo	SVO
	CP, HB, CV	3-sp		6	
	CP, HB, CV		5-sp	8 carb.	
	HB, CV		5-sp	8 carb.	20th Anniv., GT
	CP, HB, CV	4-sp		8 FI	
	HB, CV	4-sp		8 FI	20th Anniv., GT
	HB		5-sp	8 carb.	Saleen
1985	CP, HB	3-sp	4-sp	4	
	HB		5-sp	4 Turbo	SVO
	CP, HB, CV	3-sp		6	
	CP, HB, CV		5-sp	8 4-bbl.	
	HB, CV		5-sp	8 4-bbl.	GT
	CP, HB, CV	4-sp		8 TBI	
	HB, CV	4-sp		8 TBI	GT
	HB, CV		5-sp	8 4-bbl.	Saleen
	HB, CV	4-sp		8 TBI	Saleen
1986	CP, HB	3-sp	4-sp	4	
	HB		5-sp	4 Turbo	SVO
	CP, HB, CV	3-sp		6	
	CP, HB, CV	4-sp	5-sp	8	
	HB, CV	4-sp	5-sp	8	GT
	HB, CV	4-sp	5-sp	8	Saleen
1987	CP, HB, CV	4-sp	5-sp	4	
	CP, HB, CV	4-sp	5-sp	8	
	HB, CV	4-sp	5-sp	8	GT
	CP, HB, CV	4-sp	5-sp	8	Saleen

Year	Body	Automatic Transmission	Manual Transmission	Number of Cylinders	Special Models
1988	CP, HB, CV	4-sp	5-sp	4	
	CP, HB, CV	4-sp	5-sp	8	
	HB, CV	4-sp	5-sp	8	GT
	CP, HB, CV	4-sp	5-sp	8	Saleen
1989	CP, HB, CV	4-sp	5-sp	4	
	CP, HB, CV	4-sp	5-sp	8	
	HB, CV	4-sp	5-sp	8	GT
	CP, HB, CV	4-sp	5-sp	8	Saleen
	HB		5-sp	8	Saleen SSC
1990	CP, HB, CV	4-sp	5-sp	4	
	CP, HB, CV	4-sp	5-sp	8	
	HB, CV	4-sp	5-sp	8	GT
	CP, HB, CV	4-sp	5-sp	8	Saleen
	HB		5-sp	8	Saleen SC
1991	CP, HB, CV	4-sp	5-sp	4	
	CP, HB, CV	4-sp	5-sp	8	
	HB, CV	4-sp	5-sp	8	GT
	CP, HB, CV	4-sp	5-sp	8	Saleen
	HB		5-sp	8	Saleen SC
1992	CP, HB, CV	4-sp	5-sp	4	
	CP, HB, CV	4-sp	5-sp	8	
	HB, CV	4-sp	5-sp	8	GT
	CP, HB, CV	4-sp	5-sp	8	Saleen
	HB		5-sp	8	Saleen SC

Year	Body	Automatic Transmission	Manual Transmission	Number of Cylinders	Special Models
1993	CP, HB, CV	4-sp	5-sp	4	
	CP, HB, CV	4-sp	5-sp	8	
	HB, CV	4-sp	5-sp	8	GT
	CP, HB, CV	4-sp	5-sp	8	Saleen
	HB		5-sp	8	Saleen SC
	HB		5-sp	8	Cobra
	HB		5-sp	8	Cobra R
1994	CP, CV	4-sp	5-sp	6	
	CP, CV	4-sp	5-sp	8	GT
	CP, CV		5-sp	8	Saleen S-351
	CP, CV		5-sp	8	Cobra
1995	CP, CV	4-sp	5-sp	6	
	CP, CV	4-sp	5-sp	8	GT
	CP, CV		5-sp	8	Saleen S-351
	CP, CV		5-sp	8	Cobra
	CP		5-sp	8	Cobra R
1996	CP, CV	4-sp	5-sp	6	
	CP, CV	4-sp	5-sp	8	GT
	CP, CV	4-sp	5-sp	8	Saleen S-281
	CP, CV		5-sp	8	Saleen S-351
	CP, CV		5-sp	8	Cobra
1997	CP, CV	4-sp	5-sp	6	
	CP, CV	4-sp	5-sp	8	GT
	CP, CV	4-sp	5-sp	8	Saleen S-281
	CP, CV		6-sp	8	Saleen S-351
	CP, CV	4-sp	5-sp	8	Roush
	CP, CV		5-sp	8	Cobra

Year	Body	Automatic Transmission	Manual Transmission	Number of Cylinders	Special Models
1998	CP, CV	4-sp	5-sp	6	
	CP, CV	4-sp	5-sp	8	GT
	CP, CV	4-sp	5-sp	8	Saleen S-281
	CP, CV		6-sp	8	Saleen S-351
	CP, CV	4-sp	5-sp	8	Roush
	CP, CV		5-sp	8	Cobra
1999	CP, CV	4-sp	5-sp	6	
	CP, CV	4-sp	5-sp	8	GT
	CP, CV	4-sp	5-sp	8	Saleen S-281
	CP, CV		6-sp	8	Saleen S-351
	CP, CV	4-sp	5-sp	8	Roush
	CP, CV		5-sp	8	Cobra
2000	CP, CV	4-sp	5-sp	6	
	CP, CV	4-sp	5-sp	8	GT
	CP, CV	4-sp	5-sp	8	Saleen S-281
	CP, CV	4-sp	5-sp	8	Roush
	CP		6-sp	8	Cobra R
2001	CP, CV	4-sp	5-sp	6	
	CP, CV	4-sp	5-sp	8	GT
	CP		5-sp	8	Bullitt
	CP, CV	4-sp	5-sp	8	Saleen S-281
	CP, CV	4-sp	5-sp	8	Roush
	CP, CV		5-sp	8	Cobra
2002	CP, CV	4-sp	5-sp	6	
	CP, CV	4-sp	5-sp	8	GT
	CP, CV	4-sp	5-sp	8	Saleen S-281
	CP, CV		6-sp	8	Saleen S-281E
	CP, CV	4-sp	5-sp	8	Roush

Year	Body	Automatic Transmission	Manual Transmission	Number of Cylinders	Special Models
2003	CP, CV	4-sp	5-sp	6	
	CP, CV	4-sp	5-sp	8	GT
	CP	4-sp	5-sp	8	Mach 1
	CP, CV	4-sp	5-sp	8	Saleen S-281
	CP, CV		6-sp	8	Saleen S-281E
	CP, CV	4-sp	5-sp	8	Roush
	CP, CV		6-sp	8	Cobra
2004	CP, CV	4-sp	5-sp	6	
	CP, CV	4-sp	5-sp	8	GT
	CP, CV	4-sp	5-sp	8	Saleen S-281
	CP, CV		6-sp	8	Saleen S-281E
	CP, CV	4-sp	5-sp	8	Roush
	CP, CV		6-sp	8	Cobra

LEGEND

HB = fastback
CP = coupe
CV = convertible

Appendix II

1979–2004 Mustang Performance at a Glance

CID/Liters	Type	Bore/Stroke	Ind.	Compression	Horsepower	Years
FOUR-CYLINDER						
140/2.3	I-4	3.78 x 3.13	2V	9.0:1	88	'79–'86
140/2.3 Turbo	I-4	3.78 x 3.13	2V	9.0:1	131	'79–'80
140/2.3 Turbo	I-4	3.78 x 3.13	EFI	8.0:1	145	'83–'84
140/2.3 Turbo SVO	I-4	3.78 x 3.13	EFI	8.0:1	175	'84–'85
140/2.3 Turbo SVO	I-4	3.78 x 3.13	EFI	8.0:1	205	'85
140/2.3 Turbo SVO	I-4	3.78 x 3.13	EFI	8.0:1	200	86
140/2.3	I-4	3.78 x3.13	EFI	9.0:1	90	'87–'93
V-6						
171/2.8	V-6	3.66 x 2.70	2V	8.7:1	109	79
232/3.8	V-6	3.80 x 3.40	2V	8.7:1	105	83
232/3.8	V-6	3.80 x 3.40	CFI	8.7:1	120	'83–'86
232/3.8	V-6	3.80 x 3.40	TPI	9.0:1	145	'94–'98
232/3.8	V-6	3.80 x 3.40	EFI	9.36:1	190	'99–'04
INLINE 6						
200/3.3	I-6	3.68 x 3.13	1V	8.6:1	85	'79–'82
V-8						
255/4.2	V-8	3.68 x 3.00	2V	8.8:1	119	'80–'81
255/4.2	V-8	3.68 x 3.00	2V	8.2:1	120	'82
281/4.6 SOHC	V-8	3.55 x 3.54	EFI	9.0:1	215	'96–'98
281/4.6 DOHC Cobra	V-8	3.55 x 3.54	EFI	9.85:1	305	'96–'98
281/4.6 SOHC	V-8	3.55 x 3.54	EFI	9.0:1	260	'99–'04

CID/Liters	Type	Bore/Stroke	Ind.	Compression	Horsepower	Years
V-8 (continued)						
281/4.6 Roush SOHC V-8		3.55 x 3.54	EFI	9.0:1	360-379	'99-'04
281/4.6 DOHC Cobra V-8		3.55 x 3.54	EFI	9.85:1	320	'99-'01
281/4.6 SOHC Bullitt V-8		3.55 x 3.54	EFI	9.0:1	265	'01
281/4.6 SOHC Saleen S-281E	V-8	3.55 x 3.54	EFI	9.0:1	425-445	'02-'04
281/4.6 DOHC Mach 1V-8		3.55 x 3.54	EFI	10.1:1	305	'03
281/4.6 DOHC Cobra V-8		3.55 x 3.54	EFI	8.5:1	390	'03-'04
302/5.0	V-8	4.00 x 3.00	2V	8.4:1	119	'79
302/5.0	V-8	4.00 x 3.00	2V	8.3:1	157	'82
302/5.0	V-8	4.00 x 3.00	4V	8.3:1	175	'83-'84
302/5.0 AOD	V-8	4.00 x 3.00	CFI	8.3:1	165	'84
302/5.0	V-8	4.00 x 3.00	4V	8.3:1	210	'85
302/5.0 AOD	V-8	4.00 x 3.00	CFI	8.3:1	165	'85
302/5.0 AOD	V-8	4.00 x 3.00	CFI	8.3:1	180	'85
302/5.0	V-8	4.00 x 3.00	EFI	9.2:1	200	'86
302/5.0	V-8	4.00 x 3.00	EFI	9.0:1	225	'87-'92
302/5.0 Saleen SSC/SC V-8		4.00 x 3.00	EFI	9.0:1	292	'89-'93
302/5.0	V-8	4.00 x 3.00	EFI	9.0:1	205	'93
302/5.0 Cobra	V-8	4.00 x 3.00	EFI	9.0:1	235	'93
302/5.0	V-8	4.00 x 3.00	EFI	9.0:1	215	'94-'95
302/5.0 Cobra	V-8	4.00 x 3.00	EFI	9.0:1	240	'94-'95
330/5.4 DOHC Cobra RV-8		3.55 x 4.17	EFI	9.6:1	385	'00
351/5.8 Saleen S-351V-8		4.00 x 3.50	EFI	9.0:1	400	'95-'99
351/5.8 Cobra R	V-8	4.00 x 3.50	EFI	9.0:1	300	'95

Appendix III

1979–2004 Mustang Costs for Common Parts

Some people make the mistake of choosing one car over another because it has a lower purchase price, only to see the cost of replacing worn-out parts doubles or triples their initial investment.

Fortunately, the late-model Mustang enjoys tremendous support from a network of specialty shops and catalog dealers across the country, which makes locating affordable parts easier than for any other marque. Whether your intentions are to modify or preserve a 1979 or later Mustang, many companies offer the parts and, in many instances, technical advice you need.

This chart was assembled with the help of Latemodel Restoration Supply (www.50resto.com) in Robinson, Texas. It gives the prices of hundreds of the most popular Mustang parts as they apply to the years indicated. For purposes of modification and upgrading, much of this equipment can be interchanged between years if desired by the owner.

Powertrain parts relate to the V-8 engines unless otherwise indicated. Since any company's prices are subject to change, use this list only as a guideline for estimating how much money a potential purchase might need to meet your standards of restoration or modification.

'79 Rear wheel cylinder		$25
'79-'81 Turbo hood emblem		$10
'79-'82 Steering wheel	$100 core charge	$270
'79-'82 Hood scoop grille		$33
'79-'82 Ford emblem	rear hatch	$8
'79-'83 Rearview mirror		$43
'79-'84 Power rack and pinion steering	19:1 ratio	$200
'79-'85 Ignition coil		$60
'79-'85 Fuel pump	exc. EFI	$30
'79-'85 Alternator		$60
'79-'85 Fan shroud	repro	$80
'79-'86 Console coin tray		$37
'79-'86 Arm rest pad		$65
'79-'86 A/C vent registers		$20
'79-'86 Dash pads	repro	$190
'79-'86 Side marker		$13
'79-'86 Headlight retaining ring	exc. SVO	$40
'79-'86 Marchal fog lamp lens		$110
'79-'86 Front brake rotor		$40
'79-'86 Master cylinder	remanufactured	$30
'79-'89 Oil pressure sending unit		$20
'79-'90 Front fender	repro	$85
'79-'90 Front fender	original	$280
'79-'91 Starter		$60
'79-'93 Front seat belt buckle		$47
'79-'93 Outside door handle kit		$27
'79-'93 Electric window motor		$70
'79-'93 Window crank handle		$10
'79-'93 Inside door handle bezel		$23
'79-'93 Door lock actuator kit		$90
'79-'93 Lock cylinder and key		$25
'79-'93 Hatchback quarter window molding pair		$100
'79-'93 Hatch weatherstripping		$27
'79-'93 Trunk weatherstripping		$23
'79-'93 Sunroof weatherstripping kit		$150
'79-'93 Door weatherstripping kit		$40
'79-'93 Vacuum canister		$25
'79-'93 Antenna kit	black	$37
'79-'93 Antenna kit	stainless	$23
'79-'93 Antenna rod		$14
'79-'93 Rubber fender-to-hood bumpers		$2
'79-'93 Hood latch assembly		$25
'79-'93 Wiper arm and blade kit		$40
'79-'93 Wiper arm		$15
'79-'93 Windshield washer nozzle		$9
'79-'93 Trunk lid	convertible and coupe	$170
'79-'93 Floor pan		$115
'79-'93 Smog pump		$60
'79-'93 Crankshaft pulley		$70
'79-'93 Water pump pulley	GT/LX	$45
'79-'93 Distributor cover		$10
'79-'93 Smog canister		$65
'79-'93 Heater core	A/C	$30
	exc. A/C	$35
'79-'93 Radiator bracket	left	$30
	right	$60
'79-'93 Radiator		$110
'79-'93 Rear brake drum		$35

'79–'93 Power steering pump		$100
'79–'93 Front lower control arms	pair	$200
'79–'95 Pushrods	set of 16	$40
'79–'95 Harmonic balancer		$80
'79–'95 Radiator cap	16-pound	$6
	13-pound	$9
'79–'95 Thermostat	180-degree	$16
	195-degree	$7
'79–'96 Fuel cap		$20
'79–'04 Carpet		$99
'80–'93 Rear wheel cylinder		$40
'80–'95 Temperature sending unit		$8
'81–'86 Fuel tank	exc. EFI	$130
'81–'88 Four-piece T-top weatherstripping kit		$230
'82 Steering wheel	$100 core charge	$270
'82–'85 Air cleaner inlet tube		$25
'82–'93 Clutch fork		$25
'83 Steering wheel	$100 core charge	$270
'83 Hood scoop grille		$55
'83–'84 Front bumper cover	LX repro	$170
'83–'84 Tail lamp lens		$110
'83–'86 Hood	repro	$170
'83–'86 Fuel tank sending unit		$90
'83–'89 Tilt wheel lever		$6
'83–'89 Radiator core support		$180
'83–'93 Convertible top boot		$80
'83–'93 Convertible glass rear window		$125
'83–'93 Convertible top		$150
'83–'93 Convertible top headliner		$135
'83–'93 Convertible sun visor	pair	$50
'83–'93 Convertible top motor		$200
'83–'93 Front inner splash shield		$90
'83–'93 Air check valve		$50
'83–'93 Motor mount	convertible	$47
'83–'95 Coolant temperature sensor		$30
'83–'95 Ignition coil		$55
'84 Front bumper cover	GT repro	$400
'84–'85 Headlight retaining ring	SVO	$8
'84–'86 Steering wheel	(SVO) $100 core charge	$300
'84–'86 SVO intercooler-to-hood seal		$40
'84–'86 SVO emblem	SVO	$8
'84–'86 SVO master cylinder		$90
'84–'91 Rearview mirror		$38
'84–'93 LX deck lid emblem		$11
'84–'93 Fuel tank	EFI	$140
'85–'86 Front bumper cover	LX repro	$170
'85–'86 Front bumper cover	SVO repro	$400
'85–'86 Rear bumper cover		$120
'85–'86 Tail lamp lens		$80
'85–'93 Belt tensioner		$73
'85–'93 Fuel tank shield		$130
'85–'93 Power rack and pinion steering	15:1 ratio	$200
'85–'95 Hydraulic roller lifters	set of 16	$130
'86–'88 Airbox-to-throttle body inlet tube		$35
'86–'93 5.0 upper intake plaque		$60
'86–'93 PCV adapter tube		$20
'86–'93 PCV hose		$9
'86–'93 Heater tube assembly		$70
'86–'93 EFI distributor		$210
'86–'93 Battery tray		$44
'86–'93 Alternator		$150
'86–'93 Mass air meter boot		$63
'86–'93 H-pipe smog tube		$100
'86–'93 Vacuum tree		$30
'86–'93 Fan shroud	repro	$90
'86–'93 Fan shroud	original	$110
'86–'95 PCV valve grommet		$4
'87–'89 Instrument clear lens		$40
'87–'93 Console arm rest pad		$80
'87–'93 Rear console ashtray		$23
'87–'93 Emergency brake cable		$19
'87–'93 A/C control trim bezel		$22
'87–'93 Radio delete plate		$16
'87–'93 Console top panel		$65
'87–'93 Outside mirror switch		$33
'87–'93 Turn signal lever assembly		$70
'87–'93 Door speaker grille		$23
'87–'93 Hatch area speaker grille		$30
'87–'93 Convertible top switch		$50
'87–'93 Trunk latch		$50
'87–'93 Front bumper cover	LX repro	$150
'87–'93 Front bumper cover	GT repro	$140
'87–'93 Front bumper cover	LX original	$250
'87–'93 Front bumper cover	GT original	$400
'87–'93 Rear bumper cover	LX repro	$115
'87–'93 Rear bumper cover	GT repro	$140
'87–'93 Rear bumper cover	LX original	$210
'87–'93 Rear bumper cover	GT original	$250

'87–'93 Fog lamp bracket (all 3 required)	GT center	$70
	GT right	$70
	GT left	$70
'87–'93 Front fender apron		$120
'87–'93 Hood	repro	$170
'87–'93 Hood	original	$500
'87–'93 Third brake light		$45
'87–'93 Underhood insulator		$75
'87–'93 Door skin		$390
'87–'93 Quarter panel	hatchback right original	$680
	hatchback left original	$500
	convertible right original	$500
	convertible left original	$400
'87–'93 Headlight assembly	repro	$60
'87–'93 Headlight assembly	original	$73
'87–'93 Parking lamp	repro	$20
'87–'93 Side marker lamp	repro	$18
'87–'93 Fog lamp assembly	repro	$30
'87–'93 Fog lamp assembly	original	$35
'87–'93 Fog lamp lens		$18
'87–'93 Tail lamp lens		$58
'87–'93 Tail lamp assembly	LX	$170
'87–'93 Fuel tank filler neck		$40
'87–'93 Fuel tank sending unit		$83
'87–'93 Windshield washer reservoir		$40
'87–'93 Horn		$43
'87–'93 Front brake rotor		$55
'87–'93 Master cylinder reservoir and cap		$33
'87–'93 Master cylinder	remanufactured, exc. Cobra	$65
	Cobra	$100
'87–'93 Motor mount	coupe and hatchback	$65
'89–'93 Airbox-to-throttle body inlet tube		$43
'90–'93 Instrument clear lens		$40
'90–'93 Speed control switches		$65
'90–'93 Hatch cargo cover		$130
'90–'93 Radiator core support		$200
'90–'93 Oil pressure sending unit		$27
'90–'98 Steering wheel	$100 core charge	$270
'91–'93 Front fender	repro	$90
'91–'93 Front fender	original	$300
'91–'93 16x7-inch 5-spoke wheel		$140
'92–'93 Rearview mirror		$19
'92–'95 Starter		$155
'93 Front bumper cover	Cobra repro	$205

'93 Grille	Cobra	$90
'93 Rear spoiler	Cobra	$190
s'93 Upper intake plaque	Cobra	$33
'93 Water pump pulley	Cobra	$22
'93 Front brake rotor	Cobra	$60
'93–'95 Roller rockers	Cobra, set of 16	$250
'93–'04 Snake emblem	Cobra	$10
'94 Indy Pace Car deck lid emblem		$37
'94–'95 Convertible glass rear window		$165
'94–'95 Underhood insulator		$63
'94–'95 GT fender emblem		$10
'94–'95 EGR-to-header tube		$50
'94–'95 Idler pulley		$18
'94–'95 Oil pressure sending unit		$13
'94–'95 Distributor cover		$13
'94–'95 Airbox-to-throttle body inlet tube		$70
'94–'95 Radiator		$160
'94–'95 Power rack and pinion steering	14:1 ratio	$245
'94–'95 Motor mount	left	$53
	right	$84
'94–'96 Radiator core support		$200
'94–'96 Radiator-to-grille cover		$65
'94–'97 Fuel tank sending unit		$77
'94–'97 Fuse box cover		$13
'94–'98 Battery tray		$13
'94–'98 Radio and A/C bezel		$120
'94–'98 Rearview mirror		$20
'94–'98 Convertible top motor		$240
'94–'98 Front bumper cover	Cobra repro	$230
'94–'98 Front bumper cover	GT/V-6 repro	$180
'94–'98 Front inner splash shield		$40
'94–'98 Front fender	repro	$90
'94–'98 Front fender	original	$210
'94–'98 Hood	GT/V-6 repro	$200
'94–'98 Hood	GT/V-6 original	$500
'94–'98 Third brake light		$80
'94–'98 Rubber fender-to-hood bumpers		$2
'94–'98 Headlight assembly	GT/V-6	$70
'94–'98 Headlight assembly	Cobra	$100
'94–'98 Side marker lamp		$23
'94–'98 Fog lamp kit		$240
'94–'98 Pony grille emblem		$22
'94–'98 Heater core		$49
'94–'98 Clutch fork		$27

Year	Part	Variant	Price
'94-'98	Instrument clear lens		$70
'94-'00	Console arm rest pad		$70
'94-'00	Utility compartment		$18
'94-'00	Fog lamp switch		$19
'94-'00	Convertible top		$190
'94-'02	Turn signal lever assembly		$40
'94-'04	Trunk weatherstripping		$35
'94-'04	Convertible top headliner		$150
'94-'04	Factory headlight knob		$12
'94-'04	Mach 460 speaker grille		$20
'94-'04	Convertible top boot		$300
'94-'04	Convertible top switch		$20
'94-'04	Electric window motor		$110
'94-'04	Antenna rod		$12
'94-'04	Wiper arm		$35
'94-'04	Space-saver wheel and tire		$40
'94-'04	Front brake rotor	GT	$40
'94-'04	Front brake rotor	Cobra	$160
'94-'04	Outside mirror switch		$45
'94-'04	Tilt wheel lever		$6
'95-'98	SVT emblem	Cobra	$12
'95-'04	Convertible glass rear window		$165
'96-'98	Grille		$70
'96-'98	Hood	Cobra repro	$280
'96-'98	Hood	Cobra original	$500
'96-'98	Underhood insulator	GT/V-6	$60
'96-'98	Underhood insulator	Cobra	$63
'96-'98	Tail lamp assembly		$80
'96-'98	GT 4.6 fender emblem		$10
'96-'01	Engine oil cooler	Cobra	$200
'97-'98	Radiator core support		$200
'97-'04	Radiator-to-grille cover		$25
'98-'04	Fuse box cover		$10
'99	Hood scoop	35th Anniversary Edition	$130
'99	35th anniversary fender emblem		$13
'99-'00	Headlight assembly		$130
'99-'01	Hood	Cobra repro	$350
'99-'01	Underhood insulator	Cobra	$63
'99-'01	Fog lamp bezel	Cobra	$17
'99-'01	Tail lamp assembly	Cobra	$150
'99-'01	SVT Cobra emblem	Cobra	$11
'99-'04	Instrument clear lens		$30
'99-'04	Leather steering wheel		$160
'99-'04	Convertible top motor		$185
'99-'04	Front bumper cover	GT/V-6 repro	$200
'99-'04	Front bumper cover	Cobra original	$300
'99-'04	Front bumper cover	V-6 original	$400
'99-'04	Front bumper cover	GT original	$470
'99-'04	Grille		$90
'99-'04	Front fender	original	$210
'99-'04	Hood	GT/V-6 original	$500
'99-'04	Hood	Cobra original	$500
'99-'04	Third brake light		$75
'99-'04	Underhood insulator	GT/V-6	$57
'99-'04	Rubber fender-to-hood bumpers		$5
'99-'04	Radiator core support		$290
'99-'04	Fog lamp kit		$205
'99-'04	Tail lamp assembly	GT/V-6	$70
'00	Front splitter	Cobra R original	$500
'00	Hood	Cobra R repro	$320
'00	Hood	Cobra R original	$500
'01	SVT emblem	Cobra R	$8
'01	Bullitt deck lid emblem		$20
'01	Bullitt pedals	automatic and manual trans	$90
'01	Bullitt fuel door		$80
'01	Bullitt 17x8-inch wheel		$160
'01	Bullitt door scuff plate		$70
'01	Bullitt shift knob		$35
'01	Bullitt shifter trim bezel		$70
'01-'04	Fog lamp switch		$20
'01-'04	Convertible top		$200
'01-'04	Headlight assembly		$130
'01-'04	Hood scoop	GT	$130
'03	Mach 1 deck lid emblem		$23
'03	Mach 1 chin spoiler		$70
'03	Mach 1 grille		$50
'03	Mach 1 rocker stripes	pair	$60
'03	Mach 1 hood stripe		$60
'03	Mach 1 wheel		$150
'03-'04	Hood	Cobra repro	$320
'03-'04	Hood	Cobra original	$500
'03-'04	Outer door mirror	Cobra	$160
'03-'04	Steering wheel	Cobra	$170
'03-'04	Shifter knob	Cobra	$65
'03-'04	Wheel center cap	Cobra	$15

Appendix IV

1979–2004 Mustang Firsts, Lasts, and Highlights

1979
- new "Fox" body is 200 pounds lighter than '78 model
- new body is 4.1 inches longer than '78
- Indy 500 Pace Car replicas offered
- first year for Michelin TRX suspension package
- first year for T-roof panels
- first Mustang with MacPherson struts and four-bar link rear
- first Mustang with turbocharged engine
- first year all V-8 Mustangs receive serpentine accessories belt
- first inline six-cylinder in a Mustang since '73
- first year all Mustang V-8s received 7.5-inch rear axle

1980
- smallest V-8 in Mustang history introduced with 255 cubic inches of displacement
- 302-cid V-8 dropped from Mustang line
- first year for all Mustangs to be shod with radial tires
- first year for all Mustangs to be fitted with halogen headlamps
- first year retractable cargo cover offered as option
- final year for turbocharged 2.3-liter with carburetor

1981
- first year reclining seats were standard
- first year power windows offered in Fox series
- Cobra model dropped from line
- final year of Mustang production at San Jose, Calif., plant

1982
- 302-cid V-8 returned to Mustang line after two-year absence
- GT model returns to Mustang series after 12-year absence
- first year for "slapper" bars on rear suspension
- all Mustang engines painted gray beginning '82
- Ford begins building Mustangs for Special Service Vehicle program
- final year for a two-barrel carburetor in a high-performance Mustang application
- final year for factory hatchback louvers

1983
- turbocharged 2.3-liter returned in improved form
- first Mustang convertible in 10 years
- first five-speed transmission in a Mustang
- first appearance of electronic fuel injection (EFI) in the Mustang line (on Turbo motor)
- first appearance of Ford's electronic engine control (EEC-IV) on Mustang (Turbo)
- first four-barrel carburetor on any Mustang since '73 (5.0 V-8)
- first use of dual-snorkel air cleaner on V-8
- first appearance of upshift indicator light with gauges
- first year retractable cargo cover is standard equipment
- first year V-8 Fox cars had inline muffler (instead of transverse-mounted)
- Traction-Lok axle became standard with V-8

1984
- first year for four-speed automatic overdrive transmission
- first year 5.0-liter GT could be had with automatic transmission, but with lower horsepower
- first fuel injection on a Mustang V-8 (central fuel injection, CFI) on 5.0/AOD cars, also V-6
- first year for quad-shock rear suspension setup (V-8 and SVO)
- first year for clutch-operated starter motor bypass (all models)
- first four-wheel disc brake system on a Mustang (SVO)
- first five-lug wheel pattern on a Mustang since 1973 (SVO)
- first driver's footrest on a Mustang (SVO)
- first 16-inch wheels on a Mustang (SVO)
- first use of "trimline" brake booster (V-8 and SVO)
- first Saleen Mustang built
- SVO featured fuel calibration switch for regular or premium
- Ford located horn button at center of steering wheel (from stalk)
- 20th Anniversary GT and GT Turbo models released midyear
- final year for TRX wheel/tire/suspension package

1985
- first hydraulic roller camshaft on a Mustang V-8
- first set of headers on a modern Mustang V-8
- first use of forged aluminum headers (V-8)
- first time V-8 Mustangs came standard with power-assisted steering
- first flush-mounted headlights on a Mustang (SVO)
- first Saleen convertible
- first Saleen built with automatic transmission
- GT gets 15-inch wheels
- Ford began using industrial adhesive to strengthen its chassis welds
- final year for the four-barrel carburetor on a Mustang
- final year for 7.5-inch rear axle

1986
- first year for 8.8-inch rear axle
- first year for single version of 5.0 for manual and automatic transmissions
- first year for V-8 to draw air from passenger-side airbox
- first year for viscous engine mounts (V-6 and V-8)
- first year for true dual exhaust system on V-8 Mustangs
- first year for "third brake light" on all Mustangs
- first year for speed density management system on V-8
- 16-inch wheels become standard on Saleen Mustangs
- only year for E6AE cylinder head design
- final year for V-6 in Fox-body Mustang

1987
- platform for 5.0 engine is essentially set for next seven years
- four-cylinder benefited from electronic fuel injection
- all Mustangs receive SVO-like flush headlamps
- GT cosmetic package dramatically different from cheaper LX
- all Saleen Mustangs come standard with four-wheel disc brakes and five-lug rotors
- Saleen builds first car based on Mustang coupe

1988
- mass airflow sensor replaces speed density meter on California-bound V-8 cars
- minor V-8 camshaft modification midyear, no reported change in power rating

1989
- mass airflow sensor replaces speed density meter on all V-8 Mustangs
- 5.0L becomes its own model
- Saleen introduces 292-horsepower SSC, first 50-state certified Saleen Mustang

1990
- first driver's-side airbag in a Mustang
- first year for three-point passenger restraint in back seat
- new suspension geometry improves handling, increases tire life

1991
- four-cylinder gets dual-sparkplug head
- convertible top redesigned to sit lower in compartment when down
- V-8 Mustangs get 16-inch wheels
- Ford installs automatic transmission interlock to prevent shifting from Park without braking

1992
- Limited Edition midyear convertible released (Vibrant Red)

1993
- SVT introduces Cobra and Cobra R models
- first V-8 Fox-body Mustang to wear four-wheel disc brakes from factory
- first Mustang to wear 17-inch wheels from the factory (Cobra and R)
- second Limited Edition midyear convertible (Canary Yellow or Oxford White)
- Saleen builds nine 10th Anniversary SA-10 Mustangs
- Ford downgrade's 5.0-liter horsepower to 205
- final year for Mustangs built for Special Service Vehicle program
- final year for four-cylinder Mustang

1994
- first major redesign for Mustang since '79
- first year for all Mustangs to be fitted with four-wheel disc brakes and five-lug rotors
- first year for dual airbags (all Mustangs)
- first year for anti-lock braking system (optional)
- all Mustang V-8s receive a brace tying strut towers to firewall for stiffer chassis
- Ford offers removable hardtop for Mustang convertibles, but none are produced this year
- top engine is 215-horsepower 5.0-liter
- 3.8-liter V-6 returned to duty
- Cobra puts out 240 horsepower
- Cobra gets 13-inch front discs
- SVT begins tradition of white-faced gauges with Cobra
- all Cobra convertibles built this year are Indy 500 Pace Car replicas
- Saleen introduces S-351 with handbuilt 351-cid engine
- S-351 becomes first Mustang built with 18-inch wheels

1995
- SVT offers Cobra R with 351-cid engine
- Ford offers single-year GTS model, de-contented GT
- removable hardtops are delivered, but as Cobra option only
- final year for 5.0-liter Mustang motor

1996
- first year for SOHC 4.6-liter "modular" engine in Mustangs (GT)
- first year for DOHC 4.6-liter engine (Cobra)
- first year for aluminum-block V-8 in Mustang line (Cobra)
- first appearance of OBD-II engine management system
- first year for Borg-Warner T-45 five-speed transmission
- first year for 4R70W automatic transmission
- only year "Mystic" paint offered on Cobras
- all V-8 Mustangs get brake booster fed through steering pump
- stiffer block for V-6, other improvements make for 150 horsepower
- Saleen adds S-281 to model line

1997
- Ford redesigned the radiator and grille opening for better airflow
- Saleen equips all S-351s with six-speed transmissions

1998
- SVT introduces Cobra wheel similar to five-spoke that appeared on '95 R

1999
- first year for 260-horsepower 4.6-liter in GT
- 3.8-liter V-6 is boosted to 190 horsepower
- Traction Control offered as an option
- all V-6 and GT models receive "35th Anniversary" fender badge
- all Mustangs receive special trunk "escape" handle
- Mustang decklids, door skins and hoods made of plastic
- SVT installs first independent rear suspension on a production Mustang (Cobra)
- Cobra's DOHC engine fails to make advertised 320 horsepower, all are recalled
- Saleen gains certification to install superchargers through company facilities
- Saleen produces 10 SA-15 anniversary cars
- final year of Saleen's S-351 production

2000
- SVT introduces single-year 5.4-liter Cobra R
- no street Cobra was produced this year
- air conditioning became standard equipment in all Mustangs
- first six-speed manual transmission in a production Mustang (Cobra R)
- Saleen sells record number of cars (974)

2001
- GT models received non-functional scoops and vents
- Traction Control becomes standard GT equipment
- Ford introduces single-year Bullitt special edition

2002
- Saleen introduces S-281E model with hand built 4.6-liter and supercharger

2003
- Pony group option lets V-6 buyers dress their cars like a GT
- Ford improved front impact safety equipment in all Mustangs, gets five-star rating
- Mach 1 introduced

Index

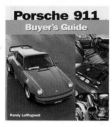
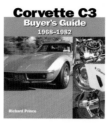

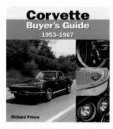